MW00529039

On Account of Sex

LANDMARK LAW CASES & AMERICAN SOCIETY

Peter Charles Hoffer
N. E. H. Hull
Williamjames Hull Hoffer
Series Editors

For a complete list of titles in the series, go to www.kansaspress.ku.edu.

PHILIPPA STRUM

On Account
of Sex

Ruth Bader Ginsburg and the
Making of Gender Equality Law

UNIVERSITY PRESS OF KANSAS

© 2022 by Philippa Strum

All rights reserved

Published by the University Press of Kansas (Lawrence, Kansas 66045), which was
organized by the Kansas Board of Regents and is operated and funded by Emporia State
University, Fort Hays State University, Kansas State University, Pittsburg State University,
the University of Kansas, and Wichita State University.

Library of Congress Cataloging-in-Publication Data

Names: Strum, Philippa, author.
Title: On account of sex : Ruth Bader Ginsburg and the making of gender
equality law / Philippa Strum.
Description: Lawrence, Kansas : University Press of Kansas, 2022. | Series:
Landmark law cases and American society | Includes bibliographical
references and index.
Identifiers: LCCN 2021057718
ISBN 9780700633432 (paperback)
ISBN 9780700633449 (ebook)
Subjects: LCSH: Women's rights—United States—Cases. | Ginsburg, Ruth
Bader, 1933-2020—Influence. | Women judges—United States—Biography. |
Women lawyers—United States—Biography.
Classification: LCC KF4758 .S775 2022 | DDC 347.73/2634—dc23/eng/20220408
LC record available at https://lccn.loc.gov/2021057718.

British Library Cataloguing-in-Publication Data is available.

Printed in the United States of America

10 9 8 7 6 5 4 3 2

The paper used in this publication is acid free and meets the minimum requirements of
the American National Standard for Permanence of Paper for Printed Library Materials
Z39.48–1992.

For Alexa Lauren Weiss
for whom RBG helped pave the way

CONTENTS

EDITORS' PREFACE

This is a book about access: access to the courts for women whose equality under law was routinely dismissed or undervalued; access to legal remedies that were, before Ruth Bader Ginsburg and her cohort arrived, nearly invisible; and access to Ginsburg's story. Although perhaps better known as a crusading and beloved member of the Supreme Court, Ginsburg's most important contribution to American law and American life may have lain in the years prior to her appointment to the Court of Appeals for the District of Columbia and then to the US Supreme Court. In these years, while she taught civil procedure and other subjects at Columbia Law School, she formulated and helped argue a series of cases that opened the door to genuine equality for women.

Professor Strum, the author of this book, is well known to readers of the University Press of Kansas's Landmark Law Cases series. Her volumes on the *Skokie* case, *Whitney v. California*, and *Mendez v. Westminster* garnered accolades from academic and general readers alike. Currently, Strum is a Global Fellow at the Woodrow Wilson International Center for Scholars and was the center's former director of the Division of United States Studies as well as Broeklundian Professor of Political Science Emerita, City University of New York.

Strum follows Ginsburg (and the court) from case to case, exploring and explaining how Ginsburg and her allies at the American Civil Liberties Union crafted the new feminist jurisprudence. Strum brings people into the story, employing many of the players' own accounts. And the reader knows where Strum stands—alongside Ginsburg. As Strum writes of the beginning of Ginsburg's brief in *Reed v. Reed* (1971), "Just as the court had erred on the subject of race but had corrected its mistake in recent years, the brief suggested, it could do the same on the subject of sex. Pulling no punches, Ginsburg told the justices that the court had contributed to societal inequality for decades."

This is a book that no one who wants to know more about Ruth Bader Ginsburg, the rights of women, and the US Constitution can afford to miss.

ACKNOWLEDGMENTS

As always, it took a village, and some of its denizens have been pressed into service for more than just this project. Their willingness to help with yet another manuscript puts me even more deeply in their debt.

The villagers include Jill Norgren, who has cheerfully plowed through rough and second drafts of mine for decades and who did so again for this book. I cannot wish anything better for a scholar than the colleague and friend she has been and is. The Red Line Group—Marie Therese Connolly, Mary Ellen Curtin, Matthew Dallek, and Robyn Muncy—came together at the Woodrow Wilson International Center for Scholars in 2007, and we have been critiquing one another's manuscripts since then. Their friendship and encouragement have been a source of support and joy for me for well over a decade. Harry Hirsch and John Ferren read through drafts once more, and they, too, are among the people I rely on. I can't imagine sending a manuscript off to a publisher before all these villagers have vetted and improved it.

Two other fellow authors gave me generous and invaluable advice. Patricia O'Toole critiqued a very early draft of two chapters, and Patrick Youngblood cast his critical eagle eye over the entire next-to-final draft.

Claire Moses, who knows more women's history than I ever will, shared her expertise for that aspect of the book. Terra Weiss read and provided helpful comments for five chapters.

As has been the case for more than two decades, my thanks go to the Woodrow Wilson Center, my scholarly home. It gives me space and resources without asking anything other than collegiality in return, which is a rare blessing. I am particularly grateful to our talented librarians: Janet Spikes, Michelle Kamelich, and Katherine Wahler.

Thanks are owed as well to the librarians in the Law Library and Manuscripts Division of the Library of Congress. Their expertise and their willingness to be as helpful as possible even when the library was closed during the pandemic are remarkable.

It was a great pleasure as well as enlightening to speak with some of Ruth Bader Ginsburg's former students and colleagues—Jane Booth, Brenda Feigen, Elizabeth Langer, Margaret Moses, Kathleen Peratis,

Patricia Ramsay, Susan Deller Ross, and Mel Wulf—and I thank them for their accessibility and their patience.

I was privileged to interview RBG at various times over more than four decades. I first spoke with her in 1979, when she was still working on the American Civil Liberties Union (ACLU)'s Women's Rights Project, and then I interviewed her repeatedly beginning in 1994, when she was the junior justice on the Supreme Court. She later vetted the manuscript of my book about the *VMI* case and reminisced again about her days at the ACLU. We last spoke early in 2020, when she agreed to be interviewed once again and to look at the draft of this manuscript when it was completed. First the pandemic and then her death made neither of those things possible, of course, and I regret that this book did not have the benefit of more of her memories and insights. I am grateful to her for making it possible for me to see otherwise unavailable documents in the Supreme Court library and for her permission to use her papers in the Library of Congress.

Finally, thanks go to the always professional and ever-patient staff at the University Press of Kansas: Senior Editor David Congdon, Managing Editor Kelly Chrisman Jacques, Andrea Laws, Derek Helms, Suzanne Galle, and Penelope Cray.

Introduction

The marble plaza in front of the United States Supreme Court was a sea of black. Somberly garbed mourners filled the plaza itself, while others stood in hushed rows on the imposing set of steps leading up to the massive bronze front door. Inside the building, the doors to the courtroom were draped in black. Across First Street NE, the flags above the US Capitol flew at half-staff.

It was September 23, 2020. Five days earlier, Justice Ruth Bader Ginsburg died of metastatic pancreatic cancer. It was her more than one hundred former clerks who lined the courthouse steps as officers of the Supreme Court Police carried her casket into the building's Great Hall. They were there to mourn the first woman justice to be memorialized in the nation's highest tribunal.

Television cameras in the Great Hall enabled the world to watch as Rabbi Lauren Holtzblatt and Chief Justice John Roberts eulogized the late justice. Rabbi Holtzblatt, whose husband had clerked for Justice Ginsburg, would officiate two days later, when another memorial ceremony was held inside the US Capitol. There, Justice Ginsburg lay in state, the first woman and the first Jewish American to do so.

There was an unprecedented outpouring of grief and respect across the nation. Flags were lowered in state capitols from Maine to Georgia. Citizens demonstrated quietly in towns, state capitols, and courthouses throughout the country, from Sacramento, California, to Boise, Idaho, and Concord, New Hampshire. Little girls, walking beside their parents, were dressed as the justice in her frilly white judicial collars and oversized round glasses. Little boys carried homemade signs with crayoned sketches of the justice affectionately known as RBG. New York City renamed the Brooklyn Municipal Building for her; a Rutgers University residential building in Newark, New Jersey, became Ruth Bader

Ginsburg Hall. Elsewhere in the world—Canada, France, Spain—prime ministers and presidents joined in the tributes.

Ginsburg had been a fine judge, unswerving in her calls for justice and human rights. Some of the dissents she wrote during her final years on the Supreme Court may well become guideposts for future decisions. That, however, did not differentiate her from other former members of the nation's highest court. What made her distinctive was not her distinguished career as a jurist but her work in the 1970s, long before she became a member of the Supreme Court. Turning to those years, Rabbi Holtzblatt eulogized Ginsburg as a prophet. "It's the rare prophet," she said at the Supreme Court ceremony, "who not only imagines a new world but also makes that new world a reality in her lifetime."

That is what Ginsburg did: imagine a world, or at least a nation, in which women possessed the legal opportunity to do everything done by men. It was her phenomenally successful work as an advocate for equal rights for women that led to the extraordinary expressions of grief and to the celebrations of her life. And it is that work that this book is about: the landmark cases that played a crucial role in changing the laws of the United States.

The story of those cases would be incomplete without some background information about the way in which Ginsburg became a women's rights advocate and how that affected her litigation strategy. Every story about the law, after all, is as much about the people in it as it is about legal doctrines. This book, however, is in no way meant as a biography of Ginsburg in her prejudicial years. Similarly, an important part of the tale concerns the American Civil Liberties Union, which enabled Ginsburg to bring the gender equality cases, and the evolution of that organization into one supportive of women's rights—but this certainly is not a history of the ACLU either. Instead, the primary focus is on the cases themselves.

A book of this length necessarily involves choices about what to include and what to leave out. Among the things for which space was inadequate are the contributions of dozens if not hundreds of other women, men, and civil society organizations to the push for legal gender equality in the years covered here. I mention some of them but apologize for having to leave to others the full story of how important they were. Ginsburg, as she would have been the first to say, did not do it alone.

A final note: I hope the way case names are presented is not confusing to the reader. The accepted style, which I follow, is to italicize case names. Sometimes Ginsburg and others referred to cases without using italics, or by underlining them, and where I quote from those sources, I use the style in the original.

In 1978, Ginsburg gave a keynote address at a West Virginia University women's conference. Looking back into American history, she told the conferees that "the Constitution was viewed by jurists until well past this century's midpoint as a virtually empty cupboard for sex equality claims." What follows is the story of how that changed.

CHAPTER I

Beginnings

There were some 160,000 lawyers in the United States in 1933, but only about 3,400 of them—less than 2.5 percent—were women. So no one could predict, when Joan Ruth Bader was born on March 15, 1933, a rainy wind-lashed day in New York City, that she would someday join their ranks. In fact, she almost didn't.

Joan Ruth was the second child of Celia Amster Bader, a Queens homemaker and bookkeeper, and Nathan Bader, a small businessman. Both parents were Jewish immigrants: Nathan from Russia; Celia, from Poland (although, as she arrived in her mother's womb and was born in the United States, she was not technically an immigrant). Celia graduated from a New York high school at age fifteen, but her family was poor, boys took precedence over girls, and Celia had to give up her hopes for more education and go to work so her brother could attend college.

A year after Joan Ruth's birth, the Baders' six-year-old daughter, Marilyn, died from spinal meningitis. The grief-stricken parents moved their family away from a place of sad memories and to a new home in Brooklyn. Their surviving daughter, soon known as Ruth because there were too many Joans in her kindergarten class, became a true Brooklynite. "I went to Ebbets Field religiously" to cheer for the Brooklyn Dodgers, she would remember. Sports fervor didn't prevent her from excelling in the local elementary school: She graduated from PS 238 at the top of her class. At James Madison High School, she again earned high grades, but she also found time for baton twirling on the school cheerleading squad and playing cello in the school orchestra (she played the piano as well).

Ruth was one of the top students picked to speak at Madison's graduation ceremony on June 27, 1950. She didn't get to the graduation, however, because two days earlier, tragedy struck the Bader household once again. Celia Bader lost a years-long battle with cancer. She remained a guiding force in her daughter's life nonetheless. When Ginsburg was nominated to the US Supreme Court, she said about herself and her mother, "I pray that I may be all that she would have been had she lived in an age when women could aspire and achieve and daughters are cherished as much as sons."

Ginsburg frequently spoke about other important influences in her life. One was books. Celia Bader instilled a love of reading and learning by taking her daughter to the public library every Friday afternoon and allowing her to choose the three books she would devour that week in addition to her schoolwork. Ginsburg remembered being inspired by the poet Emma Lazarus, because of her love for humankind, and Henrietta Szold, the feminist who founded the Jewish women's charitable health organization called Hadassah. The little girl became a believer in human rights quite early. An editorial she wrote as an eighth grader in 1946 lauded the new United Nations Charter and placed it in a line of important documents such as the Ten Commandments and the Declaration of Independence.

Some influences were a matter of simple chance, as were some of the teachers she encountered and a particularly important blind date. The teachers were at Cornell University, which she attended on scholarships from 1950 to 1954. One day, she went to the office of Robert E. Cushman, the noted scholar with whom she took a constitutional law course, hoping that he could help her make sense of the House Un-American Activities Committee's 1950s hearings into alleged Communists. Realizing her potential, Cushman asked the young student to become his research assistant and eventually suggested that she consider going to law school. While at Cornell, she also took a course in European literature with Vladimir Nabokov, whom she credited, along with Cushman, with having taught her to write succinctly. Nabokov, she said, "changed the way I read, the way I write." His teaching would stand her in good stead once she began litigating. When writing a brief, she said, "You have to keep it simple. You have to remember that judges are overwhelmed with reading cases briefs, so it was my aim to try to write a brief that . . . could be made the opinion of the court."

The blind date that proved to be so consequential was with fellow Cornell student Martin D. Ginsburg, known as Marty. He became first her best friend and then her husband. "I had the great good fortune to marry a man who thought my work was as important as his," she would say, describing him as the only man she dated who was interested in her brain. They married in 1954, a week after her graduation from Cornell, continuing a love affair that ended only with Marty's death in 2010. "I have had more than a little bit of luck in life," she wrote later, "but nothing equals in magnitude my marriage to Martin D. Ginsburg." The newly married couple moved to Fort Sill, Oklahoma, where Marty fulfilled his two-year army service obligation and their daughter, Jane, was born.

The Ginsburgs had long planned to go to graduate school together once Marty's army service was over. He was a year ahead of Ruth in school, so he would begin graduate school earlier. Their first choice was the Harvard Business School, which Marty favored, but they discovered that it would not admit women. The Harvard Law School, however, had begun accepting women in 1950. The idea of going there appealed to Ruth; her work with Professor Cushman had made her think that lawyers could be consequential and that a career in the law might be a way to contribute to society.

And so, because of the Business School's disdain for women, Ruth Bader Ginsburg got the legal education that would set the stage for her to become one of the nation's most consequential attorneys.

She entered Harvard in the fall of 1956, one of ten women in a law school class of roughly 500 (one woman dropped out after the first year, so the number is usually given as nine). Ginsburg would note later that women were then less than 3 percent of American lawyers and that they were as much of an anomaly at the Harvard Law School as they were in the legal profession at large. Their secondary status was reflected in something as seemingly trivial as bathrooms. The law school held classes in two buildings, but only one of them, Austin Hall, had a women's room, and it was down in the basement. (Nancy Boxley Tepper, one of the only women in the class before Ginsburg's, remembered it as a janitor's bathroom.) "That made it pretty tough if you were taking a class in the other building, in Langdell, worse if you were taking an exam," Ginsburg recalled. "Yet we never complained. That was just the way it was."

The paucity of women's rooms was but one indication of the law school's resistance to the presence of women in what had formerly been exclusively the ranks of men. The male students gave the female students derogatory nicknames; the criminal law professors deliberately embarrassed them by calling upon them to describe rape cases in intimate detail. Because there were so few women, "most sections had just 2 women, and you felt that every eye was on you," Ginsburg remembered. "Every time you went to answer a question, you were answering for your entire sex. It may not have been true, but certainly you felt that way. You were different and the object of curiosity."

Erwin Griswold was the dean of the law school when Ginsburg arrived in Cambridge. Every year, he held a dinner for the new female students, assigning a male faculty member as an escort for each woman. It didn't occur to Griswold that a woman student might be married or, as Ginsburg was when she arrived at Harvard, the mother of a fourteen-month-old child. After dinner in Ginsburg's year, the group retired to the Griswolds' living room. Ginsburg was seated next to her escort, the legal scholar Herbert Wechsler. Smoking was still fashionable then, and Ginsburg held their joint ashtray on her lap as Griswold asked each of the women why they were in law school, "occupying a seat that could be held by a man." As Ginsburg remembered,

> I rose when called on, and there went the cigarette butts, spread about the rug in front of me. . . . If only I had a button to push, so I could vanish through a trap door! . . . I mumbled something about my husband being in the second-year class and how important it was for a wife to understand her husband's work. I didn't mean to say that, but that's what came out.

(Years later, Ginsburg came to believe that Griswold actually favored having women at the law school and asked the question to gather ammunition when he was challenged by other faculty members.)

Ginsburg thrived at Harvard in spite of that contretemps, earning grades so high that she was invited to serve on the *Harvard Law Review*, the prestigious journal published by the law school's best students. When she was chosen as one of its editors, she decided to take her mother-in-law to the *Review*'s annual banquet at the Harvard Club in Boston. The club, however, maintained a strict men-only policy and refused to make an exception for anyone other than the two women students who had been elected to the law review.

When Marty graduated from Harvard in 1958, he landed a job with a

New York City law firm, and Ruth transferred to Columbia Law School for her final year. There, she earned grades that once again put her at the top of her class. She was one of a dozen women in a class of roughly three hundred and the only woman in her class to make law review.

That record made no difference when it came to getting a job. She applied to law firm after law firm, signing up "for every interview I could get," but none wanted a woman. Marty Ginsburg remembered that one firm told her, "We had a woman once, but she didn't work out." Ginsburg would later say she had three strikes against her: She was a woman, Jewish, and a mother.

Top law school students commonly clerk for a judge after graduation. The distinguished legal scholar Gerald Gunther, one of Ginsburg's Columbia professors, considered her to be "a brilliant student" who "demonstrated extraordinary intellectual capacities." Charged with obtaining clerkships for graduating Columbia Law students, Gunther might well have considered Ginsburg to be an obvious choice. When that proved not to be true, with one federal judge after another declining to hire a woman, he turned to Judge Edmund L. Palmieri of the federal district court in Manhattan. Palmieri hired only Columbia clerks recommended by Gunther, but, he said, he had no place for a woman with a four-year-old child. Gunther told Palmieri that if he didn't hire Ginsburg, Gunther would never again send him any other potential clerk. The professor suggested a compromise: Palmieri would hire Ginsburg, but Gunther would arrange for another (male) Columbia graduate to take leave from his Wall Street firm if Ginsburg didn't work out.

She did "work out" and clerked for Palmieri for two years. The male backup presumably remained at his firm.

Once Ginsburg had completed her clerkship with Palmieri, the logical next step was to apply for a US Supreme Court clerkship, as did many young lawyers who had clerked for a lower court judge. Albert M. Sacks, another of her former Columbia professors, tried to get her a clerkship with Justice Felix Frankfurter, but Frankfurter was horrified at the idea of a woman lawyer working in his chambers. Fortunately, a quite different kind of opportunity appeared. Columbia's law school had created a Project on International Procedure that examined codes of procedure in other countries in order to educate American attorneys about them. The project's director invited Ginsburg to work for it as a research assistant for a year while she learned Swedish and then to go to Sweden to study and write about the Swedish code with a Swedish judge as her coauthor. Ginsburg took the job, and in 1962, now reasonably proficient in Swedish, she began living intermittently in Stockholm. One result was the more than a dozen articles and books about the Swedish legal system that she wrote over the next few years.

Ginsburg's Swedish experience had an even more significant effect on her. "My eyes were opened up in Sweden," she later said. Unlike the situation in the United States, women made up about a quarter of law students, and the country was immersed in a discussion about why women should have two jobs—workplace and home—while men had only one. The Swedish government began to take measures to undo sex-role stereotypes, introducing parental leave for men and affirmative action for both sexes. At the same time, Ginsburg read feminist Simone de Beauvoir's *The Second Sex*, which she called "an eye-opener." She would mentally file the book and the Swedish model away for later use: "I put it all on a back burner until the late 60s when the women's movement came alive in the United States."

Ginsburg returned to the United States for good in 1963—and found a country in transition. The 1950s was the era of the civil rights revolution. One outcome of the marching and demonstrating and litigating by Black Americans and their allies was the Supreme Court's landmark *Brown v. Board of Education* decision of 1954, declaring that racial segregation in public schools was unconstitutional. The civil rights movement, along with *Brown* and its progeny, helped awaken many Americans to the damage done by policies of exclusion. Exclusion stigmatized; exclusion denied equal opportunities for employment and participation in civic life, as well as for education. Suddenly, equality and equal opportunity were part of the national conversation. Women activists were determined to include gender inequalities in the discussion, and in the next few years, many of them would set their sights on the workplace.

By the 1960s, the reality of life had changed from what it was decades earlier for many American women. Forty percent of all women over the age of 16 were in the paid workforce. That number included 30 percent of married women and 39 percent of women with children aged six to 17. More women than ever were going to college; 53 percent of those who graduated held paid jobs. Employment outside the home was no longer the domain of women who had to work for economic reasons—although many of them did, as the post–World War II inflation had made a second income necessary for many families. Historian William Chafe noted that by the 1960s, "a growing number of women appeared to value a job for its own sake and for the personal rewards it conferred. . . . The home remained a central focus of female life, but it had ceased to be the only focus."

Women were now freer to take control of their employment and other aspects of their lives by planning their pregnancies. On June 23, 1960, the federal Food and Drug Administration approved the sale of an oral contraceptive. Within two years, 1.2 million American women were using "the pill." By 1965, that number had grown to 6.5 million, and one out of every four wives under the age of forty-five had used it. The effect on women's aspirations was nothing short of revolutionary. Their control of a society that still treated women very differently from men, however, was not as great, and many clamored for the government to do something about it.

In 1961, President John F. Kennedy, bowing to growing public sentiment, appointed former first lady Eleanor Roosevelt as chair of a new President's Commission on the Status of Women. Its report, *American Women*, was published in 1963. The voluminous document detailed the extent to which American women were deprived of equal rights and equal opportunities. Simultaneously, Congress finally enacted the 1963 Equal Pay Act, which had been introduced in one form or another since the 1940s. The first federal law to ban sex discrimination, it mandated equal wages for men and women doing equal work. It was limited in scope and largely honored in the breech, but it was indicative of changing social mores. That same year, Betty Friedan published *The Feminine Mystique*, a powerful indictment of the "separate spheres" ideology that left so many American women out of public life and confined to a private one that was less than fulfilling.

The year 1963 also witnessed the March on Washington and Dr. Martin Luther King Jr.'s stirring "I Have a Dream" speech. Congress, beginning to catch up with the civil rights movement and what was still a contested but increasingly powerful new societal focus on equality, started to debate the proposed 1964 Civil Rights Act. Title VII of the act, as originally written, prohibited employment discrimination on the basis of race, color, religion, and national origin—but not sex.

That was not acceptable to some of the newer women legislators who had entered Congress in the last decade. Like Congresswoman Martha Griffiths, who had been elected from Michigan in 1955, they initially hoped that the Supreme Court would use the Fourteenth Amendment to begin striking down statutory gender inequality. That had not happened. "There never was a time when decisions of the Supreme Court could not have done everything we ask today," Griffiths would tell Congress in 1970, speaking in favor of the proposed Equal Rights Amendment. (The text of the proposed amendment is, "Equality of rights under the law shall not be denied or abridged by the United States or by any state on account of sex.") "The Court has held for 98 years that women, as a class, are not entitled to equal protection of the laws," Griffiths said. "They are not 'persons' within the meaning of the Constitution." She was referring to the Equal Protection Clause of the Fourteenth Amendment to the US Constitution, enacted in 1868 following the Civil War. The amendment says in part, "No State shall . . . deny to any person within its jurisdiction the equal protection of the laws." Back in 1963, believing that the legislature would have to do what the court would not, Griffiths and her colleagues maneuvered successfully to include the word "sex" in Title VII.

Title VII created the Equal Employment Opportunity Commission, with a mandate to investigate claims of employment discrimination. The new commission focused on race discrimination and paid little attention to sex discrimination. Herman Edelsberg, its executive director, called the addition of "sex" in the law a "fluke" that was "conceived out of wedlock." The commission's lack of interest in the workplace problems that women faced was so flagrant that a primarily but not exclusively female group of participants in the 1966 federally sponsored Third Annual Conference on the Status of Women walked out of the conference and, gathering in a nearby hotel room, created the National Organization for Women. Other civil society organizations devoted to gender equality followed in the next few years.

Things were slowly changing in the society at large and, in a small and very incomplete way, so were law schools. In 1963, soon after Ginsburg returned to New York from Sweden, Columbia law school professor Walter Gellhorn told her that the Rutgers University law school in Newark was looking for someone to teach civil procedure. She got the job, which also involved teaching comparative law and federal jurisdiction. After some months at Rutgers, Ginsburg discovered that in spite of the Equal Pay Act and Title VII, the law school was paying her less than a male colleague. When she complained to the dean, his explanation was, "You know, Ruth, he has a wife and two children to support and your husband has a well-paid job in New York." To him, paying men more was only fair. The possibility of wives playing a significant or even major part in a family's economic well-being did not occur to him—or to many others of his generation. And when Ginsburg became pregnant, she could not be certain he would approve of a professor who would soon give birth. She was working on a year-to-year contract, and Title VII notwithstanding, "my concern was if I revealed my pregnancy, that would be the end of my job." Her mother-in-law wore clothes that were a size larger, and Ginsburg dressed herself in those until a new contract was in hand and she felt she could safely tell her colleagues about the pregnancy.

As were her colleagues, most of Ginsburg's students at Rutgers were men. "When I began teaching law in 1963, few women appeared on the roster of students, no more than four or five in a class of over one hundred." The numbers of women gradually increased, both because changing conceptions of sex roles were affecting some young women's career aspirations and because in 1968, federal law was revised so that men were no longer able to avoid the Vietnam War draft by enrolling in graduate school. Law schools that had previously kept potential women students at a minimum were suddenly anxious about the flow of tuition money and began to recruit them. By the 1969–1970 school year, women composed 13 percent of the students at the Rutgers Law School, which was ahead of many others in admitting women and racial minorities. The first-year class of 320 included more than sixty women. (There would be even more women after 1972, when an amendment to federal law forbade educational institutions that received federal funds—which meant most institutions of higher education—from discriminating on the basis of sex.)

It proved to be a critical mass. The women arrived well aware of, and part of, the women's movement, and in 1969 some of them asked Ginsburg if she would consider teaching a course on women and the law. By then, Ginsburg had been promoted to full professor with tenure and could safely embark on something new to the law school. Deciding to read everything that had been written on the subject, she quickly discovered that there was in fact relatively little. Instead, there was a series of Supreme Court decisions demonstrating disinterest in gender equality at best and, at worst, hostility to the very idea.

*   *   *

> "The paramount destiny and mission of woman are to fulfil [*sic*] the noble and benign offices of wife and mother. This is the law of the Creator."

Those were the words of US Supreme Court Justice Joseph B. Bradley in 1873, concurring with the court's ruling in *Bradwell v. Illinois* that Illinois had a constitutional right to prevent women from becoming lawyers. There was no question that Bradley reflected the attitude of most Americans, as well as the members of the legal profession. Social mores and the law were clear: Women belonged in the home; men, out in the world.

Belief in separate spheres of activity for men and women, with women relegated to the private domestic sphere and public life reserved for men, was built into the American political ideology from its earliest days. Back in 1776, before there even was a United States, Abigail Adams admonished her husband, John, a leader of the American revolutionary movement and a future president, to treat women fairly. "In the new Code of Laws which I suppose it will be necessary for you to make," she famously wrote to him, "I desire you would Remember the Ladies, and be more generous and favourable to them than your ancestors." Far from remembering "the Ladies," however, Adams and the other Founding Fathers hewed to the society's gender norms and wrote a Constitution based on the assumption that women would have no political role. Adams was scarcely alone in his views, of course. In 1816, Adams's great friend Thomas Jefferson wrote to a correspondent, "were our state a pure democracy, in which all it's [*sic*] inhabitants should meet together to transact all their business, there would yet be excluded from their deliberations . . . women; who, to prevent depravation of morals, and ambiguity of issue, could not mix promiscuously in the public meetings of men." The other groups Jefferson mentioned as unfit to participate in a democracy were infants and slaves.

Ginsburg would quote Jefferson's words when she began litigating before the Supreme Court, citing him as indicative of the way women had been trivialized throughout American history. "Until the latter half of the 19th century," she noted, "married women could not contract, hold property, sue in their own names, or even control their own earnings." The Supreme Court didn't see much wrong with that, and it made its feelings clear when in 1873 it decided the Bradwell case, in which Justice Bradley penned his view of women's place.

Myra Bradwell was a highly successful businesswoman who owned and ran an Illinois printing and binding company. She had studied law with her husband, a county judge. (In those days, when there were very few law schools in the United States, most would-be lawyers studied with an established attorney and then took a bar exam.) In 1868, Bradwell's familiarity with the law led her to create and publish the *Chicago Legal News*. Within a decade, it was the country's most widely circulated legal newspaper.

In 1869, deciding to apply for a license to practice as well as publish material about the law, Bradwell took and passed the state bar exam with high honors. Following Illinois law, she then applied to the state supreme court for her license. The court turned her down. Sorry, the judges said; no women allowed.

An outraged Bradwell appealed to the US Supreme Court. Another section of the Fourteenth Amendment to the US Constitution reads in part, "All persons born or naturalized in the United States . . . are citizens of the United States, and of the State wherein they reside. No State shall make or enforce any law which shall abridge the privileges or immunities of citizens of the United States." Bradwell contended that one of the "privileges" protected by that part of the Fourteenth Amendment was the right to choose one's work, and that as an American citizen she was entitled to the privilege of working in her chosen profession. Not so, said the Supreme Court; the amendment did not preclude each state from deciding on the qualifications necessary to practice a profession. Justice Bradley added his assertion that the law was best left to men.

So, according to the Supreme Court, was the ballot box. Just a few years after its decision in *Bradwell v. Illinois*, the justices weighed in again on the matter of women in the public sphere. This time the case involved Virginia Minor, a Missouri resident, who on October 15, 1872, attempted unsuccessfully to register to vote in the presidential election. Both Minor and her husband, Francis, were committed suffragists who thought the time was right to bring a test case about voting. *Minor v. Happersett* (Happersett was the official who refused to register Minor) was in fact brought by both Minors because, under the laws of the time, a married woman could not sue independently. Happersett relied on the Missouri constitution, which said, "Every male citizen of the United States shall be entitled to vote." Federal law, however, outweighs and can be used to overturn state law. Like Myra Bradwell, Francis Minor, a lawyer who argued the case himself, invoked the Fourteenth Amendment's Privileges and Immunities Clause to argue that the US Constitution gave Virginia Minor a right to vote. The state courts of Missouri disagreed. So did the US Supreme Court.

Chief Justice Morrison Waite acknowledged that Minor was indeed a citizen. He went on at great length to demonstrate that women could be citizens, suggesting, perhaps, that there might be some doubt about it. He cited the historical exclusion of women from the polls, however, as he held for a unanimous court that citizenship in the United States had never included the right to vote. The Constitution explicitly left requirements for suffrage up to the states, Waite wrote. Missouri had acted well within its power by limiting the suffrage to men, as had all the other states that did so. "If the law is wrong," he concluded, "it ought to be changed; but the power for that is not with us." Or, as Ginsburg later described what the court told Virginia Minor in 1875, "You are a citizen. But so too are children. And who would think that children should have the right to vote?"

Minor reacted to the decision by petitioning for an exemption from property taxes, arguing—again unsuccessfully—that if she could not vote, she should not be subject to taxes. "The fact is," the *Richmond* [Missouri] *Democrat* chided in 1879, "Mrs. Minor has a husband to do the voting for the family. . . . The husband is the legitimate head and protector of the family, and a woman unsexes herself when she attempts to assume his duties."

At the time the court decided Virginia Minor's case, almost all of the states deprived women of the right to vote, asserting that the female sex had no place in the public sphere. In fact, however, the nation's economic well-being depended on many women coming out of their homes. The court's decisions, and the popular conception of women as homebodies, took no notice of the extent to which women were actually in the public sphere—as workers rather than voters. This came to the court's attention in 1908, when it heard from attorneys for Curt Muller.

Mr. Muller was the proprietor of Muller's Grand Laundry in Portland, Oregon. The Supreme Court had held in 1905, in the case of *Lochner v. New York*, that laws establishing maximum work hours violated the right of employees to contract for as many hours as they and their employers chose. Two years earlier, however, Oregon passed a law establishing a maximum of ten hours' work a day for women employed in manufacturing, mechanical establishments, and laundries. It did so after an attempt to establish maximum hours for both male and female workers failed in the state legislature. Joe Haselbock, who ran the Grand Laundry for Mr. Muller, broke the Oregon law when he required Mrs. Elmer Gotcher to work more than ten hours. (It was common in those days for a married woman to be known by her husband's name rather than her own—another sign of female dependence—so Emma Gotcher's first name does not appear at all in the proceedings.) A state court found Muller guilty of violating the law and imposed a fine of ten dollars. Incensed, he appealed on the grounds that maximum hours laws were unconstitutional. The Oregon Supreme Court affirmed his conviction, and Muller then took his case to the US Supreme Court.

Oregon hired attorney Louis Dembitz Brandeis to represent the state before the high court, and the brief that he submitted in the case not only changed the course of American legal history but became central to the kind of litigation gender equality advocates would bring in the 1970s. Instead of the usual brief with numerous pages of legal arguments, Brandeis limited his legal argumentation to two pages. Next came fifteen pages of excerpts from state and foreign laws limiting women's hours, to demonstrate that such maximum hours laws were not unusual and were considered rational in many jurisdictions. The bulk of the brief, however, consisted of ninety-five pages citing US state and European reports documenting the negative effect that long working hours had on women's health and the well-being of their families. The brief and Brandeis's oral argument before the court were centered on societal facts and urged the justices to take note of what was actually happening in society rather than limit themselves to legal precedents and treatises.

The Brandeis approach worked. The court upheld the Oregon law, with Justice David Brewer writing for himself and all his brethren. The view of women that illuminated his opinion, and presumably that of the other justices, is worth quoting here.

That woman's physical structure and the performance of maternal functions place her at a disadvantage in the struggle for subsistence is obvious. This is especially true when the burdens of motherhood are upon her. Even when they are not, by abundant testimony of the medical fraternity, continuance for a long time on her feet at work, repeating this from day to day, tends to injurious effects upon the body, and, as healthy mothers are essential to vigorous offspring, the physical wellbeing of woman becomes an object of public interest and care in order to preserve the strength and vigor of the race. . . . It is impossible to close one's eyes to the fact that she still looks to her brother, and depends upon him.

Oregon won its case, but at the cost of the Supreme Court declaring in effect that women were inferior and dependent creatures whose well-being was at the same time necessary for the preservation of the race. Ginsburg would nonetheless use the example of the Brandeis brief to great advantage. "While the *Muller* decision was a precedent I sought to undo, the method Brandeis used to prevail in that case is one I admired and copied," she wrote, adding, "The aim of the Brandeis brief was to educate the Judiciary about the real world in which the laws under inspection operated."

The real-world actuality that the court ignored was that there had always been American women in the paid workforce. Mrs. Gotcher's colleagues in Muller's laundry were women, as were immigrant women and poorer women in the paid workforce throughout the United States. Black women had always worked outside their homes, most of them first as slaves and then as paid workers after the Civil War. So had Mexican American women, toiling in the fields and the homes of more privileged families throughout the Southwest.

But it was not only poorer women who were working in the public sphere. The bulk of what came to be called the Brandeis brief actually was written by two women in professional jobs. Josephine Goldmark was Brandeis's sister-in-law, and Florence Kelley was the secretary general of the National Consumers League. Kelley, who had served as chief factory inspector for the state of Illinois, also held a law degree. Goldmark had taught at Barnard College and would go on to publish numerous works about women and children. Much of the information in the brief was compiled by Pauline Goldmark, another Brandeis sister-in-law. Her career included serving as the manager of the Women's Service Section of the US Railroad Administration. All three of the women, then, were involved in public policy-making.

They were far from the only ones. In 1869, the Wyoming Territory granted suffrage to women, as did the Utah Territory in 1870, the state of Colorado in 1893, and Idaho in 1896. Women were running for and winning local office in many states. In 1887, for example, Susanna Salter of Argonia, Kansas, became the first woman in the country to be elected as a mayor. Lucy Flower was elected as a trustee of the University of Illinois in 1894. Two years later, Dr. Martha Hughes Cannon took her seat in the Utah State Senate, three other women were elected to the state legislature of Colorado, and Esther Johnson was elected to the city council of Gaylord, Kansas. After the US Supreme Court declined in Myra Bradwell's case to admit women lawyers to practice before it, attorney Belva Lockwood persuaded Congress to enact an 1879 statute requiring the court to admit women. Back in 1872, while *Bradwell v. Illinois* was working its way through the courts, Illinois passed a bill providing that no one could be excluded from any occupation because of sex. Alta Hulette, who drafted the bill, became Illinois's first licensed woman lawyer. In 1907, Catharine McCulloch was elected as Illinois's first woman justice of the peace. There were seventy-five women lawyers in the United States in 1880; by 1900, the number had grown to 1,010. According to the US Census Bureau, in 1890, 4,557 American women were practicing medicine. By 1900, the numbers had increased to 7,387; by 1910, to 9,015. Women professionals were still very much a minority, but the trend was clear: Women were doing more and more of the jobs once considered the sole domain of men.

All that happened before the Supreme Court heard *Muller v. Oregon*, but it in no way affected the justices' belief that women were delicate creatures in need of the protection of men and the state. "Doubtless there are individual exceptions," Justice Brewer wrote, but they did not change the fact that "she is properly placed in a class by herself, and legislation designed for her protection may be sustained even when like legislation is not necessary for men."

It was possible to see protective legislation for women as a victory for workers, back in the years when American courts routinely struck down maximum hour and minimum wage laws, but protective legislation also limited women's access to well-paid jobs. In 1924, for example, the Supreme Court upheld a New York law that prohibited restaurants from employing women between 10 p.m. and 6 a.m. That, the court noted in *Radice v. New York*, kept women from being employed "as singers and performers, attendants in ladies' cloak room and parlors . . . in dining rooms and kitchens" during those hours. The court did not mention that those were the hours when wages and tips were likely to be highest. Justice George Sutherland wrote for the court in upholding the law. The state had argued that "night work of the kind prohibited . . . injuriously affects the physical condition of women, and . . . threatens to impair their peculiar and natural functions." Sutherland agreed. "Considering their more delicate organism," it was not unreasonable for the state to decide that women needed the protection of the state—and men could have a monopoly on well-paying jobs.

Only a year earlier, in *Adkins v. Children's Hospital*, the Supreme Court had struck down a law that mandated minimum wages for women and children in the District of Columbia. Justice Sutherland rather astonishingly declared for the court that recent developments such as the passage in 1920 of the Nineteenth Amendment, which gave women the vote, made such legislation unnecessary. "The ancient inequality of the sexes," he wrote, "has continued 'with diminishing intensity.' In view of the great—not to say revolutionary—changes which have taken place" since the *Muller* decision, "in the contractual, political and civil status of women, culminating in the Nineteenth Amendment, it is not unreasonable to say that these differences have now come almost, if not quite, to the vanishing point." So women were helpless creatures in need of protection by the government when it came to the number of hours they could work but not when a law guaranteed them a decent working wage.

This seemingly contradictory behavior by the court is explained by the justices' insistence on the doctrine of liberty of contract. Beginning in 1905, in the case of *Lochner v. New York* mentioned earlier, the court had utilized the doctrine to strike down reformers' attempts to protect workers by enacting maximum hours and minimum wage laws. The decision in *Muller* was therefore an outlier, and a court determined to protect employers rather than workers was equally determined to safeguard "liberty of contract." That accounts for Sutherland's view that "while the physical differences [of men and women] must be recognized in appropriate cases, and legislation fixing hours or conditions of work may properly take them into account, we cannot accept the doctrine that women of mature age . . . require or may be subjected to restrictions upon their liberty of contract which could not lawfully be imposed in the case of men under similar circumstances."

Sutherland's contorted reasoning notwithstanding, by the time the court decided the *Atkins* and *Radice* cases in 1923 and 1924, there were indeed small but telling changes in what the society would permit at least some women to do. Four women had been elected to the US House of Representatives. Nine women, in addition to the trailblazing Belva Lockwood, had argued before the Supreme Court. Two of those women, Annette Abbott Adams and Mabel Walker Willebrandt, were assistant attorneys general of the United States. None of that altered the justices' perceptions. Like much of the society they served, the men on the Supreme Court saw women in policy-making positions as anomalies, quite as rare and exotic as unicorns. Ginsburg would one day comment, dryly, "Ratification in 1920 of the Nineteenth Amendment, which secured to women citizens the right to vote, stimulated no dynamic change in constitutional interpretation."

That remained true for many years more. In 1948, the Supreme Court decided a case that began when Valentine Goesaert, a widow who wanted to continue running the bar in Dearborn, Michigan, that she inherited from her late husband, challenged a state law that forbade any woman to tend bar unless she was the wife or daughter of the male owner of a licensed liquor establishment. Women had been bartenders in Michigan and elsewhere during World War II, when many men were serving in the armed forces, but once the war ended, the all-male Michigan Bartenders Union decided that the women should go home. The bartenders told legislators that "liquor alone causes enough trouble, why add women?" and in 1945 Michigan changed its laws to protect the livelihood of male bartenders from the competition of women. Goesaert brought suit on behalf of herself, her daughter Margaret, and more than twenty other

Michigan women bartenders and bar owners, claiming that the statute violated the Fourteenth Amendment.

Goesaert's case was based on the Equal Protection Clause. The clause would become the foundation for the cases brought by Ginsburg in the 1970s, but that was very much in the future when the Supreme Court decided *Goesaert v. Cleary.* Justice Felix Frankfurter wrote for the majority of the justices in holding the line for tradition and a view of women's morals as requiring protection by the state. Noting that there had been "vast changes in the social and legal position of women," Frankfurter nonetheless declared that Michigan had acted reasonably when it passed the law. "The fact that women may now have achieved the virtues that men have long claimed as their prerogatives, and now indulge in vices that men have long practiced," he asserted from his paternalistic perch, "does not preclude the States from drawing a sharp line between the sexes. . . . The Constitution does not require legislatures to reflect sociological insight, or shifting social standards, any more than it requires them to keep abreast of the latest scientific standards."

It was exactly the need for the Constitution to "reflect . . . social standards" and social realities that would become the basis for the cases that Ginsburg would bring to the Supreme Court in the 1970s. She would characterize the *Goesaert* decision as reflecting, instead, "an antiquarian male attitude toward women—man as provider, man as protector, man as guardian of female morality."

It is worth remembering that Justice Frankfurter exhibited that "antiquarian" attitude in daily life as well as in his jurisprudence, when in 1960 he turned Ginsburg down as a possible law clerk. It is equally notable that Valentine Goesaert was represented before the Supreme Court by Detroit attorney Anne R. Davidow. Whether Frankfurter considered the fact that a women attorney argued the case to be a virtue, or one of the vices, is unclear.

Women in the Jury Box

The Sixth Amendment to the Constitution guarantees any person accused of a crime the right to be tried by a jury. It says nothing, however, about who can or should sit on such a jury.

The Supreme Court addressed that issue in 1879 in *Strauder v. West Virginia*. A Black man who was convicted for the murder of his wife challenged the verdict because West Virginia law excluded everyone but white men from jury service. That, he argued, violated his Fourteenth Amendment right to the equal protection of the laws. The court agreed that the exclusion of Black men violated the Equal Protection Clause but, in doing so, indicated that it was constitutional for women to be excluded. The Fourteenth Amendment forbade the state from discriminating on the basis of race or color but not gender, the court declared. "We do not say," Justice William Strong wrote for the court, "a state may not prescribe the qualifications of its jurors, and, in so doing, make discriminations. It may confine the selection to males" as well as to such other categories as property holders or "persons having educational qualifications."

The federal government has one court system, and in addition each of the states has its own. In 1946, in the case of *Ballard v. United States*, the Supreme Court held that women could not be excluded from federal juries. Justice William O. Douglas wrote in *Ballard* that "the two sexes are not fungible" and that limiting juries to men not only injured the defendant in a case but did damage as well to "the jury system, to the law as an institution, to the community at large, and to the democratic ideal reflected in the processes of our courts." The decision, however, applied only to federal courts, and the states were still free to exclude women from juries.

Women in Florida, as well as in some other states, worked to change that. By 1961, forty-seven states had declared women eligible for jury duty in state and local courts. Only Alabama, Mississippi, and South Carolina refused to recognize female jury service in those courtrooms. Eighteen states, including Florida, accorded women an absolute exemption, as did the District of Columbia.

No woman had served on any jury in Florida until 1949. In 1943, a woman member of the Florida legislature introduced a bill to require women to serve just as men did. Appalled opponents said they did not want "their wives and sisters exposed to the embarrassment of hearing filthy evidence," and the bill was voted down. Six years later, the legislature passed a compromise law providing that women's names could be added to the jury pool, but only if a woman wanting to serve went to the county courthouse and registered with the clerk of the circuit court. Men were automatically added to the pool, without registering. Most women did not register, and it is likely that many did not even know of the opportunity to do so.

That was the situation in 1957, when thirty-three-year-old Gwendolyn Hoyt was tried for murder. She had suffered years of mental and physical abuse at the hands of Clarence Hoyt, the high school boyfriend she married when she was seventeen. Gwendolyn would testify that a few months before the case began, Clarence

> went into a rage and he started to throw things around in the kitchen and [began] scooping things off counters and then he went into the living room and was tipping over chairs and tables and broke our lamps and then he went into our bedroom and he threw our night stand into the living room . . . he went after me and he tore my dress off . . . and he threw me from the door on to the bed and he started to choke me and said he would kill me.

He was repeatedly unfaithful and, at the time of the murder, had left his wife to live with his latest mistress. On the evening of September 19, 1957, he nonetheless decided to pay a visit to the modest one-story Hoyt home in Tampa and relax on the living room couch. Gwendolyn pleaded with him to return to her and their three children, and when he refused, she grabbed a broken baseball bat and hit him. She claimed that she had aimed at his arm but, when she realized she had hit his head and he was seriously wounded, she telephoned for the family doctor. He refused to come. Gwendolyn then called an ambulance. Clarence arrived at the hospital bleeding profusely and barely conscious and died some hours later.

Gwendolyn, who had a history of epilepsy, pled temporary insanity. The all-male six-man jury deliberated for only half an hour before finding her guilty of murder in the second degree. Her appeal, *Hoyt v. Florida*, eventually reached the US Supreme Court, where her attorney argued that the Florida practice of automatically registering male but not female voters had deprived her of a jury of her peers and therefore of the equal protection of the laws. "We don't know what women would have done on that jury," attorney Herbert Ehrmann told the justices. "But shouldn't she have had a chance of having a woman on the jury who would have said: 'Now, wait a minute. The woman saw her home, her husband and father of her child going?' Wasn't she entitled to have people who think like that on the jury?" George R. Georgieff, the Florida assistant attorney general who appeared for the state, countered that there were "classic differences" between men and women. Women "have functions to perform that no ascension up the scale can change. They bear our children. They are the ones that rear them, not the men. This is their function." The implication was that one function was all they could handle.

In 1961 the Supreme Court ruled, unanimously, that Florida had acted reasonably. There was no constitutional right, Justice John Marshall Harlan II wrote, "to a jury tailored to the circumstances of the particular case, whether relating to the sex or other condition of the defendant." Florida had acted "in pursuit of the general welfare" by letting a woman choose not to serve on a jury "unless she herself determines that such service is consistent with her own special responsibilities." That was because "despite the enlightened emancipation of women from the restrictions and protections of bygone years, and their entry into many parts of community life formerly considered to be reserved to men, woman is still regarded as the center of home and family life." Justice Harlan applauded "the continuing validity of this Court's dictum in *Strauder v. West Virginia* . . . to the effect that a State may constitutionally 'confine' jury duty 'to males,'" noting that it was a stance that the court had maintained "for more than eighty years." The court had seen nothing in those years to make it change its collective mind.

Three of the justices who would be known as great civil libertarians—Chief Justice Earl Warren and associate justices William O. Douglas and Hugo Black—concurred in the decision, which effectively validated the separate spheres theory once again. As Ginsburg wrote years later, with some restraint, "evening up the rights, responsibilities, and opportunities of men and women was not on the agenda of the Warren Court." It appeared that Hoyt would have to serve her sentence of thirty years of hard labor, and she was taken off to prison—although, as the justices could not know, she would be released on parole after having been incarcerated for under three years.

When the case went to the US Supreme Court, the Florida affiliate of the American Civil Liberties Union (ACLU) submitted an amicus ("friend of the court") brief on her behalf. It was the first amicus brief filed by the ACLU in a sex discrimination case. The primary author was Dorothy Kenyon, one of the first women to graduate from New York University's law school and a fierce advocate for women's rights. Kenyon was a longtime member of the board of directors of the national ACLU, which paid for the work that went into the writing and filing of the brief. Ginsburg, who would take Kenyon as one of her role models, commented in 1989 about the *Hoyt* decision that "the Justices did not comprehend the differential treatment of men and women in jury selection and other contexts as in any sense *burdensome* to women." When she began litigating before the Supreme Court in 1971, Ginsburg listed overturning *Bradwell, Muller, Goesaert*, and *Hoyt* as among her primary goals. She would also refer to the *Hoyt* case in 1993, on the first day of the hearings to confirm her nomination to the US Supreme Court, when she was asked to speak about the cases that had the most meaning for her.

Kenyon lamented the inability of the justices, along with many other men and women, to understand that minimizing women's public role was a burden rather than a gift. That inability was no longer universal. A *Washington Post* editorial about the Hoyt case, for example, opined that "the most enlightened jurisdictions now make women as welcome in the jury box as they are in the voting booth. The few states that are still holding out against feminine jurors would do well to correct this deficiency." It noted that the 1957 Civil Rights Act had codified women's eligibility for jury service in the federal courts, following the lead of the court's decision in the *Ballard* case.

Still, ideas about women's difference seemed almost hardwired into American thinking. In 1966, Congresswoman Martha Griffiths attempted to push Congress to make federal jury service not merely permissible but as compulsory for women as it was for men. New York City congressman Emanuel Celler, a seeming champion of women's rights who had long advocated permitting women to sit on federal juries, arose and mused aloud, "Frankly, I am caught between the urging of the gentlewoman from Michigan and a male constituent, who expects a hot meal on the table when he returns from work. Is it the gentlewoman's desire to come between man and wife?" As historian Linda Kerber has noted, "No one worried about who cooked Gwendolyn Hoyt's dinner."

* * *

The relationship between the Supreme Court and the society at large is a complicated one. There are times when the court is seemingly out in front of the public, as in its famous "separate is not equal" dictum in *Brown v. Board of Education* (1954) or its declaration in *Obergefell v. Hodges* (2015) that same-sex marriage is constitutionally protected. A closer look, however, suggests that the court is for the most part an extremely conservative institution that takes what appear to be radical steps only when a clear legal framework has been laid and there is a growing if far from universal agreement that it is time for change. "Courts," legal historian Richard Klarman has noted, "are never at the vanguard of social reform." By 1954, there was not only a vibrant civil rights movement; there were also a number of Supreme Court precedents that stopped short of declaring separate education to be unequal but clearly laid the groundwork for that decision. The same was true in 2015, when there was not only a solid body of legal precedents but a marked change in society's attitudes toward homosexual rights. As of 1961, the court sensed no such sentiment about sex discrimination in the body public.

One might think of a movement for social change as a train, with the Supreme Court as a car somewhere in the middle. The engine and the first few cars represent a shift in societal attitudes, and along with it comes mobilization for action. After a while, that pulls the elected lawmakers along. Next comes the Supreme Court, which reflects what has already happened and helps push the train further. Legal scholar David Cole summed up the constitutional situation at the time of the *Hoyt* case and in the years immediately following by writing, "The legal situation in the late sixties and early seventies mirrored the social framework; men saw women as different from men, and men's laws kept women different from men." It was precisely in those years that the question for Ginsburg became not only what she might teach about gender and the law but, in addition, how that legal situation might be changed. Her answer led her to a new beginning, which became a new beginning for women's constitutional rights as well.

CHAPTER 2

The Pedestal and the Cage

Ginsburg decided to accept her students' request to create a course on women and the law. Putting it together was not easy, because there was almost nothing useful in the very limited literature on the subject. She realized that she would have to provide her own materials, as did the few other law professors around the country who wanted to introduce a similar course. That is why, in 1971, Ginsburg became the faculty advisor of the *Women's Rights Law Reporter*, the first such journal in the country. A Rutgers law student named Elizabeth Langer had hosted the journal in her apartment a year earlier and was told that she could move it to the law school if, among other things, she found a faculty advisor. Ginsburg agreed to take on the job as soon as she was asked. Langer was pleasantly surprised, as until then her infant journal "had no money, no faculty, no backing," but "she went where other people wouldn't go. She took a leap." Once Ginsburg signed on, "everything fell into place," Langer added. The journal (which celebrated its fiftieth birthday in 2020) quickly began publishing scholarly articles that could be used in courses while giving students experience in conducting research about gender and the law. In 1974, Ginsburg, Herma Hill Kay, of the University of California's Berkeley Law School, and Kenneth Davidson, of Yale Law School, published the country's first sex discrimination casebook for use in law schools.

At the same time that her students asked to study women and the law, Ginsburg began dealing with sex discrimination in the world outside the classroom. The American Civil Liberties Union (ACLU) has statewide affiliates across the country. Stephen Nagler, the executive director of the New Jersey affiliate, was already using Rutgers students and faculty in some of the affiliate's work. Knowing that Ginsburg taught procedure (not to mention that she was one of only two women on the law school faculty), he asked her to handle cases that involved something new to the affiliate: women alleging that they were being denied due process because of gender discrimination. In the late 1960s and early 1970s, complaints began coming in from teachers who were being forced to give up their jobs when a pregnancy began to show. "After all," Ginsburg commented sarcastically, "the children must be spared the thought that their teacher had swallowed a watermelon." Next came cases of other kinds of gender discrimination, such as those from women whose employers provided family health insurance only for male employees and from parents whose daughters were denied admission to publicly financed educational programs that were available to boys. Ginsburg took the cases and usually won a settlement. She agreed to volunteer for the ACLU "more because it was a respectable way of getting litigation experience than out of ideological reasons, I will admit," she recalled, but the ideology was not far behind.

Many things had come together for Ginsburg by 1969: the refusal of law firms and federal judges to acknowledge her abilities when she graduated from law school, her experience in Sweden, the pay disparity for women law school professors, the raised consciousness of her Rutgers students, the plight of her ACLU clients, the publication of *The Second Sex*, and, of course, the changes that were in the societal air. Whether or not she thought of herself as such, Ginsburg was now an activist in the women's rights movement. "I was lucky to be in the right place, at the right time" she would say about the new turn in her life. "Women generations before said the same things my generation was saying, but they did so at a time when no one, or precious few, were prepared to listen." "Since 1969," she told an interviewer in 1976, "everything that I've done has centered around women's rights."

As she worked on her New Jersey ACLU cases, Ginsburg turned to her students for help. That would later become a hallmark of her litigation before the Supreme Court. The best law school students are always eager to gain "real-world" experience in addition to their studies, and litigators who work for the public interest are always in need of willing personnel. The course on women and the law that she began teaching in the spring of 1971 would enable students to do research on gender discrimination in the law, providing data that would inform her arguments.

They, and Ginsburg, were about to get an opportunity to work on the law in a larger field. And Ginsburg was about to embark on her first major gender equality case.

The story behind the case began in 1968, when a Colorado man named Charles E. Moritz claimed a $600 deduction on his federal tax return for "household help for invalid mother." A full-time editor whose work required him to travel, Moritz had spent $1,250 in 1968 for the care of his mentally impaired and wheelchair-bound eighty-nine-year-old parent. The Internal Revenue Service disallowed the claim, because Section 214 of the Internal Revenue Code limited the deduction for dependent care to "a taxpayer who is a woman or widower, or . . . a husband whose wife is incapacitated or is institutionalized." Moritz appealed to the Tax Court, arguing that the denial amounted to sex discrimination. An unmarried woman was covered by the law; he, a bachelor, was not. "If I were a dutiful daughter instead of a dutiful son, I would have been granted the deduction," Moritz wrote in the papers he filed for himself. "This makes no sense." The Tax Court disagreed and denied his appeal. Distinctions among people benefiting from a law "are within the grace of Congress," Judge Norman O. Tietjens wrote, and since the law treated Moritz in exactly the same way as all other unmarried male caretakers, he had not been deprived of due process.

Marty Ginsburg, by then a specialist in tax law, read about the *Moritz* decision at home one evening in 1970. He walked into the room where his wife was working and suggested that she look at it. Doubting that she'd be interested in a tax case, she read it anyway. As Marty remembered, she immediately understood it as an instance of flagrant sex discrimination, and her response was a smiling, "Let's take it!" Ruth firmly believed that gender stereotypes embodied in the law hurt both sexes, arbitrarily shunting them into unrealistic boxes. Charles Moritz's case would give her the opportunity to make that clear. The Ginsburgs hoped Moritz would agree to let them represent him in appealing the decision to the Court of Appeals for the Tenth Circuit, the federal appeals court that covers Colorado as well as a number of other western states. Seeking institutional backing, the Ginsburgs turned to the ACLU. What neither of them knew was that by 1970 the national organization had been gradually moving toward taking a major role in the fight against sex discrimination.

* * *

Back in 1961, when Dorothy Kenyon submitted the ACLU's amicus brief to the US Supreme Court in Gwendolyn Hoyt's jury case, it was the culmination of her decades-long effort to push the organization to oppose discrimination against women. During World War II, with women a vital part of the paid workforce, she had persuaded the organization to create a Committee on Discrimination against Women in Employment. In 1945, again at her urging, the organization adopted a statement that "the right to work is rapidly becoming for most women as important an economic right as it has always been for men." It was the ACLU's first comprehensive statement about women's rights. Kenyon went on to chair the ACLU's Women's Rights Committee and then its Equality Committee, using both forums to push the organization to fight against sex discrimination. During the 1940s and 1950s, Kenyon functioned as what historian Susan Hartmann has described as the ACLU's "resident expert on women's rights." In the late 1950s and early 1960s, inspired by the civil rights movement's use of the Fourteenth Amendment's Equal Protection Clause to litigate for equality, Kenyon became convinced that it could also be used on behalf of women. That led to her brief in Gwendolyn Hoyt's case. The ACLU's equality work, however, was still devoted primarily to race, not sex.

Kenyon acquired a vital ally in 1965, when Pauli Murray joined the ACLU's national board. Murray, a fifty-five-year-old Black attorney who had long experienced both racial and gender discrimination, was a member of the Committee on Civil and Political Rights of the President's Commission on the Status of Women. In that capacity, she wrote a report that advocated bringing sex discrimination cases with Brandeis-style briefs that would present the realities of women's situation to courts and place their claims about discrimination firmly in the Fourteenth Amendment's Equal Protection Clause.

Building on her report, Murray and Mary O. Eastwood—a Department of Justice lawyer who, like Murray, was a member of the committee as well as one of the founders of the National Organization for Women—penned an article titled "Jane Crow and the Law: Sex Discrimination and Title VII." Its thesis was that

> sex discrimination can be better understood if compared with race discrimination and that recognition of the similarities of the two

problems can be helpful in improving and clarifying the legal status of women.... That manifestations of racial prejudice have been more brutal than the more subtle manifestations of prejudice by reason of sex in no way diminishes the force of the equally obvious fact that the rights of women and the rights of Negroes are only different phases of the fundamental and indivisible issue of human rights.

Just as the Supreme Court of the 1950s had to be pushed to interpret the Equal Protection Clause as a bulwark against racial discrimination, they asserted, so a concerted effort to get the justices to apply the clause to sex discrimination should now be mounted. It was what Kenyon had been telling the ACLU for years. It was also the tactic that would subsequently be used by Ruth Bader Ginsburg. The analogy between race and sex would be a hallmark of her litigation strategy.

Murray gave Kenyon a copy of the article, and the two of them got to work to convince the ACLU staff and board that gender equality litigation ought to be an organizational priority. In 1965, the ACLU sued Lowndes County, Alabama, for systematically keeping Black men, and women of all races, off juries. It was in keeping with the ACLU's focus to that date that the organization challenged the exclusion of Black men, but it was because of Kenyon's nonstop efforts that the ACLU was ready to add the exclusion of women to its case. She and Murray wrote the section of the ACLU's brief dealing with women and appended "Jane Crow and the Law" to it. The three-judge district court that heard the case of *White v. Crook* found both practices to be unconstitutional and specifically held that keeping women from jury service violated the Equal Protection Clause. It was not the total vindication for the *Hoyt* decision that Kenyon would have liked, as the states still had the power to make female but not male service voluntary rather than compulsory, but it was a big step in the right direction.

By the late 1960s and early 1970s, a component of committed feminists had been added to the ACLU board, which had always had some women members but had been dominated by men. In addition to Kenyon and Murray, it now included women activists such as Faith Seidenberg, a leader of the National Organization for Women (NOW) whom Ginsburg considered a luminary of the drive for gender equality; Wilma Scott Heide, chair of the NOW board of directors; Margie Pitts Hames, the vice president of the Georgia Women's Political Caucus, who would argue a companion case to *Roe v. Wade* before the Supreme Court; and Suzy Post, one of the founders of the Kentucky Women's Political Caucus. Still, the women on the board had an uphill job in raising the consciousness of their fellow directors. In September 1970, for example, the board was set to discuss the question of whether it should support the Equal Rights Amendment. After receiving their materials for the meeting, Kenyon and Murray sent a telegram to the entire board. "Board materials include paper on Equal Rights Amendment written by four men law professors and (inadvertently) not one syllable from any women," it said. "We are aghast at such gallant effrontery. Hell hath no rage greater than a woman scorned. Beware of more materials."

Fortunately, it was not just the women of the ACLU who were determined to work on gender discrimination. Melvin Wulf, who became the organization's legal director in 1962, coincidentally knew Ginsburg from summer days when they were both youngsters at Camp Che-Na-Wah. He, older than she, was a waiter, and she was one of the campers assigned to his table. Wulf went on to become a lawyer and an advocate for the rights of women as well as racial minorities. In 1970, he was joined at the ACLU by Aryeh Neier, the organization's new thirty-three-year-old executive director. Surveying the enormous changes in American racial equality law that were in part the work of the Warren Court, Neier commented, "Nothing seemed beyond the reach of litigation." The ACLU was able to undertake its civil rights cases in the 1960s in part because of grants it received from private foundations for special projects. Neier saw that as a model for future ACLU work in other areas, and "one of the issues I particularly wanted to deal with was the question of women's rights."

The ACLU held summer conferences every two years that brought together staff and lay leaders from both national headquarters and ACLU affiliates around the country. Dorothy Kenyon, Pauli Murray, Suzy Post, Faith Seidenberg, and other ACLU women formed an ad hoc committee on women's rights at the June 1970 biennial and persuaded the assembled leaders to adopt a resolution opposing various forms of sex discrimination. The national board followed in the autumn of 1970 by voting to put women's rights at the top of the organization's agenda and asking affiliates to give women's rights "a high priority in funding and litigative activity." It asked Kenyon's Equality Committee to prepare a plan of action for the national office.

When the Ginsburgs asked Mel Wulf about the possibility of making Charles Moritz's appeal an ACLU case, therefore—with Ruth Ginsburg sending him a copy of the Tax Court's decision and telling him that it was "as neat a craft as one could find to test sex-based discrimination against the Constitution"—they were preaching to the choir. If the decision could be overturned, Ginsburg wrote to Wulf, "an important foothold will be secured for women's rights cases." Wulf quickly agreed, and three days later he told her the ACLU would finance the case.

As the organization's legal director, Wulf was listed along with both Ginsburgs as an author of the brief in *Moritz v. Commissioner of Internal Revenue*. It was, however, essentially Ruth Bader Ginsburg who wrote it. While it was the first brief she had ever written in a case before a federal court, it did not read like a beginner's effort. She consulted Norman Dorsen, a seasoned litigator and ACLU general counsel who would later become ACLU president. It was, he wrote to her, "one of the very best presentations I have seen in a long time." Ginsburg would call it "the grandmother brief," as it was "a model for briefs I later filed in the Supreme Court."

Most of the brief dealt with the constitutional issue. The Fourteenth Amendment's Equal Protection Clause binds only the states, not the federal government, but, as the brief pointed out, it was well established law that the Fifth Amendment's Due Process Clause ("No person shall . . . be deprived of life, liberty, or property, without due process of law") incorporated the right to equal protection of the laws. That meant that the federal government could differentiate between people—in effect, treat them unequally—only if the differentiation did not violate the Constitution. The court, Ginsburg wrote, had already looked carefully at laws that classified people when it decided racial discrimination cases, and she repeatedly referred to what she saw as the legal parallel between race and sex. It was true that cases such as *Goesaert v. Cleary*, the 1948 bartender case, had held that legislatures could treat women differently than men. Similarly, however, the court had held in cases such as *Plessy v. Ferguson* (1896) that legislatures could treat Black Americans differently than white Americans. "Today, of course," Ginsburg wrote, "a classification based on race, creed or national origins is 'suspect' or 'invidious' and a very heavy burden of justification is demanded of a legislature which draws such a distinction." Just as the court had undone *Plessy* when it handed down its decision in *Brown v. Board of Education* in 1954, she argued, so it could update its reading of the Equal Protection Clause as it applied to women.

How, then, was a court to evaluate whether a classification was constitutionally justified? Again referring to and quoting from race discrimination cases, the brief asserted that if a law affects "fundamental rights or interests . . . or when the statute classifies on a basis 'inherently suspect,' the courts will subject the legislation to the most rigid scrutiny." That meant, to Ginsburg, that the court should approach sex-based classifications the way it treated race-based classifications, establishing that they were "suspect" classifications. If a court considered a classification to be "suspect," its assumption was that the law was unconstitutional, and the burden of proof was on the government to prove otherwise.

That assumption was quite different from the way courts treated most laws that were attacked as unconstitutional. The standard in those cases was reasonableness, she wrote: "Does the classification . . . bear a reasonable and just relation to the permissible objective of the legislation?" "Reasonableness" was a far less stringent standard than "suspect," putting the burden of proof on the complainant, which is why Ginsburg would argue in this and some of her subsequent gender discrimination cases that the courts should apply the more difficult "suspect" test.

Ginsburg recognized that she was advocating something new for the courts and didn't really expect that they would immediately apply the suspect classification test to sex discrimination. As was mentioned earlier, law and courts are inherently conservative, based as they are on what is, not what could be. Major changes in the law, Ginsburg understood, required a step-by-step strategy. She had nonetheless come to hope that a series of cases would gradually get the courts there. In the *Moritz* brief, she began laying out her reasoning. "No longer shackled by decisions reflecting social and economic conditions or legal and political theories of an earlier era," lower courts had begun striking down laws discriminating against women. "The trend is clearly discernible," she went on. "Legislative discrimination grounded on sex, for purposes unrelated to any biological or functional difference between the sexes, ranks with legislative discrimination based on race, another condition of birth." But wasn't this a case where a man, rather than a woman, was being discriminated against? "While instances of discrimination against women dominate the rapidly developing case law in this area, the constitutional sword necessarily has two edges. Fair and equal treatment for women means fair and equal treatment for members of both sexes." The "constitutional guarantees of the due process and equal protection apply to all *persons*, a class in which men and women share full membership." That assertion would become a hallmark of Ginsburg's litigation: Distinctions between the sexes "for a purpose unrelated to any biological or functional difference" hurt men as well as women and so should be treated with suspicion by the courts.

Because of her doubt that the court would go so far as to declare sex a "suspect classification," Ginsburg would argue that even if the "reasonableness" or "rational basis" test was applied, the distinction between men and women in the *Moritz* case was unconstitutional. There, Marty Ginsburg's familiarity with tax law came in extremely handy. He pointed out that in the 1920 tax case of *F.S. Royster Guano Company v. Virginia*, the Supreme Court had held that classifications "must be reasonable, not arbitrary, and must rest upon some ground of difference having a fair and substantial relation to the object of the legislation, so that all persons similarly circumstanced shall be treated alike." There was nothing reasonable about treating single never-married men differently from single never-married women if the object of the law in the *Moritz* case was, as the *Congressional Record* showed, to grant relief to "taxpayers who, if they are to be gainfully employed, must provide care for physically or mentally incapacitated dependents." Before appealing to the Tax Court, Ginsburg noted, Charles Moritz had asked the Department of the Treasury, of which the Internal Revenue Service is a part, about the reasons for the sex-based categories of people eligible for the deduction. John S. Nolan, the deputy assistant secretary in charge of the Tax Section, had responded in effect that he didn't understand them either.

If the court of appeals accepted the view that the distinction was irrational, then what was the appropriate remedy? Should it strike the provision of the tax code, undoing the deduction for everyone? That was of course not the Ginsburgs' purpose. "The last thing we wanted was for the Court to say the law was bad," Ginsburg said, looking back at the case. "The law was just fine, but you just forgot someone. Include the category you left out and then the law became constitutional." It was, she noted "the first time that we dealt with the extension issue," arguing that a law that discriminated unfairly against either of the sexes should be extended to cover both rather than be overturned.

Oral argument in the case was scheduled for October 28, 1970. The Ginsburgs flew to Denver and met the night before with Moritz, with whom they had communicated only by mail and telephone. Moritz, who had thought he was getting a crank call when Marty Ginsburg first contacted him about taking the case, had promised the Ginsburgs that he would see the case through even if the government offered to settle. Marty's background in tax law led him to predict that such an offer would be made. After seeing the Ginsburgs' docketing brief, in which they urged the court to hear the case, the government had indeed offered to settle for one dollar. The Ginsburgs, however, wanted to make this a test case. Now they and the government would face off in court. Marty took the first twelve minutes of oral argument to discuss the tax law; Ruth, the second half to make the constitutional argument. It was her first presentation before a federal court. If they won, it would be another first: No court had ever overturned a provision of the US tax law.

James H. Bozarth argued for the government that Congress, as a matter of "legislative grace," had the right to decide upon whom to confer tax deductions. Deciding to allow this one for women but not men was rational, as women historically had earned less than men and were therefore in greater need of government help. Moreover, he said, the deduction was meant only for people who could have cared for the disabled parent themselves, had they not had to work. The implication was that women could be assumed to be competent caretakers, but men could not.

The court of appeals handed down its ruling more than a year later, on November 22, 1972. It was a complete victory for the Ginsburgs. It was of course a victory for Moritz and the growing drive for legal gender equality as well, but its greatest consequence may have been for Ruth Bader Ginsburg. The case, Marty wrote, "fueled Ruth's early 1970s career shift from diligent academic to enormously skilled and successful appellate advocate."

"It is true that deductions are a matter of legislative grace and that they must be authorized by a clear provision under which the taxpayer must qualify," Judge William J. Holloway Jr. wrote for himself and the two other judges who heard the case. "However, if the Congress determines to grant deductions of a general type, a denial of them to a particular class may not be based on an invidious discrimination." The distinction here "is not one having a fair and substantial relation to the object of the legislation dealing with the amelioration of burdens on the taxpayer." Instead, the law "made a special discrimination premised on sex alone, which cannot stand." The court held, accepting the Ginsburgs' extension argument, that "the benefit of the deduction generally provided by the statute should be extended to the taxpayer." Instead of striking the entire provision down, the court mandated that it be interpreted for the benefit of Moritz and other men in his position.

Congress had amended the law in December 1971 to cover unmarried men as well as unmarried women, but it was effective for taxable years only after that and so didn't affect Moritz's case. The government was nonetheless determined to overturn the court of appeals decision, worried that it would be used to challenge yet other laws that differentiated between men and women. Deciding to appeal to the US Supreme Court, the Department of Justice put together a team headed by Solicitor General Erwin Griswold, Ginsburg's former Harvard Law School dean. The brief that the department submitted to the Supreme Court argued that the tax law's distinction between men and women was valid, given the well-documented fact that women "usually assume the burden of care of dependents" and "usually work on lower pay scales and at lower paying jobs than men." Griswold added that negating the distinction between the sexes would have the unfortunate effect of "cast[ing] a cloud of unconstitutionality" upon a huge number of other federal laws that were sex-related.

To demonstrate the disruption such a decision would cause, Griswold turned to the Department of Defense. Computerized data was still in its early days and personal computers did not yet exist, so Griswold relied upon the Department of Defense's huge mainframe to provide him with a list of federal statutes that differentiated on the basis of sex. The list of more than eight hundred federal laws, as Ginsburg later commented, was "a treasure trove" and "a road map, a pearl beyond price." She noted that "over the balance of the decade, in Congress, federal courts, and the Supreme Court, aided by the ACLU's Women's Rights Project, I successfully urged the unconstitutionality of those statutes." Or, as Marty

Ginsburg would write, "with Dean Griswold's help, Mr. Moritz's case furnished the litigation agenda Ruth actively pursued" throughout the remainder of her years as a litigating attorney.

* * *

The Supreme Court declined to hear the *Moritz* case, which left the court of appeals decision in place. It is unclear why Judge Holloway and his colleagues had taken so long to issue their ruling, but by the time they did, it was almost ignored in the excitement about a much more consequential holding that had been handed down exactly one year earlier. It came in the case of *Reed v. Reed*, for which Ruth Bader Ginsburg had written her first full Supreme Court brief.

Sally and Cecil Reed were a divorced couple living in Boise, Idaho. They had an adopted son, Richard, known as Skip, and over the years each had custody of him at different times. By 1967, when Skip was a teenager, he was living with Sally but was under a court order to spend weekends with his father and the father's second family. Skip disliked being at his father's house, and on one fateful weekend, he called his mother and begged to come home. Under the court order, there was nothing she could do. Skip went down to the basement and killed himself with his father's hunting rifle.

A grieving Sally filed a petition to be the administrator of Skip's estate, not wanting Cecil, whom she blamed for her son's death, to take possession of Skip's few personal belongings. Cecil filed his own competing petition. The probate court judge who heard the case found for Cecil, on the basis of an Idaho statute that said, "Of several persons claiming and equally entitled" to administer an estate, "males must be preferred to females."

Sally had supported herself after the divorce by looking after disabled people in her home and ironing, baking, and babysitting. She used her small earnings to hire an attorney to take the case to the probate court. When she asked him to appeal its decision, he said that she had no chance of winning and refused to continue. So did sixteen other lawyers she approached, but she finally found Allen Derr, an attorney who thought the case was worth pursuing. He filed an appeal with a state district court, claiming that the automatic preference for men violated the Fourteenth Amendment's Equal Protection Clause. The court agreed, but in February 1970, its decision was reversed by the Idaho Supreme Court.

Sally Reed wanted to appeal that holding to the US Supreme Court. Her funds were running out, however, and Derr could not afford to do all the necessary work without pay. The Idaho Supreme Court ruling was reported in *U.S. Law Week*, which covers important cases from around the nation. Marvin Karpatkin, an ACLU volunteer general counsel, read about it there and went to Mel Wulf. "This is the case that will turn the Supreme Court in a new direction," Ginsburg recalled his saying. It was the kind of case Dorothy Kenyon and Pauli Murray had been pushing the ACLU to pursue, seeking to use the Equal Protection Clause to challenge sex discrimination. The ACLU told Derr it would be glad to come into the case as an amicus curiae (friend of the court) and cover expenses. The first step was to petition the Supreme Court for certiorari (a place on its calendar), which can be granted by any four of the nine justices. In the spring of 1971, the court granted certiorari to *Reed v. Reed*.

The New Jersey ACLU's sex discrimination cases and the *Moritz* case had whetted Ginsburg's appetite for gender equality litigation. She had told Mel Wulf earlier that if the Supreme Court granted certiorari in *Reed*, she would be glad to work on the case. "Have you thought about whether it would be appropriate to have a woman co-counsel in this case?" she had written to him, enclosing a copy of her brief in *Moritz* and suggesting that "some of this should be useful for *Reed v. Reed*." Wulf agreed that it certainly would be wise as well as appropriate to have that particular woman on the case. As Ginsburg remembered, "I asked if I could write the brief. . . . *We* will write the brief," Wulf replied, and so the two of them got to work. "He wrote some parts, and I wrote other parts. Then we exchanged our drafts."

* * *

An attorney about to write a brief attacking a law that discriminated on the basis of sex had a variety of questions to consider. The justices would be familiar with all the cases effectively limiting women's participation in the public sphere, including Gwendolyn Hoyt's jury case of only ten years earlier. Should the brief attempt to distinguish those precedents from the issue in *Reed*, or should it argue that the earlier decisions were wrong? And if the latter seemed a desirable approach, what would be the basis for that claim? To what extent should the brief include societal facts as relevant to the argument? Was there a line of cases in other areas of the law to which the litigator could turn, in the way a tax case had provided an important precedent in *Moritz*? Should the approach be that the justices could surely see that there was no rational basis for giving Cecil Reed an automatic preference—the "reasonableness" test—so that the court could decide this case alone without reference to the issue of gender discrimination in a multiplicity of other laws? Was there a chance that if the brief made the larger claim about all sex-specific laws, the justices might be unwilling to accept the one about the Idaho statute? Or should the brief go for broke and insist, as the one in *Moritz* did, that the court should give the same level of skeptical scrutiny to laws that allegedly discriminated against women as it did to laws that differentiated on the basis of race?

In addressing these questions, Ginsburg had two models to follow. The first, which she had relied upon in *Moritz*, was the Brandeis brief: marshaling societal realities and insisting that laws had to be in keeping with their evolution. That would suggest that the earlier decisions were well past their sell-by date and deserved a place in the trash bin of history. The second model was the one used by the National Association for the Advancement of Colored People (NAACP) in its litigation against segregation. "We definitely copied Thurgood Marshall's method," Ginsburg said about her gender equality cases. "He was my model as a lawyer. . . . I took a step-by-step, incremental approach." She admired the way that in the cases leading up to *Brown v. Board of Education*, Marshall "didn't tell the court in the first case you have to declare a separate but equal in any and all circumstances unconstitutional. He had building blocks, so we copied that."

"Building blocks" meant leading the justices, case by case, to a recognition of the unconstitutional harm gender discrimination did to women. That was so even when laws seemed, as the court thought was the situation in *Hoyt*, to benefit women by not requiring them to serve on juries, or when the court in *Goesaert* agreed that women should not be exposed to the perceived immorality of bars. Ginsburg was all too aware that when she and Wulf began working on the brief, "the Supreme Court never saw a gender-based classification it didn't like or regarded as unconstitutional." The reason, she believed, was that most of the men in the courts at that time didn't associate discrimination in its unpleasant sense with the way women were treated. They thought of themselves as good husbands and good fathers. They genuinely believed that women had the best of all possible worlds. Women could work if they wanted to; they could stay home if they wanted to. . . . The challenge was to educate the men on the bench.

That is why, Ginsburg wrote, "as an advocate in gender discrimination cases in the Seventies, I thought of myself as akin to a grade school teacher." Her lesson for the justices was that disadvantaging people on the basis of their identity, whether it was race or sex, pigeonholed them as less than equal citizens and was therefore unconstitutional.

Ginsburg and Wulf had to consider what they knew about the justices on the Supreme Court. The court sometimes speaks with one voice, as if it was a monolithic institution. It more frequently does not, demonstrating that the personalities of the justices, perhaps their ideologies, and certainly their various understandings of the commands of the law, differ. What might they expect from each of the men who sat on the court?

Chief Justice Warren Burger was appointed to the Supreme Court in 1969 by President Richard M. Nixon. A longtime Republican Party activist, he had gained a reputation as a law and order judge while serving on the Eighth Circuit Court of Appeals. He was generally considered to be a conservative politically, as was Justice Harry Blackmun, another Nixon appointee as well as Burger's friend from their boyhood days in St. Paul, Minnesota. Blackmun, who had also served on the Eighth Circuit, was a newcomer to the court: He had taken his seat in 1970, only a year before *Reed* would be argued. It was widely assumed that Blackmun would follow the chief justice's lead in deciding cases, and in fact, journalists had taken to describing Burger and Blackmun as the "Minnesota twins."

The longest-serving members of the court were William O. Douglas and William J. Brennan Jr. Douglas, appointed by President Franklin D. Roosevelt in 1939, and Brennan, appointed by Eisenhower in 1956, had gained reputations as supportive of civil liberties and civil rights. Potter Stewart, another Eisenhower appointee (1958), was known as a centrist jurist who emphasized judicial restraint. Byron White was the only justice appointed by President John F. Kennedy (1962) still on the court. A former professional football player and strong JFK supporter as well as a brilliant lawyer, he was a hard-to-pigeonhole pragmatist in his approach to the law.

Thurgood Marshall was also now one of the justices, having been appointed by President Lyndon B. Johnson in 1967. It was still an all-male bench, however, as it had been since it first met in 1790. Marshall was the first Black American to serve on the court; all the others were white, and none was young. Chief Justice Warren Burger was in his sixties, as were Brennan, Blackmun, and Marshall. The comparatively younger men—Potter Stewart and Byron White—were in their mid-fifties. William O. Douglas, the oldest as well as the most senior member, was seventy-three. (The case would be heard by only seven rather than the usual nine justices. Associate Justices Hugo Black and John Marshall Harlan II both resigned in September 1971. Their successors, Justices Lewis Powell and William Rehnquist, were not nominated by President Nixon until October and were not confirmed until later that year, after oral argument in *Reed*.)

The justices' ages were not surprising, as elevation to the nation's highest court normally comes as the capstone of an attorney's career, not the beginning. The question, however, was whether men of their years would appreciate the relatively new realities of the 1970s and the role of women in it. Perhaps Marshall, who knew what it meant to be discriminated against, could be counted on. Justices Douglas, Brennan, and Stewart had been on the court when it held against Gwendolyn Hoyt. Douglas and Brennan were nonetheless generally considered to be liberal; Stewart, less so. What that would mean in the context of *Reed* was unclear.

A very mixed clue appeared on January 25, 1971, just months before Ginsburg and Wulf began work on *Reed*. The court handed down a per curiam decision (a decision by the entire court, with no specific author noted) in the case of *Phillips v. Martin Marietta Corporation*. It was brought by Ida Phillips, who had applied to Martin Marietta for a position as a factory assembly-trainee and was told that the corporation did not hire women with preschool children. It did, however, hire men with such children. Title VII of the 1964 Civil Rights Act required businesses to consider job applicants who had equal qualifications without regard to their sex. Both the federal district court and the court of appeals nonetheless found for Martin Marietta, holding that as women constituted some 75–80 percent of the people hired for the position, there had been no discrimination based on sex. It made no difference to the courts that none of the women who were hired had preschool children or that many of the men did.

The Supreme Court sent the case back for further consideration. Both of the lower courts had granted summary judgment; that is, they decided on the basis of written submissions by the parties but without a trial. The justices said the issue that should be addressed in a fuller process was whether not having preschool children was what the 1964 Act called "a bona fide occupational qualification reasonably necessary to the normal operation of that particular business or enterprise." Could the corporation, in other words, demonstrate that women with preschool children could not possibly do the job but men could?

Justice Marshall filed a concurring opinion saying that while he agreed that the case should be returned to the lower courts, "I fear that in this case, where the issue is not squarely before us, the Court has fallen into the trap of assuming that the [Civil Rights] Act permits ancient canards about the proper role of women to be a basis for discrimination." Marshall may have written the concurrence because while the court's ruling made it seem that the other justices refused to assume that motherhood of little children automatically disqualified a potential employee and were open to claims about sex discrimination, the demeanor of some of them during oral argument suggested otherwise. Chief Justice Burger had voted against the court's hearing the case at all and made sexist jokes to the young male lawyer arguing on behalf of Phillips. A number of the justices indulged during oral argument in what Mel Wulf described as "locker-room humor." So while Marshall's concurrence suggested that at least one of the justices was a probable vote for Sally Reed, there was reason for concern. Additionally, while the court had decided *Phillips* on the basis of the Civil Rights Act, Ginsburg and Wulf wanted to make the broader constitutional equal protection argument that had so far failed in every gender discrimination case in the court's history.

Preparation of a case that will be heard by the Supreme Court requires enormous labor—more than could be supplied by Wulf and Ginsburg alone. As they went to work, Ginsburg once again turned to law students, relying on what she called their "grand aid." This time they came from Rutgers, New York University, and Yale. One of them worked with Ginsburg to put together a list of the laws that treated women differently, or what Ginsburg called "a true sign of the time, a sampling of laws of the kind that then riddled the statute books of the U.S. and all 50 states." That would become the appendix to the brief.

If the Ginsburgs' brief in *Moritz* was the "grandmother," the ACLU brief in *Reed* was the "mother." "You can see a strong resemblance between the Moritz brief to the Tenth Circuit and the Reed brief in the Supreme Court," Ginsburg said later. All of what might be called the "daughter" briefs, to continue the analogy—that is, all of the Supreme Court briefs that Ginsburg filed in the next few years—essentially tracked the one in *Reed*. The details of course differed with the facts of each case and with the progression of cases, as Ginsburg would draw on the justices' decisions in earlier cases to support the later ones. The template, however, was *Reed*, and so it provides a view of Ginsburg's strategy and her thinking about how best to change the law.

The brief, which ran to sixty-four pages without the appendix, was designed to give the justices the elementary school education Ginsburg thought they needed. It included the usual list of relevant cases and laws, and citations of law review articles, but Ginsburg went beyond those. Chastising the Supreme Court for its past decisions as misguided when written and clearly antiquated in the 1970s, the brief suggested a way for the court to redeem itself. In true Brandeis brief style, it discussed what was actually happening in society and invited the justices to come into the late twentieth century.

The *Report of the President's Commission on the Status of Women* was cited. So were works such as Caroline Bird's *Born Female: The High Cost of Keeping Women Down*, Simone de Beauvoir's *The Second Sex*, statistics on women's employment compiled by the Departments of Labor and of Health, Education, and Welfare, and Elizabeth Janeway's *Man's World, Woman's Place: A Study in Social Mythology*. Leo Kanowitz's *Women and the Law: The Unfinished Revolution* stood side-by-side with Blackstone's *Commentaries on the Laws of England* and Justice Oliver Wendell Holmes's *Collected Legal Papers*; quotes from Henrik Ibsen's *A Doll's House*, John Stuart Mill's *The Subjection of Women*, and former Swedish prime minister Olof Palme's "The Emancipation of Man"; and William L. O'Neill's *Everyone Was Brave: The Rise and Fall of Feminism in America*. The brief, which referenced even more than the titles listed above, drew on biology and philosophy as well as law. It was, in a word, eclectic. It was also a carefully crafted introductory essay on the history of women in the United States, complete with a survey of law review articles and lower court decisions that put social realities in the context of recent or desired changes in the law.

The brief examined women's current roles in society, demonstrating both that they were as capable as men of serving as executors of an estate and the reality that they were still the subject of widespread discrimination. Women earned 40.3 percent of all bachelor's degrees earned in 1967, along with 34.7 percent of master's degrees and 11.9 percent of doctorates. Women were 20 percent of all accountants, 10 percent of bank officers, and 33 percent of statisticians. Thirteen thousand women were officers in the armed forces. The Idaho legislature's and its courts' opinions that men were better qualified as administrators was "simply untenable in light of these statistics."

Nonetheless, the brief stated, "the status of women in the labor force is separate and unequal" and "almost two-thirds of this country's adult poor are women." Women could not remedy the situation by themselves. "American women have been stigmatized historically as an inferior class and are today subject to pervasive discrimination." Like other groups such as Black and Hispanic Americans that the Supreme Court had "assisted toward full equality . . . women lack political power to remedy the discriminatory treatment they are accorded in the law and in society generally." Here, the analogy between race and sex that Pauli Murray had made so clear was crucial. "Legislative discrimination grounded on sex, for purposes unrelated to any biological difference between the sexes, ranks with legislative discrimination based on race," the brief asserted. "It was once settled law that differential treatment of the races was constitutionally permissible," and the justices were urged to recognize the "kinship" between race and sex discrimination. "Prior to the Civil War, the legal status of women in the United States was comparable to that of blacks under the slave codes," and in spite of the Nineteenth Amendment that gave women the right to vote, "woman's place as subordinate to man is still reflected in many statutes regulating diverse aspects of life." That was evident in the list of statutes that Ginsburg's student had compiled for the appendix and that Ginsburg summarized in the body of the brief.

Just as the court had erred on the subject of race but had corrected its mistake in recent years, the brief suggested, it could do the same on the subject of sex. Pulling no punches, Ginsburg told the justices that the court had contributed to societal inequality for decades. "Where racial discrimination is concerned, the Court's refusal in *Plessy v. Ferguson* . . . to declare the practice unconstitutional, reinforced the institutional and political foundations of racism." Similarly, the twentieth-century court's decisions in *Muller, Goesaert,* and *Hoyt* supported "perpetuation of the treatment of women as less than full persons within the meaning of the Constitution," and "prior decisions of this Court have contributed to the separate and unequal status of women in the United States." The court, she wrote unflinchingly, bore a burden of responsibility for helping to keep women unequal. It had seen the error of its ways where race was concerned, handing down rulings that made race a "suspect classification." Government laws and regulations that differentiated on the basis of race were assumed to be unconstitutional under the Equal Protection Clause, and the burden was on the government to show that it had a "compelling interest" that justified the differentiation. It was time, the brief argued, for the Supreme Court to apply the same standard to laws classifying people on the basis of sex. "Designation of sex as a suspect classification is overdue."

That was the "going for broke" part. "The initial strategy, pursued in Reed and Frontiero [a later case, to be discussed in chapter 3], was to argue for strict scrutiny of gender distinctions, in part by drawing an analogy between sex- and race-based classification," Ginsburg would recall, using the terms "strict scrutiny" and "suspect classification" interchangeably. "We never expected the Court to reach the suspect criterion issue when decision didn't require that giant step." But that was another piece in the justices' education: getting the idea out there, in the hope that it eventually would be accepted.

Meanwhile, knowing the court would not yet go that far, the brief offered what the justices could consider an acceptable alternative. "At the very least," the court could impose the "rational basis" test on a law challenged as discriminating against women, requiring the government "to prove it rational." That would be what the brief labeled "an intermediate test," midway between the automatic assumption that a law was constitutional and the "strict scrutiny" standard that a law was not. If adopted, it would mean that "rather than require the party attacking the statute to show that the classification is irrational, the Court should require the statute's proponent to prove it rational." Idaho could not prove its law to be rational, the brief continued, as "biological differences between the sexes bear no relationship to the duties performed by an administrator," and all the evidence marshaled in the brief demonstrated that women as a class were as able to perform those duties as were men.

Fortunately for Ginsburg (and Wulf, although the guiding intellect behind the brief and most of the work on it was hers), she could point to an array of recent lower court decisions that struck down discriminatory laws, such as a Louisiana requirement that unmarried women but not men had to live in a state college dormitory, a Virginia law forcing pregnant teachers to leave the classroom, a New Jersey statute excluding women from bartending, and a New York law preventing policewomen from taking an examination for promotion to sergeant. Those cases were all cited, but the one quoted at length was the decision of the California Supreme Court in *Sail'er Inn v. Kirby*, handed down in May 1971. It overturned a California law, similar to the one the Supreme Court had upheld in the *Goesaert* case, keeping women from tending bar. The decision itself was important to the argument in *Reed*, but what was equally important to it was the California court's holding that cases alleging discrimination against women had to be decided on the basis of the suspect classification doctrine. The court's opinion made the analogy between race and sex and, as Ginsburg would, declared that "laws which disable women from full participation in the political, business and economic arenas are often characterized as 'protective' and beneficial." The opposite was true, the California court said, and went on to use language that Ginsburg would repeat frequently: "The pedestal upon which women have been placed has all too often, upon closer inspection, been revealed as a cage."

Judge Raymond Peters was listed as the author of the court's unanimous opinion. It was actually drafted by Wendy Webster Williams, a young lawyer clerking in his chambers who would go on to become one of the country's leading experts on women and the law. She would later publish with Ginsburg and become one of her biographers. The language she wrote for Judge Peters, which unknowingly tracked Ginsburg's approach, was evidence of the way many women's rights advocates were thinking about the law. Ginsburg would be the most visible of them but, as noted earlier, she was far from alone.

Her name and those of Mel Wulf and Allen Derr were of course on the ACLU brief. So were the names of Pauli Murray and Dorothy Kenyon. Murray and Kenyon had not participated at all in the case, but Ginsburg wanted to do them homage. "People of my generation owed them a great debt," she explained, "for they bravely pressed arguments for equal justice in days when few would give ear to what they were saying." Kenyon's agreement to let her name be used was one of her last acts on behalf of women. The brief was filed in late June 1971, and Kenyon died of cancer the following February.

Ginsburg had asked Mel Wulf if he wanted a woman on the brief and, as we have seen, he did. He also wanted a woman to argue the case, particularly in light of the sexist comments from the justices during the oral argument in *Phillips v. Martin Marietta*. They might behave more properly, both he and Ginsburg thought, before a woman attorney, and her mere presence would keep them focused on the kind of gender discrimination at issue in the case. Wulf's choice was Eleanor Holmes Norton, an experienced litigator who had been the ACLU's assistant legal director before leaving it to chair the New York City Commission on Human Rights. Allen Derr, who had taken on Sally Reed's case when no other lawyer was willing to do so, had other ideas. He was similar to many relatively unknown attorneys who accepted hard cases early on and, understandably, felt they deserved the cachet of appearing before the Supreme Court. He had never argued before that court, however, and Ginsburg and Wulf were convinced he was the wrong person for the job. Extensive back-and-forth failed to dissuade Derr, and Sally Reed supported him. That is why Derr was the attorney representing Sally Reed in the oral argument.

Ginsburg was in the courtroom on October 19, 1971, squirming mentally at Derr's presentation. Mel Wulf was so appalled that he said it "may have been one of the worst in the history of the Supreme Court." Derr began by telling the court that the case had "significant significance" and that its impact could be "somewhat akin to what Brown v. Board of Education did for the Colored people." Justice Harry Blackmun, who liked to make notes giving attorneys' oral arguments a grade, marked Derr as deserving a D. Charles Stout, Derr's opponent, didn't do much better: Blackmun gave him a D+, and called their combined presentations "perhaps the worst argued case I have heard up here."

Stout, along with fellow attorney Myron Anderson, had written the brief for the other side, and it contained a surprisingly short fifteen pages of argument. They argued in it that the Supreme Court should not hear the case at all, because while it was pending, Idaho repealed the law that had kept Sally Reed from being considered as an administrator of her son's estate. The brief did not mention that the new law was not retroactive and so did not deal with Sally Reed's situation. The two men argued that *Bradwell v. Illinois* and *Minor v. Happersett* were still good law and that the race/sex analogy did not hold: "Women . . . are in a different situation from those of a disadvantaged race . . . women in the United States have the same right as men to vote and enact laws." The brief declared that the proposed Equal Rights Amendment was not a good idea—although the ERA was not at issue in the case—and that states should be left alone to deal with matters involving property. It was legitimate for laws to treat women differently, because "in all species . . . nature protects the female and the offspring to propagate the species and not because the female is inferior. . . . This [is a] prime necessity if the race is to be continued." Stout and Anderson criticized the ACLU and its amicus briefs as "more emotional than legal." All in all, their brief could have been written in the late nineteenth century.

The oral argument ended, the chief justice intoned the ritualistic "The case is submitted," and there was nothing to do but wait and see if the ACLU brief had been more persuasive than Allen Derr.

The Supreme Court did hear another gender equality case that day. It came from Illinois and was brought by Peter Stanley. Upon the death of Joan Stanley, his common law wife, their three children were taken from him and placed with court-appointed guardians. Peter and Joan had lived together intermittently for eighteen years. No one had proved that Peter was an unfit father, but under Illinois law, an unmarried father had no claim on his children. An unmarried mother or a married father, however, did, and Peter asserted that in taking his children without giving him a chance to prove his fitness, the state had deprived him of the equal protection of the laws.

The case was a bit worrisome to women's rights advocates, as it involved a rethinking of the concept of "family" and it was unclear whether the justices were prepared to go that far. As would happen throughout Ginsburg's litigation years, she had no control over the case or the order in which gender equality issues were brought to the court. *Stanley v. Illinois* was the work of Patrick Murphy, a crusading lawyer with the Chicago Juvenile Legal Aid Society. Amicus briefs were submitted by two attorneys from the Center on Social Welfare Policy and Law and by the Child Care Association of Illinois. All three organizations had been created in the mid-1960s, as had so many other pro bono ("for the good of the public") organizations devoted to equality in those heady years of the civil rights movement and the belief that equality had only to be fought for in order to be achieved. All three approached the issue from the vantage point of children's rights. Whether the case would affect the way the justices thought about the subject of gender equality, and the fate of *Reed*, was of course unknown.

Ginsburg and the other attorneys could only sit back and wait to see what the justices would do. Surprisingly, the court handed down its decision in *Reed* in only a little over a month. It was a legal bombshell.

"All We Ask of Our Brethren Is That They Take Their Feet off Our Necks"

"High Court Outlaws Sex Discrimination," the *New York Post* banner trumpeted on its first page, reporting on the decision that the Supreme Court handed down on November 22, 1971. That wasn't at all what the court did in *Reed v. Reed*, but the confusion was understandable. For the first time since the adoption of the Fourteenth Amendment in 1868, the country's highest court held that its Equal Protection Clause applied to gender as well as to race and ethnicity.

Chief Justice Warren Burger wrote the court's unanimous decision, saying that the "arbitrary preference" given to men by Idaho's probate law violated the clause. States were permitted "to treat different classes of persons in different ways," he said, but it could not create "different classes on the basis of criteria wholly unrelated to the objective of that statute." Idaho had defended the statute on the grounds of administrative convenience, as it would enable probate courts to avoid having to hold a hearing whenever a wife and a husband each filed a claim. That argument had "some legitimacy," the chief justice agreed, but the objective of managing the courts' workload had to be advanced in a manner that was consistent with the Equal Protection Clause. That was not the situation here. He took judicial notice of the fact that many estates were administered by widows, indicating that at least some women were as capable of acting as administrators as were men.

The obvious question was that if states were *sometimes* entitled to create categories of persons and to differentiate between the sexes, how would the court go about deciding which such differentiations passed constitutional muster? There, Marty Ginsburg's flagging of the *Royster Guano Company v. Virginia* tax case, the one that Ginsburg had cited in the *Moritz* litigation as well as in her brief in *Reed*, proved persuasive.

Chief Justice Burger quoted the decision in *Royster*, holding that "a classification 'must be reasonable, not arbitrary, and must rest upon some ground of difference having a fair and substantial relation to the object of the legislation, so that all persons similarly circumstanced shall be treated alike.'" He added that the question in *Reed* was whether the law bore "a rational relationship" to the state's objective of securing a capable estate administrator. That was legalese for saying that if two people were equally well qualified ("similarly situated," in the legal phrase) to perform a function, such as that of administrator of an estate, a law that arbitrarily gave preference to one over the other on the basis of sex did not meet the test of reasonableness. "By providing dissimilar treatment for men and women who are thus similarly situated, the challenged section violates the Equal Protection Clause."

Chief Justice Burger's opinion did not specifically say so, but it in fact suggested a new standard for assessing challenges under the Equal Protection Clause. Ruth Bader Ginsburg had called the "rational basis" criterion the "anything goes" test, because it was relatively easy to show that a law was not entirely irrational. What *Reed* did, by quoting the *Royster* decision, was establish that a classification had to have a "substantial relation to the object of the legislation" and could not be "arbitrary." That suggested that the court would examine the law in question to see if it met those criteria. It was far from "strict scrutiny," but it was a kind of scrutiny, and so it appeared to hint at the creation of an intermediate standard between rational basis and the more stringent one.

Ginsburg didn't know about the decision until she got on a train from New Jersey on the way back to her home in Manhattan that evening and caught sight of a headline on another commuter's newspaper. "My first reaction was total elation," she remembered. "I could hardly hold back the tears of joy."

Sally Reed had won her case. "It's a remarkable thing about the American legal system," Ginsburg would reflect, "that people like Sally Reed think they have access to justice by going to a court and explaining why they have been treated unjustly." Sally had not been in the courtroom when the case was argued, because she could not afford the airfare. Her assumption that laws were designed to treat people fairly, however, had helped make legal history.

Years later, analyzing the decision in the case she would call "the turning point" for gender equality law, Ginsburg saw the court's holding as a reaction to the new mood in the country. She thought that the passage of the 1963 Equal Pay Act and Title VII of the 1964 Civil Rights Act, along with the ongoing discussion in Congress about and support for the proposed Equal Rights Amendment (ERA), "made it difficult for jurists to repeat the traditional suppositions—that differential treatment of the sexes invariably operated benignly in woman's favor." The House of Representatives had already endorsed the ERA, and the Senate was in the process of considering it. The justices read the newspapers, she believed, and eventually caught up with the tenor of the times. She did regret that the *Moritz* case hadn't reached the Supreme Court at the same time as *Reed* (it was of course still pending before the court of appeals). That, she thought, would have enabled the justices to see that gender classifications based on outmoded stereotypes hurt men as well as women.

Ginsburg wrote to a colleague that the fact that the chief justice was the author of the opinion, and that the decision was unanimous, would make it a particularly strong precedent. She could not know then that the justices' papers, along with the more obvious clue implicit in the unusually short time between oral argument and the decision, would indicate that the jurists found it to be an easy case. Justice Harry Blackmun, for example, had made a note to himself while *Reed* was being considered, referring to it as "a very simple little case." He had also ruminated, "All in all, I am inclined to feel that sex can be considered a suspect classification ... There can be no question that women have been held down in the past in almost every area."

It appeared that at least some of his colleagues, however, were far from ready to declare sex a "suspect classification." If there was a downside to the decision, that was it: the court had opted for the relatively easy-to-achieve criterion of an enhanced version of "reasonableness," rather than putting gender classifications in the category that would have led the courts to treat such differentiations with suspicion. Mel Wulf, the legal director of the American Civil Liberties Union (ACLU), was upset about that, but Ginsburg did not find it surprising. She had been certain that "it would take more than a single case to move the Court" to the suspect classification test, and she didn't expect the justices to take that "giant step" if they could decide the case without it. "Real change, enduring change," she was wont to say, "happens one step at a time." The point of arguing for suspect classification anyway was to lay the groundwork: to plant a seed in the justices' minds in the hope that it would sprout when they were presented with other cases later on.

Exactly what the decision in *Reed* meant for gender equality law became a matter of discussion by the press and by legal scholars. "The significance of the case," a law school professor wrote in the *Missouri Law Review*, "lies in the possibility it reveals that the Court in the future will actually require evidence (even if only the opinion of a respectable body of persons), rather than finding a rational basis for sex discrimination in the canards and shibboleths, concepts and stereotypes that are being questioned in today's culture." While applauding the decision, many commentators effectively agreed with Mel Wulf in wishing the court had gone farther. Calling the decision "a significant step forward," the *Loyola Law Review* nonetheless lamented that "women cannot help but feel a sense of disappointment in the language of the opinion." "What is troublesome," the *Akron Law Review* added, "is the fact that one may contend that the Supreme Court hedged, perhaps avoided, an excellent opportunity in which to expand the constitutional scope of the Equal Protection Clause." *Time* magazine told readers that the decision "falls far short of announcing a broad general principle," and the *Boston Globe* saw it as conferring "a smidgen of equality." *The Idaho Statesman* applauded the ruling and added, "Now the legislature should look at other discriminatory laws."

The Idaho *Sun* noted that Chief Justice Burger's opinion "severely limited the impact of the decision by forbidding only discrimination that is unreasonable or arbitrary, terms which the six-page opinion did not define." The result was that "women must continue going into court on a case-by-case basis to establish whether discrimination against them 'bears a rational relationship to a state objective.'" Nonetheless, the article continued, "the decision does give them an important new legal tool with which to fight such court battles." And Ginsburg was about to get the means to use it.

* * *

In December 1971, shortly after the Supreme Court handed down its ruling in *Reed v. Reed*, the ACLU followed up on its commitment to prioritize women's rights. It had already produced a pamphlet about women's rights titled "Sexual Equality: This Is the Law," covering areas such as employment and jury service as well as reproductive rights, which the ACLU had been championing since the 1920s. Now Ginsburg and three of the board of directors' women members took a plan for a new women's rights project to their colleagues. Once the board voted in favor of it, as Executive Director Aryeh Neier recalled, he "began asking around who was well qualified to lead a project of that sort." He didn't have to look far. He had only to walk down the hall to the office of Mel Wulf, who had just worked with Ginsburg on *Reed v. Reed.* Neier quickly called to offer her the position.

Ginsburg was intrigued by the prospect of working with the ACLU on women's rights issues. She thought that the organization had sufficient resources to bring the kinds of sex discrimination cases that might overturn the Supreme Court precedents that she deplored. The ACLU was willing to put $50,000 of its own less than plentiful funds into the project, which meant that "we could go to foundations and say this organization is strongly supportive of what we're doing . . . and we need your contribution to advance our efforts." The ACLU's network of state affiliates was another plus. "That was very important in developing cases. . . . The affiliates would report on complaints they had received from women and sometimes men." The prospectus that Ginsburg wrote for the project to take to potential funders listed the offering of assistance to affiliates as the first method the project would employ. There was one additional attraction for her in the ACLU position. "ACLU involvement meant men would be working alongside women in this effort, and that was important to me." It was crucial, she said, "to include men in the effort to make women's rights part of the human rights agenda. Without the understanding of all humankind, as I see it, the effort cannot succeed."

It was not only the ACLU that wanted Ginsburg. That same month, Columbia Law School, which had hired its first woman faculty member a year earlier, made her an offer as well. She would be the first tenured woman professor at the law school, as Harriet Rabb, the previous hire, was there on a year-to-year contract basis. Teaching at Rutgers meant long commutes to Newark: she was usually at the law school until 6:00 p.m. and didn't get home until 7:30. Columbia was much closer to her Manhattan home than Rutgers, and the ACLU was based in Manhattan as well. She hammered out an arrangement with the two institutions that would let her work part-time at Columbia and part-time as director of what was now called the ACLU's Women's Rights Project (WRP), with each institution contributing to her salary. She viewed the arrangement as symbiotic, writing in the prospectus that "enlist[ing] the assistance of . . . law students in developing these cases" would be part of the WRP's methodology.

Hiring Ginsburg as a half-time director meant that someone else would have to handle the operational side of the WRP while Ginsburg strategized and litigated. Mel Wulf turned to Brenda Feigen Fasteau, a former legislative vice president of the National Organization for Women (NOW) and a founder of *Ms.* magazine. She became WRP's co-director in 1972, in charge of functions such as maintaining contact with the ACLU affiliates as they created their own women's rights agenda. The two women found an unused area in the ACLU offices on Fortieth Street and Madison Avenue and hung out a bright yellow sign, "WOMEN WORKING."

As Aryeh Neier had hoped, the project was successful in raising funds from private foundations. (ACLU policy largely precludes accepting government money.) Over the years, grants would come from a number of small foundations as well as from the Rockefeller Family Fund. The major source of funds, however, was the Ford Foundation. Under the aegis of Susan Berresford, the foundation's program officer for national affairs and later its president, Ford became crucial to women's rights litigation in the 1970s. It gave money for that purpose to the League of Women Voters; the Cleveland-based Women's Law Fund; the Center for Law and Social Policy, headquartered in Washington, DC; and Public Advocates, Inc., in San Francisco; as well as for sex discrimination cases that were brought by the NAACP Legal Defense and Educational Fund and the Mexican-American Legal Defense and Education Fund. The bulk of its contributions to gender equality litigation, however, went to the WRP (or, more indirectly, to Ginsburg's Equal Rights Advocacy seminar), to which Ford contributed $1 million over the 1970s.

Susan Berresford would note that most American foundations ignored the drive for gender equality in those years, contributing only one-fifth of 1 percent of their grants to the effort. In 1976, Ford made more than twice as many such awards as any other foundation, and it

{ *Chapter Three* }

seems fair to speculate that had Ford not directed its money as it did in the 1970s, there would have been far less gender equality litigation. Certainly, the WRP could not have brought the cases that changed the meaning of the Constitution's Fourteenth Amendment and, ultimately, affected many of the laws of the land.

Ginsburg and the WRP were involved in almost every sex discrimination case that went to the Supreme Court in the 1970s. By the end of 1979, she had participated in writing the main brief for nine cases decided by the Supreme Court, argued six of those, participated in amicus briefs in another fifteen Supreme Court cases, worked on eleven major cases the court chose not to take, and helped draft other memoranda and petitions. "Think of any Supreme Court decision on women's rights in the 1970s," Kenneth Karst has written, "and you can be sure that Ruth Bader Ginsburg was there."

Early each weekday morning, Ginsburg would leave her apartment on East Sixty-Ninth Street, cross town and go up to the Columbia Law School on Amsterdam Avenue and West 116th Street. By mid-morning, she was ready to travel downtown and back across town, arriving at the ACLU's offices on East Fortieth Street. There, she, Feigen Fasteau, and their lone office assistant would orchestrate the work that would revolutionize constitutional law.

The WRP was central to constitutional gender equality litigation, but as the other Ford recipients indicate, it was far from alone. The Women's Legal Defense Fund (WLDF), based in the District of Columbia, was organized in 1971. It initially had no paid staff and had to rely upon the services of volunteer lawyers for the cases it brought. That situation lasted until 1974, when attorney Brooksley Born gave a speech about sex discrimination in the law to the Junior League of Washington, DC. Fired up, the league responded by asking how it could help bring about a change. Born suggested sending money to the WLDF, and the league raised $30,000. That enabled the WLDF to hire Judith Lichtman, who promptly began work on the case of *Barnes v. Costle* (finally decided in 1977), the first Title VII challenge to sexual harassment in the workplace. In 1972, the Center for Law and Social Policy created its Women's Rights Project, later the National Women's Law Center, hiring attorney Marcia Greenberger as its founding president. The project became a leader in litigation based on Title VII. In the late 1960s and the 1970s, Nancy

Stearns and Rhonda Copelon of the Center for Constitutional Rights (CCR), a progressive organization founded in 1966, pushed into gender equality litigation.

All these women, along with others and the few men who were litigating for gender equality, would sign on to or help think through various cases brought by Ginsburg and the WRP, as she would cooperate with theirs. They brainstormed strategy together and signed on to each other's amicus briefs. "There weren't many of us" working on sex discrimination cases in the 1970s, Nancy Stearns would remember. "The field of women's rights law was only just developing. We all knew each other.... It was a wonderful thing to have sisters doing what we were doing and believing what we believed." Occasionally, cases were brought by older organizations like the NAACP's Legal Defense and Education Fund, which had funded the *Phillips v. Martin Marietta* employment case discussed in chapter 2, or by labor unions.

The wide variety of organizations beginning to litigate for gender equality could be a hindrance as well as a help, however. Ginsburg had a clear plan for educating the justices of the Supreme Court and leading them to agree with her interpretation of the Equal Protection Clause. Aryeh Neier, who worked at the ACLU beginning in 1963 and directed the organization from 1970 to 1978, recalled, "There never was another circumstance in my tenure at the ACLU when there was as clearly planned a litigation strategy as Ginsburg implemented in the women's rights field.... Effectively what Ginsburg was trying to do was to get the equivalent of the Equal Rights Amendment." He was impressed by "her very careful process of inching the Court along."

"Inching along" meant not only taking the right cases to the Supreme Court but also trying to make certain that the wrong ones—cases that tried to push the justices too far too quickly and were therefore likely to lose and set back the effort—were not brought. That goal was one reason Ginsburg joined the boards of other organizations in the field, such as the National Organization for Women, the Women's Legal Defense Fund, and the Women's Equity Action League. It was not an entirely successful effort, because, as she wrote in 1978, "with many groups and individuals involved, not always marching to the same tune, it is impossible to duplicate the orderly, step-by-step litigation campaign that led to Brown v. Board of Education."

"Inching along" also meant that there were some areas of discrimination that Ginsburg and the WRP would not touch, because she was certain that the moment for cases about them had not yet arrived. "We tried to figure out the issues that were ripe for change through litigation and the ones that were likely to fail," she remembered. She doubted that the 1970s courts would be sympathetic to a claim that laws differentiating between married and unmarried couples were unconstitutional, for example, because "the Court was just not ready to take it on." Veterans' preference was another such area. Returning veterans were automatically put at the head of the line for government jobs, and as women were largely excluded from the military, the result was that women were sent farther down on the list. "Yet, just when the Viet Nam war was winding down and the veterans were returning, it seemed to me that no court was going to look sympathetically on knocking down the veterans' preference."

In deciding upon the right litigation to undertake at the right time, Ginsburg looked for cases brought by women, but she also sought sex discrimination claims from men. She had argued in the *Moritz* case that arbitrary distinctions hurt men as much as women. She wanted to keep reminding the justices of that fact, so cases in which the WRP represented men became an element of its strategy. Ginsburg got the idea about seeking male plaintiffs, she wrote in a 1971 letter, from "Mill and the Swedes." The "Swedes" part came from her experience in Sweden, where the government had taken steps to overcome gender stereotyping by policies such as extending parental leave to men. "Mill" referred to John Stuart Mill, the British philosopher who argued, in his 1869 *The Subjection of Women*, that sex-role stereotyping prevented both men and women from reaching their full potential and deprived society of the talents of both. It became one of the texts of the women's movement of the late 1960s and 1970s.

Ginsburg recognized that education took place outside the courtroom as well as inside it. It was necessary to educate the public, she knew, and it was equally important to enlighten legislators. Litigation was the major weapon in her battle for gender equality, but it was far from the only one. She instinctively understood the mechanics of social change, and the role that both the citizenry and office holders played in the evolution of the law. "We tried to convey to them [the public, legislators, and judges] that . . . their own daughters and granddaughters could be disadvantaged by the way things were." Younger as well as older lawyers also had to be shown why gender equality ought to be one of their priorities. The WRP issued press releases about its cases, sometimes drawing on the ACLU's relationships with members of the media. It published a monthly newsletter and a quarterly docket of the sex discrimination cases it and ACLU affiliates brought, as well as model legal briefs. Ginsburg wrote numerous articles for law journals and spoke at conferences of law professors, students, and practitioners. She made sure to keep up with other law review articles about gender and the law. And just to make certain that the cause of gender equality was not siloed in the ACLU and treated as the domain of the WRP but not of the organization as a whole, Ginsburg became one of the organization's general counsels in 1973. That meant helping to decide which cases the ACLU would bring in any area of the law. In 1974, she joined the board of directors as well. One wonders when she slept.

Her students might have wondered as well. Margaret Moses, a student of hers at Columbia and later an internationally renowned scholar, put all of her other courses aside when Ginsburg gave her one particular assignment about Title VII. Moses worked on it for days and eventually turned in an eighty-page mini-opus. She was astonished to get it back, with comments, the very next morning. Moses subsequently went to work as WRP's clinical director, supervising later classes of students in turn, as many of them in effect became Ginsburg's junior partners and contributed to WRP cases. Ginsburg discussed her litigation strategy with her equal rights seminar students, acknowledging them when they worked on her briefs and articles and inviting them to accompany her to the Supreme Court when she argued. Her hope, she told *TIME* magazine in 1977 for an article celebrating "Ten Teachers Who Shape the Future," was that the students would become lawyers ready "to reflect and respond to the needs of the society [the law] serves."

Former students, such as Jane Booth, later an attorney for the federal government and then Columbia University's general counsel, remembered Ginsburg as so meticulous that they quickly learned the value of checking and double-checking. "Her great gift to us," Booth said, "was her perfectionist standards." Perhaps channeling Nabokov, Ginsburg taught her students as well to eliminate unnecessary wordage, as she was careful to do in her own writing. She was formal in the classroom but interested in her students and completely available outside of it, becoming a role model for dozens of young women and men who would go on to distinguished careers in the law.

* * *

There was one area in which Ginsburg could not bring cases, much as she would have liked to. The prospectus for the WRP listed cases about "reproductive control," specifically including the right to abortion, as a priority. The Ford Foundation would not fund any entity that litigated on the subject of abortion, however, and Ford funding was crucial to the WRP. That led the ACLU to create a Reproductive Rights Project that was completely separate from the WRP. There was no prohibition preventing the WRP from taking on cases of pregnancy discrimination, however, and that was one of the matters Ginsburg would deal with next.

Susan Struck was an unmarried captain in the US Air Force who served as a nurse during the Vietnam War. In 1970, she became pregnant. Air force regulations required a pregnant officer either to have an abortion or to leave the service. (It was a great irony that while abortions were illegal in much of the nation, the armed services urged them upon and made them available to its members.) Struck, a Catholic, refused to have an abortion but told the air force that she would give the baby up for adoption. She was owed sixty days leave, and she said that by using it for the period before and after the birth of the child, she would impose no financial burden on the service. The air force nonetheless ordered her to leave Vietnam and report to a base in the state of Washington for a disposition board hearing, which resulted in a ruling that she be discharged.

Struck turned to the Washington State ACLU affiliate, which was able to keep the discharge order from being enforced while she appealed to the courts. Officers with other temporary disabilities were accommodated by the service, her attorneys argued, and male officers who were responsible for a pregnancy were encouraged to remain in the air force. Both the federal district court and the Ninth Circuit Court of Appeals decided against her. (She gave birth while the case was pending before the district court and immediately surrendered the baby for adoption.)

The Washington affiliate asked if Ginsburg would take *Struck v. Secretary of Defense* to the US Supreme Court. She saw it as an opportunity to attack pregnancy discrimination on the basis of the Fourteenth Amendment. "One thing that conspicuously distinguishes women from men," she said later, "is that only women become pregnant; and if you subject a woman to disadvantageous treatment on the basis of her pregnant status, which was what was happening to Captain Struck, you would be denying her equal treatment under the law."

By the beginning of 1972, *Roe v. Wade* and its companion case *Doe v. Bolton* had been heard once by the Supreme Court and were scheduled for reargument. Ginsburg was distressed that the attorneys in both cases based their claims for abortion rights on the right to privacy. A privacy right was not specifically mentioned in the Constitution, but in the 1965 case of *Griswold v. Connecticut*, the Supreme Court had said it was nonetheless implicit in the section of the Constitution's Due Process Clause that protected individual liberties. The court's decision in *Griswold* left the right largely undefined and was so hazy that Ginsburg, along with numerous other legal commentators, considered it to be anything but a solid basis for reproductive rights.

Ginsburg believed that if she was successful in situating a pregnancy discrimination claim in the Equal Protection Clause, however, it would have a lasting effect on the law. She therefore prepared a brief in *Struck* based on the grounds of equal protection, the right to privacy in one's personal life, and the free exercise of religion guaranteed by the First Amendment. All the air force regulation accomplished, she argued, was reinforcement of separate spheres for men and women, with women primarily responsible for child-rearing "This distinction [between pregnancy and other temporary disabilities]," she wrote, "reflects arbitrary notions of woman's place wholly at odds with contemporary legislative and judicial recognition that individual potential must not be restrained, or equal opportunity limited, by law-sanctioned stereotypical prejudgments. Captain Struck ... simply asks to be judged on the basis of her individual capacities and qualifications, and not on the basis of characteristics assumed to typify pregnant women."

Reading the brief, the solicitor general of the United States was clearly worried about the possible impact of a decision favorable to Struck, because he advised the air force to repeal its automatic discharge policy and waive Struck's discharge. The solicitor general was still Erwin Griswold, the former Harvard Law School dean who had inadvertently given Ginsburg a litigation road map in the *Moritz* case. The woman he had once challenged to justify her presence at the law school had become a formidable legal foe.

The air force followed Griswold's advice, giving Struck her job and back pay. Since that made the case moot, the Supreme Court never heard it. Ginsburg was troubled by what she viewed as a Pyrrhic victory. Hoping to find another basis on which to keep the case alive, Ginsburg asked Struck whether there was anything else she wanted that the air force had not given her. Struck replied that she'd always wanted to be a pilot but women weren't allowed into the training course. The two women chuckled sadly. There was no way, in 1971, that was going to happen.

Ginsburg would call *Struck*, ruefully, "the case that got away." Had the Supreme Court handed down a decision for Susan Struck based on the Equal Protection Clause, in a sympathetic case in which a woman objected to being told to have an abortion, the long-term impact of the case might have been to solidify the constitutional right to reproductive freedom in a way that it was not in *Roe v. Wade* and its successors. The immediate result for Ginsburg, however, was that Ginsburg didn't get to argue *Struck v. Secretary of Defense*.

She had hoped to take another reproductive freedom case to the court. In 1973, she and Brenda Feigen Fasteau went into federal court in North Carolina on behalf of Nial Ruth Cox. An unmarried Black woman from an impoverished family, Cox had been forcibly sterilized by the state in 1965. She had given birth earlier and the state, declaring that she was mentally defective although there was absolutely no indication that she was, apparently saw an opportunity to prevent an eighteen-year-old Black woman from producing more children. Cox initially demurred, but she and her family were told that if she did not have the operation, her family would be taken off the welfare rolls. The state ordered her to have a reversible operation; the doctor performing it decided to perform one that was irreversible. Five years later Cox, by then a nurses' aide in New York, discovered with horror that she could no longer bear children.

Ginsburg and the WRP brought a class action suit, which included other North Carolina women who had been forcibly sterilized, and asked for an award to Cox of $1 million. The lower courts held that Cox had not brought her case soon enough after the event and that the statute of limitations had run out. The Supreme Court declined to hear the case, and so Ginsburg made her first Supreme Court appearance in the case of a servicewoman named Sharron Frontiero rather than on behalf of Nial Ruth Cox.

Like Susan Struck, Frontiero was an officer in the air force. One year into her service, which began in 1968, twenty-four-year-old Sharron married Joseph Frontiero. Joseph, a veteran and full-time student at Huntington College, received $205 a month under the GI Bill and $30 a month from a part-time job. Sharron, a physical therapist at the Maxwell Air Force Base hospital in Montgomery, Alabama, provided the remainder of the funds for his monthly expenses of approximately $354.

The couple lived off base, as Maxwell Air Force Base did not provide on-base housing for the families of married, women air force personnel. In 1970, learning that married armed forces members living off base could apply for a supplemental housing allowance, she requested one. Her application was denied. Air force regulations, her commander informed her, automatically provided the allowance for married male members, making the assumption that their wives were dependents. A female member, however, could claim her husband as a dependent only if she provided more than one-half of his support, and that was not the Frontieros' situation: The air force also provided medical benefits for the wives and children of male members, but again required female married personnel to prove that they were responsible for more than one-half of the husband's support in order to get the benefits.

In December 1970, the Frontieros sued in federal district court. They were represented by Joseph Levin and Morris Dees, two local attorneys. Dees would soon create the Southern Poverty Law Center (SPLC), which became a leader in civil rights litigation. The case was pending when the Supreme Court handed down its decision in *Reed v. Reed*. In spite of *Reed*'s holding that administrative convenience did not justify sex discrimination, however, the three-judge district court that heard *Frontiero* ruled in 1972 for the air force. With limited funds, Levin and Dees turned to the ACLU for help.

The WRP agreed to take on the case. Ginsburg thought it a good one, as "it could easily be perceived as a straight equal pay case. Two people in the military, both the same rank, one gets more money than the other." After all, the law had mandated equal pay for equal work ever since passage of the 1963 Equal Pay Act. WRP went into the case with the understanding that it would control an appeal to the Supreme Court and that Ginsburg would represent the Frontieros in oral argument. Ginsburg emphasized the importance of having a woman present the case. Levin and Dees reneged on the deal, however, insisting—as Allen Derr had done—that they had earned the right to appear before the court. "We have carried this case from its inception and do not intend to lose control of it at this stage," Levin wrote to her, admitting that he wanted the prominence of having argued before the high court. "I am normally the easiest guy in the world to get along with . . . but let me make it clear that this is our case." He thought it unimportant for a woman to appear in oral argument. Convinced that was a mistake, but unable to reach an agreement with Levin, the WRP decided to file an amicus brief. It petitioned the court for permission to argue orally. Levin was allotted twenty minutes; Ginsburg, ten.

Aside from the jockeying over oral argument, the SPLC and ACLU attorneys had very different ideas about how to present the case to the Supreme Court. Ginsburg was determined to continue the drive to get the justices to put sex in the "suspect classification" category; Levin and Dees would aim only for an intermediate approach. It would call for strict scrutiny, without the court assuming that differentiating people by sex was automatically suspect. Ginsburg tried to persuade them, sending them a copy of her brief and writing, "We hope you will read our *Frontiero* brief with close attention . . . and rethink your position on suspect classification." They were not convinced, and when Levin stood before the justices to make his argument, he would note that the SPLC thought the court should use the "strict scrutiny" test to determine reasonableness in a specific case without presuming that all statutory classifications violated the Equal Protection Clause and were unconstitutional until proven otherwise. The SPLC brief did say that "the instant burdensome classification by sex is suspect." In other words, while *this* statute was "suspect," the SPLC was not willing to argue that all statutes that differentiated on the basis of sex fit that category.

The competing views of the appropriate test to utilize may seem legalistic and arcane, but adoption of one test rather than another would have enormous consequences. The "rational basis" test was based on the assumption that a law was constitutional if there was any rational reason for it, so the government that enacted the law had a very low burden of proof. The doctrine that came out of the *Reed* case was that sex-based classifications had not only to be "rational" but also to bear a "substantial relation to the object of the legislation" and could not be "arbitrary." "Suspect classification," with its implication that a law based on the classification might well be unconstitutional, transferred the burden of proof to the government. If "suspect classification" became the standard for judging gender equality cases, the assumption that laws categorizing by sex were unconstitutional would save proponents of equality from having to litigate on a case-by-case basis, as both federal and state law-makers would be reluctant to differentiate on the basis of sex unless they believed that the result could stand up in court. The kind of scrutiny implicit in the *Reed* doctrine—to see if a law was arbitrary—placed a higher burden on laws than the "rational basis" test, but in addition to keeping the door ajar for endless litigation, the intermediate test effectively denied the parallel between race and sex. That, as Ginsburg understood, would leave the justices—and perhaps the country—uneducated about the realities of American women's status and the stereotypical thinking that still hampered any progress toward gender equality. The ACLU brief, which was also signed by Mel Wulf, Brenda Feigen Fasteau, and Marc Feigen Fasteau, was designed to teach as well as to win a case—or, perhaps, to win a case by teaching.

"Historically, women have been treated as subordinate and inferior to men," the brief said, and without the "firm constitutional foundation for equal treatment of men and women by the law" that would be provided by adoption of the "suspect classification" criterion, "women seeking to be judged on their individual merits will continue to encounter law-sanctioned obstacles." The court was asked to adopt the criterion so that "although the legislature may distinguish between individuals on the basis of their need or ability, it is presumptively impermissible to distinguish on the basis of an unalterable identifying trait over which the individual has no control and for which he or she should not be disadvantaged by the law."

Determined to educate the justices, Ginsburg devoted some nine pages to a "Historical Perspective," demonstrating that "a person born female continues to be branded inferior for this congenital and unalterable condition of birth." She drew on a wide range of quotes, from men such as Thomas Jefferson and English legal theorist William Blackstone as well as women such as Sojourner Truth and the writers of the 1848 Seneca Falls Declaration of Sentiments, in order to illustrate the discrimination that existed throughout American history. "Men viewing their world without rose-colored glasses would have noticed in the last century, as those who look will observe today, that no pedestal marks the place occupied by most women." For further evidence, she turned to the cases that were her bêtes noires: *Bradwell v. Illinois, Minor v. Happersett, Muller v. Oregon, Goesaert v. Cleary,* and *Hoyt v. Florida.* Recalling Justice Bradley's assertion in *Bradwell* that "the paramount destiny and mission of women are to fulfil the noble and benign offices of wife and mother. This is the law of the Creator," Ginsburg commented drily that "the method of communication between the Creator and the jurist is never disclosed." She wrote of the court's decision in the *Goesaert v. Cleary* bartender case, "It was retrogressive in its day and is intolerable a generation later." Discussing the *Hoyt* case and a subsequent one in which a state was permitted to exclude women from jury service unless they volunteered, she noted, "The inference might well be drawn that full participation by women in community affairs is not yet recognized as a value worthy of 'protection' in the interest of society."

The court's decision in *Reed v. Reed*, Ginsburg went on, had sown confusion. She pointed to numerous lower court cases in the few intervening years that interpreted *Reed* in opposite ways. Judges in some cases had viewed *Reed* as mandating close scrutiny of sex-based differentials, but there were numerous others in which the judges had taken it to connote approval of the "reasonableness" test. The confusion was exacerbated by the court's 1972 decision in *Stanley v. Illinois*, the parental custody case that was argued the same day as *Reed.* By a vote of 5–2, the court held that an unwed widowed father had a right to a hearing to assess his fitness to raise his children. It cited *Reed* but did not discuss the appropriate standard for review under the Equal Protection Clause. It was time, Ginsburg now suggested, to end the uncertainly by adopting the suspect classification criterion.

The *Frontiero* brief submitted by the Department of Justice, under the aegis of Solicitor General Erwin Griswold, urged the court to apply the less restrictive reasonableness standard. "Congress could reasonably conclude," the brief said, "that the economical administration of the dependency benefits program would be better served by not requiring an individual examination of each claim for benefits by the nearly one and one-half million married male members of the services, in view of the likelihood that the wives of most members are in fact dependent on their husbands." The assumptions in the brief were twofold: that women were economically dependent on men, and that administrative convenience was a reasonable basis for treating men and women differently.

Reed, of course, rejected administrative convenience as a sufficient basis, although whether the court would always regard administrative convenience as an unacceptable rationale was less than clear. In March 1972, in the case of *Forbush v. Wallace*, the court affirmed without opinion a federal district court decision upholding an Alabama law that required a woman to use her married name on official documents. The lower court had decided the case on the basis of administrative convenience. But taking no chances that the court might now apply the rule in *Reed* to *Frontiero*, the government's brief asserted that even if administrative convenience was not a sufficient justification, the situation in *Reed* was different from the one facing the Frontieros. The fact was that men and women were equally capable of functioning as an administrator of an estate, so the categorization in *Reed* was arbitrary. Here, however, "the classification chosen by Congress . . . is based upon reasonable presumptions of dependency, which are in accord with the realities of American life."

Ginsburg was quite ready to take on what seemed to be a persistent assertion by the government that all women were dependent. She presented an array of government statistics: 42.7 percent of women sixteen years of age or older were in the labor force; 58.5 percent of them (18.5 million) were married and living with their husbands; both husband and wife were employed in 42 percent of families with two spouses; in 23.4 percent of those families, the husband earned just or less than the $6,960 that the Bureau of Labor Statistics considered would provide only a low standard of living for an urban family of four. "It is likely, then, that many married women earn enough to cover more than half of their own living expenses." If the air force did not want the administrative burden of finding out which service members' spouses were in fact dependent on them, it had the option of extending the housing and health benefits to all married couples.

The court heard oral argument in *Frontiero v. Laird* on Wednesday, January 17, 1973. (Melvin Laird was the Secretary of Defense. By the time the Supreme Court handed down its opinion in May, he had been replaced by Elliot Richardson, and so the case is now known as *Frontiero v. Richardson*.) The venue for it was one of the most imposing buildings in a city that was known for imposing structures.

The Supreme Court's four-story "Marble Palace" is on First Street NE, across from Congress. Its facade has become familiar to Americans as the background for media shots of protesters admonishing the court to do the right thing and lawyers commenting on what has gone on inside. The focal point of the building, however, is the courtroom. In 1973, it was reached by climbing broad flights of white marble steps up to the sculpted bronze main doors, past marble statues titled "Authority of Law" and "Contemplation of Justice." "Authority" is male; "Contemplation," female. (The main doors have been closed since 9/11, with visitors now required to use a side door.) The pediment above the main entrance, topping marble columns, bears nine symbolic figures. One is the "goddess of liberty," who holds the scales of justice. All the others are modeled after real people, all male. Below them is the inscription, "Equal Justice Under Law."

Inside, the long soaring marble-columned Great Hall leads to the courtroom. It is a stunning room, well suited to a house of justice. The first impression is of great size, as the courtroom measures ninety-one feet from front to back, eighty-two feet across, and forty-four feet high. It is filled with cream and crimson and with dark brown wood. The eye is drawn to the creamy marble columns on all four sides, following them up the soaring walls to the sculpted marble panels that circle the room. Mythical figures such as "Majesty of the Law," "Power of Government," "Defense of Human Rights," "Justice," and "Wisdom" grace the front and back panels. Historical figures associated with the law parade around the two sides: Moses, Hammurabi, Solomon, Confucius, Mohammed, Chief Justice John Marshall. Again, they are all male, although one can glimpse the winged female figures of "Divine Inspiration" and other embodiments of virtue and vice such as "Peace," "Corruption," and "Deceit."

The crimson of the long gold-fringed drapes and the cushions of the spectators' benches is repeated in the gold, crimson, and black-patterned carpet that draws one into the room and pulls one's attention to the raised mahogany brown bench in front. The justices reach it from behind another set of crimson and gold drapes. Between the spectators' rows and the bench is a bronze railing, marking off the section of mahogany seats reserved for members of the Supreme Court bar. Ginsburg would sit at one of the tables for the two sets of lawyers, facing a central lectern with microphones for the attorney presenting an argument. A section for the press is off to the left; another set of pews on the right, each labeled with the name of a justice, is reserved for their guests.

That was the setting when Joseph Levin rose to make the opening argument in *Frontiero*, as the side appealing a lower court decision gets to argue first. Levin concentrated on the statistics about women's vital economic role and on the unacceptability of administrative convenience as a justification for the different treatment of husbands and wives. As he had in his brief, he asked only for the use of an intermediate standard, leaving it to Ginsburg to make the case for suspect classification. Then it was her turn to make her first argument before the nine men of the United States Supreme Court. She did so on an empty stomach, worried that if she ate anything, her nerves would just make her throw it up.

The justices saw a slim, petite, thirty-nine-year-old woman, dark hair tied back, with a gold circle pin attached to her suit jacket. It, and the matching antique gold earrings she wore, had belonged to her mother. Ginsburg would wear them to her Supreme Court appearances as a good luck charm.

"Amicus views this case as kin to Reed v. Reed," she began. "The legislative judgment in both derives from the same stereotype." That opening did two things. It reminded the justices of what they had done in *Reed*, implicitly suggesting that in order to be consistent they had to do the same thing in *Frontiero*, and it signaled her determination to make them understand the persistent view of women as inferior that needed to be eliminated from American law.

Ginsburg next admonished the justices that they had an obligation to make their thinking clear, as "the Court ... writes not only for this case and this day alone, but for this type of case." State and lower federal courts were understandably confused about the standard of review in sex discrimination cases, and she offered a solution: "To provide the guidance so badly needed ... amicus urges the Court to declare sex a suspect criterion." Like race, sex was an "immutable characteristic bearing no necessary relationship to ability." Ginsburg acknowledged that the Fourteenth Amendment as written was meant to apply to race, not sex. "But why did the framers of the Fourteenth Amendment regard racial discrimination as odious?" she asked rhetorically. The answer was that "a person's skin color bears no necessary relationship to ability, similarly as appellees' concede, a person's sex bears no necessary relationship to ability." Neither did national origin and alienage, both of which the court had put in the category of cases to be decided on the basis of suspect classification, "although the new comers to our shores was not the paramount concern of the nation when the Fourteenth Amendment was adopted." The court, she noted, "has recognized that the notion of what constitutes equal protection does change."

The government had argued that women were a majority of American citizens, and therefore not in need of help from either Congress or the court. Ginsburg had an answer to that: "Surely no one would suggest that race is not a suspect criterion in the District of Columbia because the black population here outnumbers the white." Ginsburg referred to the continuing discrimination women faced in employment and education and their relative absence among policy-makers.

As for the government's claim that classification on the basis of sex did not imply inferiority, she pointed to the decisions in *Muller v. Oregon*, *Goesaert v. Cleary*, and *Hoyt v. Florida*. All those distinctions "have a common effect. They help keep woman in her place, a place inferior to that occupied by men in our society." Returning to her argument for "suspect classification," Ginsburg "wanted the Justices to begin to think in a new way . . . and I thought something attention-grabbing would help." So she ended by quoting from a favorite 1837 speech by Sarah Grimké, an abolitionist and feminist.

She spoke not elegantly but with unmistakable clarity.

She said, "I ask no favor for my sex. All we ask of our brethren is that they take their feet off our necks."

A remarkable thing happened when Ginsburg was speaking. The justices were absolutely quiet. Anyone who has seen or read about the usual process in the court knows that the justices are active participants in oral arguments. They interrupt the lawyers with such frequency that attorneys about to present have practiced ways of getting in their key points no matter how much of their allotted time the justices use up.

Joseph Levin was able to get only four minutes into his oral argument before Chief Justice Burger asked a question, and other justices soon followed. It was so unheard of for a litigator to get all the way through a presentation with no interjections from the bench that Ginsburg was left wondering if the justices considered what she had to say to be so unimportant that they saw no reason to interact with it.

They certainly jumped in when Assistant Solicitor General Samuel Huntington rose to present the government's side of the case. Arguing that the "significant majority" of the wives of "over one million married military men" were dependent on them but that the "overwhelming majority" of civilian men married to "the one or two thousand military women" were not dependent upon them, "it is rational to examine individually the few instances where a military woman might have a dependent husband." In response to a question from Justice Byron White about what would be involved if every married serviceperson had to submit a spouse's affidavit of dependence in order for the couple to qualify for the housing and medical benefits, Huntington spoke of the administrative burden. "But," Justice White continued, "how about letting the women claim—you could treat women the same as men the other way I suppose." Huntington admitted that the last Congress had considered but not passed just such a change. Justice Thurgood Marshall asked if the statistics on female dependency had changed since the statute was written twenty years earlier—a question that answered itself. Huntington replied that the classification established when the law was enacted was rational. Marshall was skeptical.

> QUESTION: So you based it on the whole general class of women and the whole general class of men, period ... And that's a rational basis?
> MR. HUNTINGTON: Yes. We submit it is a rational basis.
> QUESTION: That's a rational basis.
> MR. HUNTINGTON: Yes.

It was clear from Huntington's argument that, just as had been the case in *Moritz*, the government was worried less about a decision in *Frontiero* as such than it was about the impact of such a decision on other laws. "Denominating sex classifications as suspect would subject all statutes containing sex classifications to strict review and could result in invalidating many of them," he warned. Justice White focused on the specific statute, however, asking, "Could we just strike down that particular part of the statute of the provision" requiring women service members to prove their husbands' dependency? "That's right," Huntington replied.

Joseph Levin was given a few more minutes of argument time. Then Chief Justice Burger intoned, "The case is submitted," and the justices filed out.

CHAPTER 4

A Big Win, a Big Loss, and a Society
in Transition

Two days after oral argument in the *Frontiero* case, the justices assembled in their conference room for their usual Friday conference. There are only nine people in the room when the court's members sit down together to discuss a case. If the justices need any material during their deliberations, the most junior justice opens the door, summons one of the pages waiting outside, and takes the material into the conference room once it arrives. No one else is allowed in. The purpose of the secrecy surrounding the conference is frank deliberation. The justices want to be free to have honest, open exchanges—and, if it seems wise, to change their minds during and after conference without fear of embarrassment.

The chief justice opens the discussion of each case by laying out what he sees as the issues in it. (As this is written, there has not yet been a female chief justice.) The other justices then have the opportunity to present their views, in descending order of seniority. Chief Justice Burger began by dismissing the Frontieros' argument, declaring that the case had "nothing to do with" *Reed* and that preventing the armed forces from distinguishing between men and women could have an "enormous" negative effect. It soon became apparent, however, that he was in the minority. Seven of the justices indicated that they considered the regulation unconstitutional. Only Justice William Rehnquist sided with the chief justice.

It is the chief justice who assigns the writing of the opinion for the court when he is in the majority. When he is not, the task goes to the most senior justice in the majority. That was Justice William O. Douglas, who asked Justice William Brennan to take on the job. Brennan said during the conference that he saw no difference between *Reed* and *Frontiero*. The majority agreed, and so it appeared that the court would ignore

Ginsburg's argument for suspect classification and decide on the basis of the enhanced version of the rational basis test it had created two years earlier in *Reed*.

Brennan did rely on *Reed* when he wrote his first draft and circulated it to the other justices. Geoffrey Stone, the clerk who worked on the case for Brennan, however, was pushing him to consider a suspect classification approach instead, and Brennan became convinced that some of his brethren were ready for that as well. "As you will note," he said in the February 14 memo attached to his draft, "I have structured this opinion along the lines which reflect what I understood was our agreement at conference . . . without reaching the question whether sex constitutes a 'suspect criterion' calling for 'strict scrutiny.'" While he thought that *Reed* was sufficient grounds for overturning the provision at issue in *Frontiero*, "I do feel however that this case would provide an appropriate vehicle for us to recognize sex as a 'suspect criterion.'" If others agreed, "I'd have no difficulty in writing the opinion along those lines." He next sent around a draft incorporating the suspect classification test.

The result was a dialogue by memo among the justices. Justice Potter Stewart replied, "I see no need to decide in this case whether sex is a 'suspect' criterion, and I would not mention the question in the opinion. I would, therefore . . . substitute a statement that we find that the classification effected by the statute is invidiously discriminatory." Justice Harry Blackmun agreed.

> I have now concluded that it is not advisable, and certainly not necessary, for us to reach out in this case to hold that sex, like race and national origin and alienage, is a suspect classification. It seems to me that Reed v. Reed is ample precedent here and is all we need and that we should not, by this case, enter the arena of the proposed Equal Rights Amendment.

Justice Thurgood Marshall, however, quickly signed on to the new draft, as did Justice Byron White. Justice White indicated that he thought *Reed* "applied more than a rational test" and "I would think that sex is a suspect classification, if for no other reason than the fact that Congress has submitted a constitutional amendment making sex discrimination unconstitutional. I would remain of the same view whether the amendment is adopted or not."

Justice Lewis Powell objected at length to Justice Brennan's new draft. "My principal concern about going this far at this time," he wrote,

> is that it places the Court in the position of preempting the amendatory process initiated by the Congress. If the Equal Rights Amendment is duly adopted, it will represent the will of the people accomplished in the manner prescribed by the Constitution. If, on the other hand, this Court puts 'sex' in the same category as "race" we will have assumed a decisional responsibility (not within the democratic process) unnecessary to the decision of this case.

Wait and see, he advised, whether the discussion about ERA that was taking place in the country resulted in a consensus that "it is wise, fair and prudent to subject both sexes to identical responsibilities as well as rights."

Brennan attempted to hold the line on his approach, hoping that he could get a majority behind it. On March 6, he wrote to Powell, "You make a strong argument and I have given it much thought. I come out however still of the view that the 'suspect' approach is the proper one and, further, that now is the time, and this is the case, to make that clear." He thought that, as Justice Marshall had written in a different case, "the only rational explication of Reed is that it rests upon the 'suspect' approach." His view of the ERA ratification process, which proved to be prescient, was that "we cannot count on the Equal Rights Amendment to make the Equal Protection issue go away."

> Eleven states have now voted against ratification . . . and within the next month or two, at least two, and probably four, more states . . . are expected to vote against ratification. Since rejection in 13 states is sufficient to kill the Amendment it looks like a lost cause. . . . I therefore don't see that we gain anything by awaiting what is at best an uncertain outcome. Moreover, whether or not the Equal Rights Amendment eventually is ratified, we cannot ignore the fact that Congress and the legislatures of more than half the States have already determined that classifications based upon sex are inherently suspect.

Brennan failed to convince Powell, and perhaps the reason had less to do with Powell's desire to wait for the political process to unfold than with his queasiness about the implications of true gender equality. "If and when it becomes necessary to consider whether sex is a suspect classification, I will find the issue a difficult one," he had written in his note to Brennan. "Women certainly have not been treated as being fungible with men (thank God!)." Powell rejected the race/sex analogy, because "the reasons for different treatment have in no way resembled the purposeful and invidious discrimination directed against blacks and aliens. Nor may it be said any longer that, as a class, women are a discrete minority barred from effective participation in the political process."

Justices Blackmun and Stewart were equally unconvinced by Brennan, which meant that while at least six of the other eight justices would still vote with him, four of them would disagree that the standard should be suspect classification rather than rational basis. Brennan would command a majority of the court in favor of the Frontieros but only a plurality for suspect classification, which would therefore not become part of the court's ruling. Chief Justice Burger chimed in to protest what he saw as a misreading of *Reed*. "Some may construe Reed as supporting the 'suspect' view but I do not. The author of Reed" (who was of course Burger himself) "never remotely contemplated such a broad concept but then a lot of people sire offspring unintended!" He nonetheless changed his vote and signed on to a concurring opinion written by Justice Powell that relied on the rational basis standard. Justice William Rehnquist became the lone dissenter, not bothering to write a full opinion but merely citing the decision and reasoning of the district court.

Ginsburg would say later about fashioning the briefs that she submitted to the court, "I tried to write them so that a justice who agreed with me could write his opinion from the brief." Justice Brennan proved willing to do so, and Ginsburg would call his opinion "a joy to read." In the language used by the Supreme Court reporter, he "announced the Court's judgment and issued an opinion" that was joined by Justices Douglas, Marshall, and White. It declared that *Reed* gave "implicit" support to the suspect classification test when it rejected the state's "apparently rational explanation" of the law and concluded that "by ignoring the individual qualifications of particular applicants," it treated similarly situated men and women differently. In other words, according to Brennan's logic, striking down a statute that was reasonable—it did, after all, aid administrative convenience—meant that the court had in effect looked upon a law that differentiated on the basis of sex and ignored individual circumstances as unconstitutional.

"There can be no doubt," Brennan continued, "that our Nation has had a long and unfortunate history of sex discrimination." Picking up Ginsburg's language, which itself drew from the California Supreme Court's decision in *Sail'er Inn v. Kirby*, he noted that "such discrimination was rationalized by an attitude of 'romantic paternalism' which, in practical effect, put women, not on a pedestal, but in a cage." He quoted Justice Bradley's dictum in Myra Bradwell's case about woman's inferior status being ordained by the Creator, saying that "as a result of notions such as these, our statute books gradually became laden with gross, stereotyped distinctions between the sexes and, indeed, throughout much of the 19th century the position of women in our society was, in many respects, comparable to that of blacks under the pre-Civil War slave codes." He cited some of the authors Ginsburg relied upon in her brief and added that "women still face pervasive, although at times more subtle, discrimination in our educational institutions, in the job market and, perhaps most conspicuously, in the political arena." It was clear that he accepted her interpretation of the economic and political statistics, rather than the government's view. Recent legislation such as the Equal Pay Act and the congressional endorsement of ERA, he said, showed that "Congress itself has concluded that classifications based upon sex are inherently invidious." Then he added a sentence that, had it commanded a majority of the justices rather than only a plurality, would have revolutionized American law: "With these considerations in mind, we can only conclude that classifications based upon sex, like classifications based upon race, alienage, or national origin, are inherently suspect, and must therefore be subjected to strict judicial scrutiny."

Given that standard, it was obvious that the categories at issue in *Frontiero* had to fall. Administrative convenience, Brennan reminded the brethren and the lower courts, was not an acceptable justification. Picking up on the questioning by Justice White in oral argument, he added that since all the husband of a female service member had to do to establish his dependence was to fill out a simple affidavit documenting it, it was difficult to see how it would be a great administrative inconvenience if that requirement was extended to the wife of a male service member.

Brennan added a copious number of footnotes, again drawing on the authorities cited by Ginsburg and referring to her statistics.

Justice Powell's concurrence for himself, Chief Justice Burger, and Justice Blackmun repeated what he said in the justices' dialogue. There was no need to declare sex to be a suspect classification, "with all of the far-reaching implications of such a holding." More importantly, it behooved the court to wait and see what happened with ERA. "Democratic institutions are weakened, and confidence in the restraint of the Court is impaired," he chastised the plurality, "when we appear unnecessarily to decide sensitive issues of broad social and political importance at the very time they are under consideration within the prescribed constitutional processes." Justice Stewart limited himself to a terse sentence: "Mr. Justice Stewart concurs in the judgment, agreeing that the statutes before us work an invidious discrimination in violation of the Constitution," citing *Reed v. Reed*.

By the time the decision was handed down on May 4, 1973, Sharron Frontiero was no longer in the US Air Force. Her husband had gotten his degree and a job as an industrial hygienist at a naval shipyard in New Hampshire, and the couple had moved to Massachusetts in late 1972. They were exuberant, though, with Sharron telling the *New York Times* that her reaction to the decision was "Hot damn!" and her husband's, "We did it!"

But exactly what had been accomplished was not entirely clear.

* * *

It was easy to see why the Frontieros were excited about the outcome of their case. They had won; the air force would now give women at least some of the benefits available to men. Four of the nine justices had agreed that sex should be treated as a suspect classification.

From Ginsburg's point of view, that was exactly what went wrong. The majority of five justices rejected the race/sex analogy and refused to consider laws that differentiated among women and men as inherently suspect. It meant that the battle for constitutional gender equality would still have to be fought on a time- and resources-consuming, case-by-case basis, with no certainty as to the outcome. "The war on sex discrimination was not going to be a lightning blitz, but rather a long drawn-out struggle," a report for the Ford Foundation lamented.

Ginsburg recognized sadly that when she took her next case to the Supreme Court, it would be with the "clear [understanding] that one could not garner five votes for labeling sex a 'suspect classification.'" She would have to change her strategy if she was to persuade the court to adopt that test sometime in the future. Nonetheless, Ginsburg told an interviewer in 1975, "Frontiero v. Richardson was very important, more important than Reed v. Reed, because it hit at the line drawn most frequently in the law between men and women, a line that types males as breadwinners, females as dependent."

Ginsburg laid out a five-year plan. She went back to the list that Attorney General Erwin Griswold had unintentionally given her in Charles Moritz's tax case, and decided to target provisions of the Social Security laws that gave benefits only to widows and not to widowers. She knew what cases she wanted to see on the Supreme Court's docket next. But, as she would say ruefully, some things were beyond her control. Ginsburg, and the drive for constitutional gender equality, were about to suffer a major setback.

*   *   *

It would be convenient if a litigator for social reform had the luxury of focusing on one case from beginning to end and then turning to the next. That, however, is not usually how it works, and it was not the way it worked for Ginsburg and the Women's Rights Project (WRP). *Frontiero* was handed down on May 14, 1973. By then, the case of *Cleveland v. LaFleur* was on its way to the Supreme Court, challenging a requirement that a pregnant teacher had to take unpaid leave at the beginning of her fifth month of pregnancy and could not return until the start of the semester that began after her child was three months old. Ginsburg and the WRP were amicus in the case, which was argued by ACLU cooperating attorney Philip Hirschkop. (A "cooperating attorney" is one who works elsewhere but participates in an ACLU case.) A federal district court in Louisiana had already heard and was about to hand down its decision in *Healy v. Edwards*, which in effect asked for a ruling opposite to that in Gwendolyn Hoyt's jury case—one of the cases Ginsburg had made it her mission to overturn. Ginsburg and the WRP were directly involved in *Healy*, which they expected would go to the US Supreme Court.

In keeping with her five-year plan, Ginsburg was also hard at work on a challenge to the Social Security regulation that gave a widowed mother but not a widowed father support for child care. The case that most immediately concerned her, however, was one that she could happily have lived without.

Melvin Kahn, a widower, lived in Dade County, Florida. In 1971, he applied to the county tax assessor's office for a $500 property tax exemption, which would have lowered his tax bill by $15. The tax assessor rejected his application, as an 1885 Florida law provided the exemption only for widows, the blind, and the totally disabled. Kahn turned to the Florida affiliate of the ACLU, where attorney Bill Hoppe, certain that affording the benefit to widows but not widowers violated the Equal Protection Clause, took his case.

The county circuit court agreed with Kahn and his attorney, finding that the statute was "discriminatory and arbitrary and unconstitutional." The county appealed, and in February 1973, the Florida Supreme Court reversed the lower court's decision, declaring that the distinction was a legitimate legislative enactment. Citing *Reed*'s holding that a distinction had to have "a fair and substantial relation to the object of the legislation" in order to be valid, the court said that it did: the object was to "reduce the disparity between the economic . . . capabilities of a man and a woman." The Florida ACLU then asked the US Supreme Court to hear the case, which was named *Kahn v. Shevin*, as Robert Shevin was the attorney general of Florida.

ACLU state affiliates are empowered to accept cases without consulting the national organization, but they are supposed to check with the national office before seeking a hearing by the Supreme Court. Hoppe was new to the Florida affiliate and was unaware of the rule. The first that Ginsburg and Mel Wulf knew about the case was when they read in *Law Week* that the Supreme Court had agreed to hear it.

They were stunned, and horrified. Ginsburg was certain that the case was a loser. The justices had begun to understand that excluding women from benefits available to men was discriminatory and based on generalizations that no longer bore close scrutiny—if, indeed, they ever had. But ironically, and in part because of that understanding, they were susceptible to claims that a classification designed to help women, to compensate them in some way for past discrimination, was only fair. Ginsburg had not yet been able to teach the court that the fault lay in generalizations about all men and all women, which frequently ended up hurting both.

It was too late to keep the case from the justices, and the worst thing possible would be for it to be presented by someone not able to do so well. Wulf was shocked to see that Hoppe had declared naively in one of the documents he submitted to the court that the Nineteenth Amendment had "fully emancipated" women. Ginsburg knew she would have to take the case on herself. She began to write a brief.

There was no point in asking the justices to apply the suspect classification test. "I do not plan to urge sex as a suspect classification and the brief tries to fudge on the review standard issue," she acknowledged. Ginsburg would have to aim her argument at the justices who had flinched at suspect classification but might be persuaded if she used a lesser criterion: Justices Lewis Powell, Potter Stewart, and perhaps Harry Blackmun—who after musing sympathetically about suspect classification while the court was considering *Reed* had declined to apply it in *Frontiero*. In fact, Ginsburg worried that the justices would use the less demanding rational basis test and uphold the law. Another reason for her concern was that the court typically gave states wide discretion in the field of property tax law, which it might view as the key issue here. In addition, she thought, the statute could be seen as a form of much-needed affirmative action for women. Various American institutions had adopted policies providing affirmative action for racial minorities, and a case in which the Washington State Supreme Court had upheld the University of Washington law school's race-based affirmative action program was already on its way to the US Supreme Court. The statute at issue in *Kahn*, she realized, could be seen as analogous.

Avoiding any mention of suspect classification, Ginsburg opened her brief with an attack on the Florida law as a form of "invidious discrimination" based on an outmoded stereotype. While a widow is considered to be "economically disabled," a widower "is believed to suffer scant financial loss upon the death of his wife, and even to be relieved of the burden of supporting her." The stereotype was "hardly tenable in this latter half of the twentieth century," and Ginsburg turned to the usual statistics to demonstrate the changed financial situation of millions of American women. She quoted extensively from *Reed* and *Frontiero* in reminding the court that it had held that "lump treatment of men, on the one hand, and women on the other is constitutionally impermissible." She cited numerous lower court rulings rejecting "disadvantageous treatment of men unsupported by strong affirmative justification," the *Moritz* tax case among them. Far from benefitting women, she continued, the law "perpetuates sex stereotypes and thereby retards women's access to equal opportunity in economic life." She urged the justices not to overturn the statute but to extend the exemption to widowers as well as widows.

Some of the opening language in the brief submitted by Florida reads, deceptively, as if it had been written by the Women's Rights Project. "Although women make up an ever-increasing portion of the work force," it asserted, "they are still far behind in obtaining equality of economic opportunity." Drawing on government statistics, the state noted that the national gap between men's and women's wages was growing, not narrowing, and that 35.8 percent of Florida families headed by women fell below the poverty line, while that was true of only 9.8 percent of families headed by men. The conclusion that Florida drew from those statistics, however, was far from one that the WRP could support. The economic inequality, the state claimed, proved that there was a reasonable connection between the special treatment of widows and the law's objective of compensating for past discrimination. "Classifications based on sex are properly found to be valid when they bear a rational relationship to a proper state object," and here the objective was "to alleviate the hardship to women resulting from the inequality of economic opportunity." Just to cover all bases, the state argued that even if the court based its decision on the suspect classification test, Florida had a "compelling interest" in reducing the "economic disparity" between the sexes and "the resulting encouragement of the elderly to locate in Florida."

Ginsburg was back in the Supreme Court courtroom on the afternoon of February 25, 1974, for oral argument in the case. It was less than a triumph, and the first perhaps symbolic setback came when she stood to address the court. Ginsburg was barely five feet tall. The lectern was set much too high. "If you'd like to lower the lectern, you are quite at liberty to do so," Chief Justice Warren Burger said, and after adjusting it, she began to speak.

The argument was uncomfortably convoluted, as Ginsburg found herself having to retreat from the suspect classification stance as well as the race/sex analogy. This time, the justices were not as forgiving as they had been when she argued *Frontiero*, and they interrupted repeatedly. She told them that the case could be decided on the basis of *Reed's* enhanced rational basis test, and that it was unnecessary to extend the suspect classification test used in race discrimination cases to all sex discrimination cases. "Excuse me, I'm not too clear," Chief Justice Warren Burger interjected. "You are arguing that sex ought not to be treated as a suspect classification?" It wasn't necessary in this case, she replied, as Burger asked whether her preferred test was "suspect plus." In an unusual moment for the normally articulate attorney, she responded, "It is the classification, it is the criterion sex that is suspect, not female, but the criterion sex."

> JUSTICE BURGER: So the suspect classification can be found only with respect to discriminatory classification against a minority group; is that correct?
> MRS. GINSBURG: That is how it has been used in this court's precedent.
> JUSTICE BURGER: Traditionally up until now?

Ginsburg had told her colleagues earlier that she saw no option but "to fudge" the standard that should be used in arguing *Kahn*, and the fudging clearly was proving awkward. But she regained her footing as the colloquy continued.

> JUSTICE BURGER: In other words, you don't want it whether it [a law that benefits women] helps—even if it helps.
> MRS. GINSBURG: My question is if it ever does help.... I have not yet found any such classification in the law that genuinely helps. From a very shortsighted viewpoint, perhaps, such as this one, yes. But long run—no, I think that what women need is, first of all, a removal of exclusions and restrictive quotas. They are the only population group that today still faces outright exclusions and restrictive quotas.... But the notion that they need special favored treatment, because they are women, I think has been what has helped to keep women in a special place, and has kept them away from equal opportunity for so long.

The court adjourned after hearing Ginsburg and reopened the next morning with Sydney H. McKenzie, an assistant attorney general, making the case for Florida. He relied on the rational basis test and the states' power to choose their tax laws.

Supreme Court watchers frequently attempt to discern the way individual justices are likely to vote by listening to the questions they ask in oral argument. That attempt can be far from successful, as justices sometimes play devil's advocate. At other times, they use their platform to conduct a dialogue among themselves, and it is in those instances that the careful listener can occasionally get a sense of the way the votes are likely to go. Here, Justice William Brennan, who had come out so strongly for suspect classification in *Frontiero*, questioned McKenzie about whether the statistics didn't demonstrate that many women were "anything but . . . economically disadvantaged." Justice Stewart, who had balked at utilizing the suspect classification test, immediately jumped in to help McKenzie.

JUSTICE STEWART: Well, I think my brother Brennan is referring to the fact that widows own a great deal of the property in the country but that is because there are many, many, many more widows than there are widowers.

Justice Thurgood Marshall had voted with Justice Brennan in *Frontiero*. Noting that the Florida law dated back to 1885, he now asked whether women were not currently in a better economic position than they had been then. "I would assume," he added, "that there are some widows in the Palm Beach area that are a little better off than some widowers in the upper part of Florida." Admit, Justice Marshall challenged McKenzie, that "this is based on sex" rather than need. "It's based on sex plus the underlying recognition of factual differences between the sexes [that] are not simply a stereotype," McKenzie replied. But Marshall wasn't done. Referring to Gwendolyn Hoyt's case, he continued.

JUSTICE MARSHALL: The same constitution [Florida's] also that prevented women from serving on juries, didn't it? . . . And now they do. . . . Now, they've been persuaded to let women serve on juries, haven't they?

When Justice Marshall went on to ask what difference the fifteen dollars at issue would make to an economically distressed widow, Justice Stewart jumped in again, declaring that it "might enable her to retain the ownership of the property rather than make a distressed sale of it." As court watchers might have predicted, Justices Brennan and Marshall would vote to overturn the law; Justice Stewart, to uphold it.

Ginsburg was given a few minutes for rebuttal, and Justice Blackmun asked her if the case argued the preceding morning affected her position. The case, *DeFunis v. Odegaard*, was the one that involved the University of Washington law school's affirmative action program. Again, Ginsburg was seemingly forced into a position of backing away from the race/sex analogy.

> MRS. GINSBURG: The DeFunis case raises a very different issue. De-Funis is a program of a law school that is designed to open doors to equal opportunity, to assure a law student body with diverse backgrounds and experience and to what defy the conspicuous absence of minority groups in the profession. It is not a welfare dole, based on the assumed inferior capabilities of any population group. No rigid race line is presented, as we have here a rigid sex line. Race is merely one of the many characteristics assessed in that case.
>
> But most significantly, DeFunis involved no general law classi-fication. It's a measure addressed to a very special selection prob-lem that law schools have.

In fact, as she wrote to Bill Hoppe, Justice Blackmun's question en-abled her to spin what were supposed to be her two minutes out to seven, and she had "carefully prepared an answer to that question. I was de-lighted with the opportunity to hammer down the distinction I tried to make on Sunday." Whether that would be persuasive remained to be seen.

When the justices met in conference to discuss *Kahn*, the majority voted to sustain the Florida law. Chief Justice Burger asked Justice Wil-liam O. Douglas to write the opinion for the court. When Douglas circu-lated his first draft three weeks later, Justice Stewart immediately signed on, and shortly thereafter so did Justices Lewis Powell and William Rehnquist. Justice Brennan let Douglas know that he would be writ-ing an opinion, presumably a dissent, of his own. Justice Blackmun told Douglas he wanted to wait and see Justice Brennan's dissent and some days later, unpersuaded by it, added his name to Douglas's final version.

Justice Byron White circulated another dissent. What finally emerged was Douglas's opinion for the court, which the Chief Justice and Justices Stewart, Blackmun, Powell, and Rehnquist joined; Justice Brennan's dissent, joined by Justice Marshall; and Justice White's separate dissent.

"There can be no dispute that the financial difficulties confronting the lone woman in Florida or in any other State exceed those facing the man," Justice Douglas began his short, four-paragraph opinion. "Whether from overt discrimination or from the socialization process of a male-dominated culture, the job market is inhospitable to the woman seeking any but the lowest paid jobs." That led him to conclude that "there can be no doubt," and here he quoted from *Reed v. Reed*, "that Florida's differing treatment of widows and widowers 'rest[s] upon some ground of difference having a fair and substantial relation to the object of the legislation.'" *Frontiero* was different, Douglas said. The provision here was not a matter of administrative convenience but "a state tax law reasonably designed to further the state policy of cushioning the financial impact of spousal loss upon the sex for which that loss imposes a disproportionately heavy burden." He added that the decision was in keeping with the long-standing leeway the court gave to states to fashion their own tax laws.

Ginsburg called the opinion "a retrenchment" and "a disgrace from every point of view. . . . It is galling that Douglas sees women as appropriate objects of benign dispensation (ranked with the blind and the totally disabled) when he should know that there is no surer way to keep them down than to perpetuate that brand of chivalry." She was astounded by what she viewed as Justice Douglas's about-face from his stance in *Frontiero*, when he had joined Justice Brennan's call for strict scrutiny. It was Douglas who was known as the court's great defender of individual rights and equality. It was he who had also said that race-based compensatory treatment stigmatized, but he seemed to have no problem with equally stigmatizing sex-based compensatory laws. She hypothesized that the coincidence of *DeFunis* and *Kahn* being argued on the same day had led to the majority of the justices' equating remedial action for racial minorities with a similarly acceptable compensatory provision for women.

Ginsburg did not know then about Douglas's family situation. His father died when Douglas was six years old. His widowed mother was left almost penniless, with three young children to support. Douglas and his two young siblings took whatever odd jobs they could find in order to help out, but the family struggled with poverty for years. The experience clearly left its mark on him.

Justice White wrote in dissent that as the Florida tax break went to wealthy widows as well as those in need and "ignores all those widowers who have felt the effects of economic discrimination, whether as a member of a racial group or as one of the many who cannot escape the cycle of poverty," it was a clear violation of the Equal Protection Clause. Ginsburg called his opinion "the only one with complete integrity" and "very close to my own view of the case."

Justices Brennan and Marshall would remain Ginsburg's staunch allies. Marshall no doubt understood her step-by-step attempts to educate the justices, as that was exactly the gradual approach he and the NAACP had used in attacking segregation. Brennan and Ginsburg seemed to be in something of a balletic pas de deux, with Brennan picking up language from Ginsburg's briefs and Ginsburg using his language the next time around. In *Kahn,* drawing on the statistics she provided, he went farther than she had in her briefs and oral argument, once again calling sex a suspect classification. He agreed that remedying the historical discrimination faced by women was a compelling state interest: "No one familiar with this country's history of pervasive sex discrimination against women can doubt the need for remedial measures to correct the resulting economic imbalances." That goal could be achieved, however, without relying on outmoded stereotypes.

> The exemption is granted only to widows who complete and file with the tax assessor a form application establishing their status as widows. By merely redrafting that form to exclude widows who earn annual incomes, or possess assets, in excess of specified amounts, the state could readily narrow the class of beneficiaries to those widows for whom the effects of past economic discrimination against women have been a practical reality.

Ginsburg would always have a special place in her heart for Justice Brennan. That did not mitigate the pain and frustration of the setback in a case that would never have reached the Supreme Court had Bill Hoppe understood ACLU rules. There was no question that the decision was a serious blow to Ginsburg's hoped-for progression of cases that would lead to constitutional gender equality—or, at least, less inequality. There was little time to lament, however, as too many other important cases were already underway.

* * *

By the mid-1970s, the WRP had become a major powerhouse, in spite of having only a relatively small staff. It brought or assisted with cases at all levels of the judiciary, across the entire United States, many of them in cooperation with ACLU affiliates. The WRP had hired Patricia Beyea as its project coordinator. The position was in keeping with Ginsburg's belief that it would take a well-coordinated litigation docket and substantial educational effort to achieve legal gender equality. Beyea traveled to ACLU affiliates and regional offices, working with staff to develop programs and lay leadership as well as relationships with the media. She carried with her copies of a WRP-produced paperback booklet on women's rights, part of a larger ACLU series on rights. Beyea later recalled that once a month Ginsburg, the five other WRP lawyers, and Beyea would gather around a long table, send out for sandwiches (tuna fish was the norm), and discuss the project's agenda: What cases seemed promising? What cases that they would have liked to bring might do more harm than good, if the time was not yet right to hope for a favorable outcome? Obviously, cases like *Kahn v. Shevin* and its unfortunate precedent were to be avoided.

Occasionally, while they worked, the sounds of children's voices could be heard from next door. The women were free to bring their nursing babies and preschool children to work. The women in effect established an informal daycare center—another first for the ACLU.

The plethora of cases the WRP and other organizations were taking to the Supreme Court and to other tribunals around the country reflected a societal environment that was startlingly different from the one that existed in 1969, when Ginsburg contemplated creating a course on women and the law. Her thinking had evolved since then, and so had the society in which she operated. That year, New York University's law school became the first in the nation to offer a course on the subject. It would be followed in 1970 by Yale, Georgetown, and George Washington University, at the same time that San Diego State College created the nation's first program in women's studies. Two years later, Sarah Lawrence professor Gerda Lerner and City University of New York professor Joan Kelly created the country's first graduate degree program in women's history. Even before that, in 1969, women at the annual convention of the American Historical Association had formed a Coordinating Committee on Women in the Historical Profession, and women in other academic disciplines quickly followed suit. Historian Ruth Rosen estimated that in 1974, some one thousand colleges and universities had courses in women's studies. In 1970, Florence Howe started the Feminist Press, dedicated to printing works by women; 1972 saw the creation of the journal *Feminist Studies.*

By 1977, so many colleges and universities had programs in women's studies—"programs," meaning a whole series of courses, some of which could be taken as a major—that the National Women's Studies Association was formed. Women—and some men—across the spectrum of higher education were organizing to teach themselves and their students about the underacknowledged role women had played in society from its earliest days and to advocate for women-friendly policies in both their professions and society at large. These academics were still a minority among university faculty and other intellectuals, but they were indicative of a trend that showed no sign of letting up. Sarah Lawrence College, the Women's Action Alliance, and the Smithsonian Institution, again led by Gerda Lerner, held a fifteen-day conference on women's history in the summer of 1979. Women from forty-five different women's organizations attended.

Women in academia were far from the only ones thinking and organizing in new ways. Ginsburg's briefs from *Reed* on had summarized the continuing movement of women into the paid workforce. Most of those women held positions far removed from academia, but they were no less fervent in their drive for acknowledgment and fair treatment. The National Domestic Workers Union was founded in 1968 by Black women. In 1970, Mexican American women created the Comisión Femenil Mexicana (Mexican Women's Commission), which in 1972 developed the Chicana Service Action Center, an employment and training program. The Coalition of Labor Union Women (CLUW) was organized in 1974; 9to5, an organization of office workers, was founded in Boston a year earlier, as was Women Employed (WE), in Chicago.

The new consciousness of and about women, and a demand for equality and dignity in all areas of life, spread across the country. In the 1970s, the nation saw multiple Take Back the Night marches and the creation of Rape Crisis hotlines. Activists including Florynce Kennedy and Faith Ringgold organized the National Black Feminist Organization. In 1972, Gloria Steinem and other feminists created *Ms.* magazine. The *American Heritage School Dictionary* agreed to use "Ms." rather than "Miss" or "Mrs." as a title for women who requested it; the following year, the official US Printing Office did the same. While consciousness-raising groups were a major element of the women's liberation movement and were to be found in every state of the nation, the new consciousness became part of mainstream culture as well. In 1973, Dr. Benjamin Spock, the guru of child-rearing, declared in a *Redbook* article that caring for children was a job for men as well as women, and he promised to use gender-neutral pronouns in new editions of his best-selling guide.

The fact that Dr. Spock's article appeared in *Redbook* was telling. "Women's" magazines such as *Redbook* and *The Ladies' Home Journal* didn't give up their columns about home décor, enticing meals, and ways to attract a man, but those stories now shared space with articles about women's activism and women's job choices. The women's movement was suddenly the subject of coverage by such thoroughly mainstream publications as *TIME, Newsweek, Atlantic Monthly, Look,* and *Life.* In 1972, Helen Reddy's "I am Woman," with its iconic lines "I am woman, hear me roar, In numbers too big to ignore," was number one on the Billboard chart and won a GRAMMY Award. Television viewers could watch the widely popular *Mary Tyler Moore Show,* featuring a thirty-something career television producer, or its predecessor, *That Girl,* starring Marlo Thomas. In 1973, they might have been among the 90,000,000 viewers worldwide who watched tennis champion Billie Jean King, a twenty-nine-year-old feminist, beat Bobby Riggs in the tennis match that was billed as the "Battle of the Sexes." Or they could have picked up a copy of Erica Jong's *Fear of Flying,* with its celebration of casual female sexuality.

All of that reflected a seismic cultural shift in the United States and helped drive it forward. Like any other major cultural upheaval, it had its opponents. In a 1976 article, Ginsburg quoted from Elizabeth Janeway's *Man's World, Woman's Place:* "If there's nothing more powerful than an idea whose time has come, there is nothing more ubiquitously pervasive than an idea whose time won't go." "Feminism" was still a dirty word in many circles, and the mid-1970s would see the emergence of a strong right-wing, anti-feminist movement led most prominently by Phyllis Schlafly. Nonetheless, Congress allocated $5 million for the National Women's Conference that was held in Houston in 1977 (with Schlafly and her followers holding their own counter-conference). It was Congress, after all, that added "sex" to Title VII of the 1964 Civil Rights Act; amended the Equal Pay Act in 1972 to extend to more categories of workers and to include Title IX, which banned sex discrimination in educational institutions; and passed the 1974 Equal Credit Opportunity Act, enabling married women to apply for credit in their own names. The elected branches of the federal government had gotten the message, however incompletely and however uncomfortable it still made some of their members.

Ginsburg acknowledged that. Speaking of the women's movement, she wrote in 2013,

> We tried to get legislative change and when that didn't work, the Court was the next resort. In fact, in the '70s, the legislature and the courts were involved in a kind of dialogue. The Court would say, "This gender line is unconstitutional," and the legislature would then make amendments in that law and others like it. The Department of Justice and the U.S. Civil Rights Commission went through the entire U.S. Code to identify all of the gender-based differentials and Congress eliminated most of them.

Ginsburg's reference to the Civil Rights Commission omits her role in the process. In 1972, the commission was charged with adding instances of sex discrimination to its agenda. It turned to the Women's Rights Project, which in turn called upon Ginsburg's Columbia Law School students to identify federal laws that discriminated on the basis of sex. Fifteen of the students researched and helped draft *Sex Bias in the U.S. Code*, which was published by the Commission in 1977. *Sex Bias* criticized the Supreme Court for choosing "on numerous occasions to deny to women certain rights and privileges not denied to men" and for refusing to declare sex a suspect classification. Carol Bonosaro, director of the Civil Rights Commission's Women's Rights Unit, drew upon the report to develop Justice Department programs. The task force in the Department of Justice that was charged with developing a plan for eliminating sex discrimination in the public sector relied upon the report as well. Senator Howard Metzenbaum put a summary of the report in the *Congressional Record*.

Sex Bias emphasized that "Congress clearly must assume leadership in amending the Code and enacting legislation to promote equal opportunity." By 1977, there were members of Congress who were willing to accept the job. Things had changed dramatically since the 1960s. Back then, as Representative Don Edwards, a leading member of the House Judiciary Committee, remembered, the effort to include sex in the 1964 Civil Rights Act was "the first example, the first instance, the first time that most of us got an indication of sex discrimination in this country. We really hadn't heard about it before. We'd heard about what they—white people—did to Indians, to black people, and so forth, but not to women and, if you think about it, it's a relatively new concept that discrimination against sex should be protected by law."

In the 1950s through the early 1970s, as noted earlier, women began entering Congress in what were still miniscule but nonetheless unprecedented numbers. They were not just any women; most were explicitly feminist. As Congress has since recognized, "their feminism—their belief in the social, political, and economic equality of the sexes—shaped their agenda." In 1977, fifteen congressional women formed the bipartisan Congresswomen's Caucus, later the Congressional Caucus for Women's Issues, and began discussing issues such as Social Security and private pension reform, child care, job training for women on welfare, and government contracts for women-owned businesses.

The movement for gender equality was not only American; it was worldwide. When the National Organization for Women held its International Feminist Planning Conference in 1973, three hundred women from twenty-seven countries attended. The United Nations declared 1975 to be the International Year of the Woman.

All this was background as Ginsburg worked on the cases that reached the Supreme Court. The men of the court were not only aware of what was happening in society but were fathers, brothers, husbands, grandfathers. Some of them discovered that there were feminists—or at least women determined to lead their own lives—in the bosom of their families. William Brennan's daughter Nancy educated him about the women's movement and her own career expectations. Divorced, Nancy and her child moved in temporarily with the Brennans while she pursued her career, and the justice found himself having to leave work each afternoon to pick up his granddaughter from day care. Harry Blackmun turned to his wife and daughters for their thoughts when he was assigned the court's opinion in *Roe v. Wade*. "Judges had daughters and granddaughters and they began to recognize that some of . . . the so-called favors for women were not favors at all, but they were locking women into a small piece of man's wide world," Ginsburg would comment. For the first time, the 1974–1975 court term saw an unprecedented four women law clerks in the justices' chambers—some of them with childcare responsibilities.

In other words, to return to the analogy of the Supreme Court as somewhere in the middle of the train of social change, Ginsburg and the success of her litigation both reflected what was going on in society and added momentum to the phenomenon. The constitutional canvas on which she painted had been an unwelcoming one at first, and to some extent still was, but the societal framework was very much in her favor. She said repeatedly that she simply happened to be there at the right moment: "It was the change in society that opened the Court's eyes and made my arguments palatable when they would not have been a generation before." That greatly minimizes the importance of her enormous legal talents, but to some extent it is quite right.

CHAPTER 5

The Kidnapper, the Lieutenant, and the Widower

Ginsburg said frequently that gender stereotypes hurt men as well as women. The truth of that assertion was evident in three cases, each with a male plaintiff, that reached the Supreme Court in the mid-1970s.

In 1972, a Louisiana man named Billy Taylor was convicted by an all-male jury and sentenced to death for a kidnapping that involved robbery and rape. Both the Louisiana constitution and the state's criminal law made jury service mandatory for men, but gave women an automatic exemption unless they filed a declaration of their desire to serve. The law, in other words, was a version of the statute in Gwendolyn Hoyt's case. Taylor appealed, as Hoyt had, arguing that the exemption violated the Sixth Amendment's right to a jury representative of the community and the Fourteenth Amendment's Due Process Clause. Both the lower court and the state supreme court denied his claim. Taylor was represented by local Louisiana counsel, who appealed the case to the US Supreme Court.

In August 1973, two months after the *Frontiero* decision, the United States District Court for eastern Louisiana heard a similar case. In it, the same Louisiana constitutional provision and law were challenged by three groups of Louisiana citizens: women who said they were effectively excluded from jury service, men who contended that the exclusion of women subjected them to more frequent jury service, and women litigants represented by other women in civil litigation who argued that they were deprived of a jury of their peers. Ginsburg worked with a local attorney on the case, which was named *Healy v. Edwards* after Marsha B. Healy, one of the women, and Governor Edwin Edwards. Healy was a member of the Louisiana ACLU affiliate's board of directors, and the litigation was quite deliberately initiated by the affiliate as a test case that did not involve someone the justices might have seen as an unsympathetic convicted criminal.

Ginsburg had hoped to get a different jury case to the high court. In 1972, a Tennessee jury convicted Edna Stubblefield, a young Black woman, of murder. Stubblefield challenged her grand jury indictment and then appealed after her conviction on the grounds that Black Americans had been excluded from jury service, as had any white woman who did not register to serve. The grand jury foreman was a white man who had served in that position since 1937. As Ginsburg would note, "between 1961 and 1972, 2259 whites were called for jury duty as opposed to 47 blacks," and "only 21 women were called (only one of whom was black) but none actually served." After the Tennessee Supreme Court rejected Stubblefield's appeal, her attorneys asked the Women's Rights Project (WRP) to take on the case. Ginsburg saw it as her opportunity to overturn *Hoyt*, but the US Supreme Court refused to hear it. Now, in *Healy v. Edwards*, she had another chance.

She prepared a brief that relied heavily on the Supreme Court's 1946 decision in *Ballard v. U.S.* In that decision, it may be remembered, the court held that the exclusion of women as jurors in federal criminal trials—but not state trials—violated the Sixth Amendment's guarantee of a jury of one's peers. Ginsburg could now argue that *Reed* had established that under the Equal Protection Clause, a state law creating an unsupported sex-based classification also had to fall. The case was assigned to a three-judge federal district court in New Orleans, and Ginsburg flew there in July 1973, for oral argument.

To her surprised delight, the judges immediately told her that she'd successfully made her point in her brief and asked if she had anything to add. Relying on the brief and a very truncated oral argument, the court held on August 31 that *Hoyt* was no longer good law. Citing the Supreme Court's decisions in *Reed* and *Frontiero*, the unanimous opinion declared that the absence of women from juries deprived defendants of their right to be tried by a cross section of the community. Louisiana appealed. Ginsburg would argue the case in the US Supreme Court.

The court decided to combine the cases of *Edwards v. Healy* and *Taylor v. Louisiana* and scheduled oral argument for October 16, 1974. It would hear from Ginsburg in the *Healy* case and then from William King, Taylor's lawyer, in *Taylor*.

Louisiana assistant attorney general Kendall Vick spoke first in *Edwards v. Healy*, arguing that the case was moot, as the state had drafted an amendment to its constitution, making all male and female adult citizens eligible for jury service as of January 1975. The justices were unpersuaded, because even if the new provision went into effect for future cases, it was not retroactive, and Taylor's conviction would stand. When it was Ginsburg's turn to speak about *Healy*, she noted that the new provision, if adopted, would make all women eligible but would still let the state legislature decide what exemptions to actual jury service should be made under it. The state might, for example, give all mothers but not all fathers an automatic exemption. Like *Taylor*, the *Healy* case was not moot at all.

Ginsburg told the court that excluding women from a jury denied litigants both equal protection and due process, "because the system precludes any possibility that their cases will be tried by a jury drawn from a representative cross-section of the community." Justice Stewart questioned that.

> JUSTICE STEWART: I thought the new theory was that there's very little difference between men and women, and so wouldn't men jurors be their peers?
>
> Ms. GINSBURG: Well, I am not aware of that new theory. I subscribe and I think most people do to a theory announced by one of the justices some years ago in Ballard against the United States, that the two sexes are not fungible, that the absence of either may make the jury even less representative of the community than it would be if an economic or a racial group were excluded.

Chief Justice Burger asked whether the analogy could be made to *Kahn v. Shevin*; that is, whether the provision excusing women from juries was not a good thing for them. Not wanting to attack that decision before the justices who had voted for it, Ginsburg replied that *Kahn* involved a property tax, an area in which the court traditionally gave the states great leeway. Here, she said, the question was whether exclusion of women was fair to litigants. Justice Stewart, clearly still resistant, asked whether establishing categories of acceptable jurors didn't make sense, referring to age limitations and Louisiana's exclusion of jurors under eighteen and over seventy. "Of course," Ginsburg replied, "there is a tremendous difference between age, which is something that happens to all of us, and sex which is immutable and doesn't change. . . . You're put in that status at birth, and you can't get out of it." (It should be noted that "transgender" had not yet made its way into US law—or in the thinking of the society at large.)

In saying that *Hoyt* was no longer good law, the district court had called it "outgrown dogma." Ginsburg now criticized the assumption in *Hoyt* that requiring women to serve as jurors would hurt family stability. Testily reminding her that *Hoyt* was decided by a unanimous court (and although he did not mention it, he had participated in that decision), Justice Stewart objected, "You seem to treat [*Hoyt*] fairly cavalierly." That in turn appeared to bother Chief Justice Burger, who had not been on the court when *Hoyt* was decided. Before he ended oral argument, the chief justice commented, "I'm not sure you need any defense, Mrs. Ginsburg, but your brief and argument is much less cavalier toward *Hoyt* than the three judges of the Fifth Circuit." Apparently, Justice Stewart and Chief Justice Burger had their differences.

The various justices' papers suggest that there was nonetheless not a great deal of disagreement among them about how the two cases should be decided, and on January 21, 1975, the court handed down its decision in *Taylor*. Justice White wrote for the court, holding that under the Sixth Amendment's right to a jury trial, juries had to be drawn from a cross section of the community. "The purpose of a jury," he said, "is to guard against the exercise of arbitrary power—to make available the commonsense judgment of the community." That does not happen "if the jury pool is made up of only special segments of the populace or if large, distinctive groups are excluded from the pool." Participation by the entire community "is not only consistent with our democratic heritage but is also critical to public confidence in the fairness of the criminal justice system." The logical conclusion was that "if it was ever the case that women . . . were so situated that none of them should be required to perform jury service, that time has long since passed." He backed up his assertion with a long footnote detailing statistics about women in the labor force. *Hoyt*, Justice White declared, was no longer good law.

Because the decision was based on the Sixth Amendment's right to a trial, there was no reason for the court to get into the debate about the proper test to be used when sex-based categories were challenged under the Fourteenth Amendment's Equal Protection Clause. Justice White might have been thinking about that, however, when he added, "The right to a proper jury cannot be overcome on merely rational grounds." The court left for another day Ginsburg's Equal Protection argument in *Edwards v. Healy*.

The vote in *Taylor* was 8–1, with Justice Rehnquist protesting in dissent that no one had shown that Taylor had suffered from the absence of women on the jury that convicted him. A week later, the justices held unanimously in a *per curium* opinion (the case was *Daniel v. Louisiana*) that the *Taylor* holding was not to be applied retroactively and so had no effect on cases in which juries were empaneled before *Taylor* was decided. A few months later, on June 9, 1975, it sent *Healy* back to the district court to decide whether, in light of what by then were the changes to the Louisiana constitution and statutes, the case had become moot. It had, and so the court wrote no decision in *Edwards v. Healy*.

Ginsburg was nonetheless pleased, saying that the decision in *Taylor* helped to "put the Court back on track" after the devastating loss in *Kahn v. Shevin*. Congratulations were in order, but Ginsburg and the WRP were about to wrestle with another decision they viewed as setting the law back.

* * *

Robert C. Ballard was a lieutenant in the US Navy. By 1972, he had served as a commissioned officer for nine years. He was then turned down twice for promotion to lieutenant commander, and under US law, a male lieutenant who twice failed to be promoted during nine years of service had to be discharged. A woman lieutenant, however, had thirteen years rather than nine in which to qualify for promotion before a mandatory discharge. The monetary implications were substantial, as the retirement benefits Ballard was denied would have amounted to approximately $200,000 (over a million dollars in the 2020s). He sued, calling the difference in the treatment of male and female officers a violation of due process and equal protection.

The three-judge federal district court that heard the case relied upon *Frontiero v. Richardson*, saying that the differential was based on considerations of fiscal and administrative policy and was therefore unconstitutional. The government appealed to the US Supreme Court.

Schlesinger v. Ballard was not a WRP case, as the lieutenant was represented by Morris Dees of the Southern Poverty Law Center and California attorney Charles Khoury. (James R. Schlesinger was the secretary of defense.) The case, however, had obvious implications for Ginsburg's and the WRP's attempt to strike down differential treatment based on stereotypes. Ballard lost in the Supreme Court. The decision was handed down just a week before the justices announced their decision in the *Taylor* jury case. The results in the two cases demonstrated once again that the justices were finding it difficult to fashion a coherent approach to the question of gender equality. *Taylor* struck a blow for treating men and women equally; *Ballard* did just the opposite.

Justice Potter Stewart wrote for the five-man *Ballard* majority in holding that the situations in *Reed* and *Frontiero* were entirely distinct from those in the new case. The differential in *Ballard*, he said, was based not on administrative convenience but on "the demonstrable fact that male and female line officers in the Navy are not similarly situated with respect to opportunities for professional service." Specifically, as women were not eligible to serve in combat and on any vessels other than hospital and transport ships, they had less of a chance to compile the kind of service records that would entitle them to be considered for promotion. As a result, they needed a longer time to prove their mettle.

Justice Brennan disagreed. He insisted once again that the proper standard for judgment of a gender-based differential was "suspect classification" and a showing that there was a compelling governmental interest that could not be achieved any other way. In a footnote, he went even further, making a comment that showed him to be substantially ahead of his time.

I find quite troublesome the notion that a gender-based difference in treatment can be justified by another, broader, gender-based difference in treatment imposed directly and currently by the Navy itself. While it is true that the restrictions upon women officers' opportunities for professional service are not here directly under attack, they are obviously implicated on the Court's chosen ground for decision, and the Court ought at least to consider whether they may be valid before sustaining a provision it conceives to be based upon them.

Neither Lieutenant Ballard nor the government, as Ginsburg would point out in an article, had challenged "the discrimination that made it possible for a man to be promoted more rapidly than a woman—the drastically curtailed job training and assignments available to Navy women." That made it all the more remarkable, in 1974, for Brennan to question the exclusion of women from many navy positions. Justices Douglas and Marshall signed onto Brennan's dissent. But even though Justice Byron White also dissented, the dissenters were in the minority, and *Ballard* simply reinforced the ruling in *Kahn v. Shevin* that differential treatment was appropriate compensation for women. Ginsburg called *Kahn* and *Ballard* "backsliding." *Ballard*, she wrote, was "a tangled, idiosyncratic case . . . [that] tendered a problem peculiarly resistant to judicial solution. The Court was asked to screen in isolation, and riveted to Lt. Ballard's special situation, a small piece of a large, complex puzzle."

The puzzle was about what role women should serve in the military, and had it been up to Ginsburg, *Ballard* would never have gone to the Supreme Court. It was distressing to her that the case she saw as setting back the drive for gender equality hadn't even been thought of originally as a women's rights case, and its reaching the Supreme Court was indicative of her inability to control the litigation agenda. As she recalled one of his attorneys telling her, "Ballard came to me with his problem, and I thought and thought, what can I do to get him the extra time that he needs to qualify for the pension? And then it came to me—sex discrimination!"

But there was another case she very much wanted to go to the court, and it was one that she would call "near and dear to my heart": It was called *Weinberger v. Wiesenfeld*.

* * *

When Paula Polatschek and Stephen Wiesenfeld married on November 15, 1970, she was working as a school math teacher and he was a computer consultant. That year, Paula earned $9,808; Stephen, $3,100. She continued to be the primary breadwinner during their marriage, as her salary in 1971 was $10,686 while Stephen brought home $2,475. In keeping with the law, Social Security contributions were deducted from Paula's salary throughout those years. The Wiesenfelds had enough of an income to allow them to begin a family, and in 1971 Paula become pregnant.

On June 5, 1972, Paula Wiesenfeld died giving birth to a son, Jason Paul. A devastated Stephen decided to raise Jason by himself. He and Paula had planned for him to do the bulk of childcare while working part-time anyway, and while he tried to hire outside help as a supplement during the hours he needed to work, he found it inadequate. "I hired a nurse from Boston—she wasn't all that interested. I brought a girl from Norway—she wasn't clean," Stephen would tell Ginsburg. He knew he would not be able to spend sufficient time with his son while working full-time, and so he applied for Social Security childcare benefits. The office in New Brunswick, New Jersey, told him that under the Social Security laws he was entitled to child insurance benefits for Jason but he was ineligible for the "child in care" payments that went to a widow in his situation. The law provided a benefit only for a "mother [who] has in her care a child of [an insured] individual," but not for a father. Stephen could collect only half the amount that would have been paid to a similarly situated female survivor of a male wage earner.

A struggling Stephen read a story in a New Brunswick newspaper about widowed men. That prompted him to write a letter to the editor about what he saw as the unfairness of his situation. Phyllis Boring, a professor at Rutgers University and an officer of the Women's Equity Action League, read the letter, asked if he would consider pursuing a legal remedy, and wrote to Ginsburg about it.

Ginsburg thought that it would be a perfect case and that Stephen was the perfect plaintiff. "It's a great case and we certainly will take it if Mr. Wiesenfeld agrees," Ginsburg wrote to Boring. "If you come across any other gems like this, please let me know." She saw the case as involving "three-fold discrimination": "Discrimination against the woman as wage earner—her contributions to Social Security did not net for her family the same benefits that a man's contributions did. Discrimination against Stephen as a parent, who wanted to care personally for his child. And discrimination against the baby, who would have the opportunity for the care of the sole surviving parent if the parent were female, but not if the parent were male."

Stephen contacted Ginsburg in late 1972. Needing to be certain of her facts, she asked him for details. "My son is in my care and I intend to keep it that way," he wrote to her. He occasionally had to leave his son with his parents, while he looked desperately for work, but "the majority of his time is with me."

Ginsburg was busy preparing for oral argument in *Frontiero*, which would take place in January 1973, and she turned some of the work in *Wiesenfeld* over to the students in her Equal Rights Advocacy Project. They would join her when the case was argued in the district court and would later have the excitement of sitting at the counsel table with her when *Wiesenfeld* went to the US Supreme Court. She believed it was the perfect follow-up to *Frontiero*: a way to demonstrate once again that sex-specific classifications hurt men as well as women. She planned for it to reach the Court right after *Frontiero*, but "in a movement as diffuse as this one," she lamented once again, "a well-planned litigation campaign is impossible to arrange." The fly in the ointment, of course, was *Kahn v. Shevin*. She would have to deal with it as she shaped her argument in *Wiesenfeld*.

The federal district court in New Jersey that would hear Stephen Wiesenfeld's case was busy with a different major case, and so oral argument did not take place until June 20, 1973. In the meantime, Ginsburg worked on her brief while also juggling Edna Stubblefield's and the *Healy v. Edwards* jury cases. The *Frontiero* decision was handed down a month before oral argument in *Wiesenfeld*, which meant she could refer to it as she spoke to the district court. Jubilant about *Frontiero* and especially about Brennan's opinion in it, she wrote to Jane Lifset, her former student at Rutgers and now the New Jersey attorney with whom she was working on *Wiesenfeld*, "the decision pulls the rug out from under any tenable argument the [government] could make." She would soon learn that the three-judge district court thought so as well.

The district court decided for Stephen Wiesenfeld, agreeing with Ginsburg that under the law, the rights of three classes of people were violated. It rejected the rational basis test as insufficient and turned instead to the suspect classification standard in Justice Brennan's plurality opinion in *Frontiero*. Under it, the court said, the law clearly "discriminates against women such as Paula Wiesenfeld who have successfully gained employment as well as against men and children who have lost their wives and mothers."

The government appealed, and Ginsburg began to write her brief for the Supreme Court. As she did so, she no longer referred to "sex" discrimination. Milicent Tryon, the secretary at Columbia University who did her typing, had told her, as Ginsburg remembered, "I'm typing these briefs for you and jumping out all over the page is 'sex, sex, sex.' Don't you know that for the male audience you are addressing, the first association of the word 'sex' is not what you're talking about? So, why don't you use a grammar book term? Use 'gender.' It has a neutral sound, and it will ward off distracting associations." So "gender" discrimination it became.

It also became an argument that did not include urging the justices to adopt the suspect classification test. "The initial strategy, pursued in Reed and Frontiero," Ginsburg said, "was to argue for strict scrutiny of gender distinctions, in part by drawing an analogy between sex- and race-based classification. That tack was modified in briefing Wiesenfeld," because the votes for suspect classification simply were not there. Her omission of the suspect classification argument, however, did not mean that she wanted to give up the slow fight for it; she still wanted to keep the idea before the justices. She therefore worked closely with Elizabeth Schneider, Nancy Stearns, and Rhonda Copelon of the Center for Constitutional Rights, three stalwart feminist litigators, as they prepared an amicus brief that urged the court "to seize the opportunity presented by this case to . . . accord women the equal protection of strict judicial scrutiny." When Ginsburg was contacted by other groups wanting to join one of her cases as amici, she would coordinate with them carefully, making certain that their approaches complemented hers. "Your brief might make a suspect classification argument," she wrote to Schneider, adding, "I would appreciate seeing a draft of your amicus before you file it."

Leaving it to the amici to make the suspect classification argument, Ginsburg wrote in her own brief that the more stringent standard was unnecessary here anyway. She relied on the enhanced rational basis test implicit in *Reed* and preferred by the majority in *Frontiero*, stating that it was clearly Congress's intention "to provide for the families of deceased workers" and that there was no logical relationship between that goal and excluding a widower from the "child in care" benefits. She distinguished *Kahn* as relying on the leeway given to states in writing their tax laws and as reflecting a desire "to remedy past economic discrimination encountered by women." That was a "laudable legislative objective," she agreed, but a court had to be certain that a gender classification "does not perpetuate practices responsible for that discrimination." And the law here, she went on, "presents a classic example of the double-edged discrimination characteristic of laws that chivalrous gentlemen, sitting in all-male chambers, misconceive as a favor to the ladies." Depriving Stephen Wiesenfeld of a childcare benefit was no favor to anyone. "Surely Paula Wiesenfeld would have found unfathomable the attempt to cast a compensatory cloak over the denial to her family of benefits available to the family of a male insured," Ginsburg wrote. Nor would Paula have understood "why the infant Jason Paul Wiesenfeld can have the personal care of a sole surviving parent only if that parent is female."

Yes, Congress had ignored the phenomenon of working mothers when it enacted this provision of the Social Security law in 1939, Ginsburg acknowledged. "Congress assumed a division of parental responsibility along gender lines: breadwinner was synonymous with father; child tenderer with mother." The world had moved on since then, however, and she once again pointed to statistics about women's economic role. The Wiesenfelds' family situation was far from unique, she pointed out. In 1970, wives earned more than did their husbands in 3.2 million, or 7.4 percent, of all American families. There was no reason to treat them as anything but providers for their families.

The tone of her brief was unusually angry for Ginsburg, and it appeared that the government's arguments were the reason. The government's brief, filed in the name of Robert Bork, the solicitor general, attacked everything she had achieved in *Reed* and in her cases that followed that decision. Largely ignoring the changes that the court had accepted in interpreting the Equal Protection Clause, Bork blithely claimed that under the court's ruling in *Kahn*, the justices would have to uphold any program that purported to provide compensation for underpaid women. The race/sex analogy was rejected as frivolous. The classification involved in the *Wiesenfeld* case "serves the legitimate, compassionate governmental objective of ameliorating the harsh economic circumstances of women." The brief asserted that the reason for the differential in the Wiesenfelds' earnings was that Stephen was a student—which, Ginsburg pointed out, was simply not true. Besides, the government claimed, women collected more benefits under the Social Security system than did men and paid less into the system. The cost of extending the benefit to fathers would throw the program into debt and would therefore require either an increase in taxes or a decrease in everyone's benefits.

Frontiero, as well as numerous cases in other areas of the law, Ginsburg replied, made it clear that while "fiscal economy is a commendable goal . . . it may not be achieved by invidious exclusions of persons guaranteed by the Constitution the equal protection of the laws." In fact, the government had admitted in a footnote that the additional cost would not be substantial but that it was worried about "closely analogous provisions" in other laws. That seemed to echo the government's argument in Charles Moritz's tax case, when it professed horror at the specter of men and women being treated equally by a profusion of laws, as well as the government's equally failed argument in *Frontiero*. Far from being "compassionate," the differential merely reflected "the assumption that it is less important for a child to be cared for by its sole surviving parent when that parent is male rather than female." Ginsburg quoted Justice Brennan's language in *Frontiero* about a pedestal and a cage, noting that a large number of lower courts had implicitly accepted that assertion in striking down other legislation based on outmoded stereotypes: excluding policewomen from taking the exam for promotion to sergeant, for example, and banning female high school students from sports teams. She reminded the court of congressional and presidential actions that acknowledged women's substantial economic roles and prohibited gender discrimination in the workplace.

Ginsburg was as contemptuous of the government's arguments as she was angry about them. "Now that it's no good to discriminate against women," she told an interviewer in 1976, "they rationalize every gender line as a help to women." They used that approach in *Wiesenfeld*: "'Since the benefits go to mothers, this has to help women.' Then they just ignore the reality."

Deputy Solicitor General Keith A. Jones spoke for the government when the court heard oral argument on January 20, 1975. He began by conceding that "the traditionally permissive rational basis standard of review" might not be appropriate whenever a claim of sex discrimination was made. What the court was now doing, Jones said, was demand "that sex based classifications must rest upon some substantial reasonable basis." There was one here. The court had acknowledged in *Kahn* that women were traditionally underpaid, and so it was reasonable for Congress to recognize that "the probable need of widows is greater than that of widowers." Jones reiterated the argument that the Social Security system was legally mandated to remain in actuarial balance, and as women already received more than their fair share of benefits under it, extending additional benefits to men would be an unacceptable strain on the system's viability.

Ginsburg began her presentation by speaking at some length about the Wiesenfelds. Her approach reflected her belief that the justices had to be made to see the real-world people and the potential real-world consequences involved in gender discrimination cases. Here, with Stephen sitting at the counsel table—she wanted the justices to see a man who was hurt by gender classifications—she made that point by describing the way all three Wiesenfelds were discriminated against by the law.

> MRS. GINSBURG: In 1972, Paula died giving birth to her son Jason Paul, leaving the child's father Stephen Wiesenfeld, with the sole responsibility for the care of Jason Paul. For the eight months, immediately following his wife's death and for all but the seventh month period thereafter, Stephen Wiesenfeld did not engage in substantial gainful employment. Instead, he devoted himself to the care of the infant, Jason Paul. . . . There could not be a clearer case than this one of the double-edged swords in operation of differential treatment accorded similarly situated persons based grossly and solely on gender.
>
> Paula Wiesenfeld, in fact the principal wage earner, is treated as though her years of work were of only secondary value to her family. Stephen Wiesenfeld, in fact the nurturing parent, is treated as though he did not perform that function. And Jason Paul, a motherless infant with a father able and willing to provide care of him personally, is treated as an infant not entitled to the personal care of his sole surviving parent.

"All the plaintiffs represented by the ACLU's Women's Rights Project were real people with a story, a life story that was engaging and entirely genuine," Ginsburg said later. "Stephen's case so moved me. He was devastated by his wife's death and he was really determined to bring up Jason himself." She wanted the men in the robes to understand that men, or at least some men, could be as involved in childcare as could women. This time, the justices permitted Ginsburg to speak at length before anyone interrupted.

In *Frontiero*, she went on to remind them, "the Court evidenced a concern to analyze gender classifications with a view to the modern world and to be weary of gross, archaic, overbroad generalizations." In fact, "the prime generator of discrimination accounted by women in the economic sector is the pervasive attitude, now lacking functional justification, that pairs women with children, men with work." Ginsburg dismissed the classification in the statute as no more than "law-reinforced sex-role pigeon-holing defended as a remedy." She emphasized that Paula had contributed the required percentage of her wages as Social Security taxes, so the benefit was something the family had earned, not a gift. As for the government's claim that extending the benefit to fathers would destroy the system, she pointed out both that the benefit would be available only to what would probably be the relatively small proportion of fathers who would choose to do full-time childcare and that the benefit ceased once the family's income reached a certain limit.

The time allotted to the case expired, and Ginsburg raced back to New York to teach her class at Columbia. (Jane Booth, one of her students, remembered that the students were so certain that she would need time to decompress after oral argument, and so would cancel class, that many of them had not even done the reading for the day.) At the justices' conference later that week, Chief Justice Burger assigned the opinion for the court to Justice Brennan. When the court announced its unanimous decision on March 19, 1975, it was a resounding victory for Ginsburg.

Brennan's opinion relied on *Frontiero*, calling "the gender-based distinction" in the Social Security law "indistinguishable" from the one the court struck down in that case, and dependent on "a virtually identical 'archaic and overbroad' generalization." This law was even more "pernicious" than the one in *Frontiero*, in two ways. Under the law challenged in *Frontiero*, the servicewoman was at least given an opportunity to demonstrate that her husband was dependent on her. Here, however, the law gave Stephen Wiesenfeld no opportunity to prove his dependence on his wife. In addition, as social security taxes were deducted from Paula's salary, she was forced to contribute even though her family would not receive the same protection that the family of a similarly situated male worker would receive.

The legislative history of the law made it clear, Brennan declared, that Congress's purpose was "to provide children deprived of one parent with the opportunity for the personal attention of the other," and "given the purpose of enabling the surviving parent to remain at home to care for a child, the gender-based distinction . . . is entirely irrational." He cited Ginsburg's brief in noting that most male workers probably would not opt for full-time child-care and probably would earn too much to be eligible for the benefit, so the system would not be in fiscal jeopardy and the classification was entirely "gratuitous."

The vote was 8–0. (Justice William O. Douglas had suffered a stroke at the end of 1974 and took no part in the case.) Justices Powell and Rehnquist each wrote a short concurrence. Brennan described the case as involving women's rights; Powell, joined by Chief Justice Burger, as a matter of fairness to men; Rehnquist, as a victory for children's rights. Among them, as Ginsburg would comment, they "covered all the bases." It was the only time in Ginsburg's litigation career that Rehnquist would vote to strike down a classification based on gender. Years later, when she became a member of the Supreme Court, Rehnquist, who by then was chief justice, asked Ginsburg if Stephen had really raised Jason. She was able to assure him that yes, Stephen had.

Brennan's opinion in *Wiesenfeld* had once again picked up on Ginsburg's arguments, as she had utilized his earlier language in her brief. The ballet of the two continued. Brennan was now also referring to "gender"; the government, in both its brief and oral argument, was relying on "sex." By the time the decision was announced, Ginsburg, anticipating, or perhaps simply hoping for the result, was busy planning attacks on other parts of the Social Security law that differentiated unfairly between men and women: "In fact, we had the basic papers for [the next case] already prepared in Wiesenfeld."

"Justices Back Widower's Equal Rights," the *New York Times* headlined, calling *Wiesenfeld* as much a victory for women's rights as for men. The decision, the first-page article said, was "the first time the Court had insisted on equal treatment in a sex discrimination case when such a ruling would be very expensive to the Government." The article was accompanied by a picture of two-and-a-half-year-old Jason, held by a smiling Stephen, clutching a telephone and supposedly being informed about what the family had won. Syndicated columnist James Kilpatrick declared in the *Miami Herald* that "Brennan's denunciation of discrimination by reason of sex was just about wholesale." "The trend is unmistakably clear," Kilpatrick continued. "Unless the state or the federal government can come up with compelling reasons to justify sexual discrimination, such discrimination cannot survive."

Ginsburg became fond of many of her clients, but she remained particularly close to the Wiesenfelds. She had first met Stephen in person on the train to Trenton, as they traveled to the district court for oral argument, and the two became friends. Once the Supreme Court decision was handed down, the Ginsburgs hosted a victory party at their apartment, with Stephen and Jason in attendance. Before it, Ginsburg and her nine-year-old son, James, bought copies of some of James' favorite early childhood books as a present for Jason. Stephen testified at her Senate confirmation hearing when Ginsburg was nominated to the Supreme Court in 1993. She in turn copresided at Jason's wedding in 1998. And when Stephen decided in 2014 to remarry, Ginsburg performed the wedding in the same Supreme Court building in which she had successfully argued his case almost thirty years earlier.

Wiesenfeld was a great victory. "Tears came to my eyes when I read the decision," Milicent Tryon wrote to Ginsburg. "I cried too!" Ginsburg replied. "Wiesenfeld may put a stop to uncritical recitation of Kahn to uphold classifications considered 'benign' to women," she told a law student. Nonetheless, the trend that James Kilpatrick wrote about was interrupted in a major way when the justices were confronted with an issue they found confusing. It had to do with pregnant women.

The Court Grapples with Pregnancy

"Something about reproductive health makes politicians and local officials lose their reasoning faculties," journalists Nicholas Kristof and Sheryl WuDunn write in *Tightrope: Americans Reaching for Hope*. They might have added, "and something about pregnancy makes judges lose their reasoning faculties as well." That certainly is the impression one gets in reviewing the Supreme Court's decisions in the pregnancy-related cases of the 1970s.

Ginsburg had long believed, as did most other attorneys working in the field, that a major obstacle to gender equality in employment was the courts' and legislatures' attitude toward pregnancy. That applied to the right to have children free of government interference as well as the right to decide not to have them. Most private employers had very mixed attitudes toward work and motherhood, and that, too, limited women's lives. From 1973 on, the Women's Rights Project (WRP) was involved in a series of cases challenging the way both government and private employers treated pregnancy in the workplace. The results were mixed at best; at some times, a total disaster.

The armed forces was one of the workplaces that the WRP looked at. Ginsburg had cared deeply about the case of Susan Struck, the US Air Force captain who had been forced to leave the service when she became pregnant. Ginsburg's brief in the case had declared, "Heading the list of arbitrary barriers that have plagued women seeking equal opportunity is disadvantaged treatment based on their unique childbearing function." The result in Struck's case was mixed, because while in 1973 the air force quickly responded by changing its regulation, its doing so kept the case from being heard by the Supreme Court. Civilian workplaces were also a problem. Mary Ellen Schattman was an employee of the Texas Employment Commission who was forced to leave when she was seven months pregnant. Ginsburg asked the Supreme Court to hear her case, but at the same time that *Struck* was mooted, the justices refused to give Mary Ellen Schattman's appeal a place on their calendar. The WRP reacted by publishing a paper titled *The Right to Be Pregnant* and by looking for a case that might make it onto the all-male court's docket.

There was in fact one such case that was already on the court's calendar. It was *Cleveland v. LaFleur*, mentioned earlier, challenging Cleveland's mandatory leave rule for pregnant teachers. The case was brought by the Women's Law Fund of Cleveland, which thought that the Due Process Clause provided better grounds for an appeal than the Equal Protection Clause. They proved to be correct. The justices held in favor of Jo Carol LaFleur, but did so on the basis of due process and the right to privacy they found in that clause rather than equal protection. "This Court," Justice Potter Stewart wrote for the seven-justice majority, "has long recognized that freedom of personal choice in matters of marriage and family life is one of the liberties protected by the Due Process Clause of the Fourteenth Amendment," and he cited abortion rights cases. Those cases reflected the right "to be free from unwarranted governmental intrusion into matters so fundamentally affecting a person as the decision whether to bear or beget a child," he added. What Cleveland had done was "penalize the pregnant teacher for deciding to bear a child," which violated her right to personal choice.

Ginsburg and the WRP were amicus in the case. Ginsburg's brief made the equal protection argument, but Justice Stewart did not mention the Equal Protection Clause. One of Justice Harry Blackmun's clerks, reading Stewart's draft opinion, wrote to Blackmun, "The words sex discrimination are nowhere mentioned, believe it or not." While Ginsburg was "delighted" at the outcome of the case, she knew that the omission of equal protection had serious consequences for future pregnancy-related claims of sex discrimination. It appeared that the justices, and perhaps much of society, thought of the kind of gender equality mandated by the Equal Protection Clause, on the one hand, and pregnancy itself, on the other, as occupying completely different legal silos. The state of gender equality law, she wrote in 1974, "is euphemistically described as muddled. The problem is that a majority has never faced up to the basic issue in this area: may government prescribe or allocate social functions on the basis of sex, rather than the individual's ability or

{ *Chapter Six* }

preference. Instead, cases have been handled on an ad hoc basis. . . . The Court's future course seems to me unpredictable."

The justices' rulings were not only unpredictable; they reflected the difficulty the all-male court had in grappling with the matter of pregnant women and the workplace. That became clear when the court decided *Geduldig v. Aiello.*

The plaintiffs in the case were Carolyn Aiello, a California hairdresser, and three other women. Under a system to which workers contributed a percentage of their earnings, the California Unemployment Insurance Code provided insurance for workers with disabilities. That included disability stemming from skiing accidents, cosmetic surgery, hair transplants, prostate gland surgery, sickle cell anemia, circumcision, and almost every imaginable disability that might affect one's workplace capability. There were two exceptions. The first was that institutionalized alcoholics, drug addicts, and sexual psychopaths were not covered. The second applied to pregnant women, who were ineligible for the disability insurance program until twenty-eight days after the end of pregnancy, when they presumably were "normal" workers again. All four women had contributed to the plan. Aiello was unable to work because of an ectopic pregnancy, and two of the other women suffered pregnancy complications as well. Jacquelyn Jaramillo, the fourth plaintiff, had a normal pregnancy and delivery. While the case was pending, California changed its law to cover women who suffered pregnancy-related disabilities but not normal pregnancies. By the time the case reached the Supreme Court, the other three women were therefore eligible for the system's disability insurance, but Jaramillo was not.

The case was argued in the Northern California federal district court by Wendy Webster Williams, the young attorney who had drafted the district court opinion in the *Sail'er Inn* women bartenders case when she was clerking for Judge Raymond Peters at the California Supreme Court. She was now in the process of cofounding Equal Rights Advocates, a California-based organization dedicated to achieving rights for working women and men. Williams grounded her argument in the Equal Protection Clause, stating that discrimination based on pregnancy was sex discrimination and asking the courts to apply strict scrutiny to the case.

The three-judge district court that heard the case declined to discuss the varying possible tests under the Equal Protection Clause because it found that the law was unconstitutional even under *Reed's* enhanced rational basis standard. California had argued in part that pregnancy-related disabilities were particularly expensive and that the exclusion of pregnancy was necessary to preserve the insurance system's fiscal integrity. "The denial of benefits for pregnancy-related disabilities seems to have its roots in the belief that all pregnant women are incapable of work for long periods of time, and therefore, they will submit large disability claims," the district court wrote, but "a realistic look at what women actually do even in our society belies the belief that they cannot generally work throughout pregnancy." The Constitution demanded that "each pregnant woman be considered individually." If the state's concern was truly fiscal, rather than a matter of outmoded stereotypes, there were methods other than an "irrational" classification for maintaining fiscal stability: the percentage that workers paid into the system could be raised, for example, or a cap could be put on all benefits. The arbitrary nature of the classification made it unconstitutional.

The state appealed, and Williams flew to Washington to argue the case before the US Supreme Court. (As Dwight Geduldig was the director of the California Department of Human Resources, the case was named *Geduldig v. Aiello*.) The justices heard it only two months after they handed down their decision in *LaFleur*, so there was reason to hope they would act similarly in *Geduldig*. Ginsburg and the WRP submitted an amicus brief, which was joined by the National Organization for Women and the Center for Constitutional Rights. In it, Ginsburg argued, as she had in Susan Struck's case, that the classification rested on and reinforced traditional conceptions of women's family roles. It also prevented a woman from exercising her right to decide whether or not to bear a child. As she wrote in her brief on behalf of Mary Ellen Schattman, the unequal treatment of pregnant women "created a very real threat of economic blackmail": give up the idea of motherhood or lose your job. The system created a self-fulfilling prophecy. "If women are treated by the state and their employers as detached from the work force when pregnancy disabled them, denied disability compensation and other employment-related benefits, it is not surprising that some succumb to the disincentives barring the way to return, and to appellant's stereotyped version of women's place post-childbirth." She urged the court to apply the suspect classification standard, but maintained that the California system had to fall even under the compelling interest test.

The pregnancy workplace discrimination that Ginsburg and Williams and so many others were attacking was spread throughout the American economy. Airlines like Delta, Northwestern, and United forced women flight attendants, known then as stewardesses, to leave their jobs as soon as they became pregnant. Large corporations such as E. I. duPont de Nemours, with more than 111,000 employees, and General Mills, with more than 40,000, required pregnant workers to leave. So did such disparate organizations as Westinghouse Electric, banks, police departments, and toy factories. "The presumption," a group of feminists wrote in the *Yale Law and Policy Review*, was that "motherhood and a commitment to one's job are incompatible."

The men of the Supreme Court appeared to agree. On June 17, 1974, they ruled in *Geduldig* by a vote of 6–3 that excluding pregnant women from disability coverage was not sex discrimination. "It is clear that California intended to establish this benefit system as an insurance program that was to function essentially in accordance with insurance concepts," Justice Potter Stewart wrote for the court. California had the laudable goals of making the program self-sufficient and keeping the required contribution at no more than 1 percent so as not to burden lower-paid workers unduly. Covering pregnancy would place a great burden on the program, and California had therefore made the rational policy decision to exclude it. There was no violation of the Equal Protection Clause. "There is no evidence in the record that the selection of the risks insured by the program worked to discriminate against any definable group or class. . . . There is no risk from which men are protected and women are not. Likewise, there is no risk from which women are protected and men are not." He added in a footnote, "The program divides potential recipients into two groups—pregnant women and nonpregnant persons. While the first group is exclusively female, the second includes members of both sexes." Or, to paraphrase, there was no sex discrimination because anyone who was pregnant, male or female, was excluded from coverage.

Justice Stewart did not attempt to distinguish the court's holding in *LaFleur*, in which he had written the majority opinion; in fact, he did not mention *LaFleur* at all. It was left to Justice William Brennan, writing in dissent for himself and Justices Thurgood Marshall and William O. Douglas, to remind his brethren that only women became pregnant.

> By singling out for less favorable treatment a gender-linked disability peculiar to women, the State has created a double standard . . . a limitation is imposed upon the disabilities for which women workers may recover, while men receive full compensation for all disabilities suffered. . . . In effect, one set of rules is applied to females and another to males. Such dissimilar treatment of men and women, on the basis of physical characteristics inextricably linked to one sex, inevitably constitutes sex discrimination. . . . The saving of welfare costs cannot justify an otherwise invidious classification.

The court's decision, Brennan continued, was contrary to its precedents in cases such as *Reed v. Reed* and *Frontiero v. Richardson*—both of which Justice Stewart said had no bearing on the California case.

The Equal Employment Opportunity Commission (EEOC) is the federal agency charged with enforcement of Title VII of the Civil Rights Act of 1964. As Brennan pointed out, the Commission's *Guidelines on Discrimination Because of Sex*, published in 1972, specifically identified pregnancy discrimination as an aspect of sex discrimination. He might have added that every federal court of appeals that heard cases of alleged pregnancy discrimination had unanimously held that such discrimination was sex discrimination.

Women's rights advocates and lawyers were shocked at the ruling. "Criticizing Geduldig has since become a cottage industry," legal scholar Sylvia Law commented, pointing to a host of law review articles. "About all the Supreme Court accomplishes by its semantic approach in *Aiello* is to suggest that it does not take sex discrimination very seriously," Diane Zimmerman, one of Ginsburg's students, wrote in the *Columbia Law Review*. An article in the *South Texas Law Journal*, titled "Barefoot and Pregnant," called the *Geduldig* decision "three steps backward." Ginsburg would later comment, with understatement, that "Burger Court decisions relating to pregnancy in the employment context display less than perfect logic and consistency."

There was no doubt that in addition to being somewhat incomprehensible, *Geduldig* was a major blow. It came only two months after the equally disturbing decision in *Kahn v. Shevin*, the Florida widower's tax case. Advocates wondered: Was the court about to back away entirely from the forward movement that had begun with *Reed*? What exactly was going on in the justices' minds?

The confusion was only deepened the following year when the court handed down its decision in a case challenging a Utah unemployment law that denied benefits to women during their last three months of pregnancy and for six weeks after delivery. The Utah Supreme Court, hearing the case of *Turner v. Department of Employment Security*, had held that the law was constitutional and issued a ruling that must have left many people gasping.

> Should a man be unable to work because he was pregnant, the statute would apply to him equally as it does to her. What she should do is to work for the repeal of the biological law of nature. She should get it amended so that men shared equally with women in bearing children. If she could prevail upon the Great Creator to so order things, she would be guilty of violating the equal protection of the law unless she saw to it that man could also share in the thrill and glory of Motherhood. . . . In the matter of pregnancy there is no way to find equality between men and women. The Great Creator so ordained the difference, and there are few women who would wish to change the situation.

That was apparently a bit much for the US Supreme Court, even for the justices who had been in the majority in *Geduldig*. "The Utah Supreme Court's opinion makes clear that the challenged ineligibility provision rests on a conclusive presumption that women are 'unable to work' during the 18-week period because of pregnancy and childbirth," the court wrote in a short per curiam opinion. "It cannot be doubted that a substantial number of women are fully capable of working well into their last trimester of pregnancy and of resuming employment shortly after childbirth." Citing its decision in *LaFleur*, the court found the Utah law to be a violation of the Equal Protection Clause, doing so without hearing oral argument.

The *Turner* case was initiated by the Utah affiliate of the ACLU. When it reached the US Supreme Court in 1975, it was handled by the Women's Rights Project. By then, Ginsburg had decided she needed to spend less time on administration and more on litigation and teaching both her students and the general public. She also wanted to focus on her new role as one of the ACLU's general counsels, charged with reviewing all of the national organization's cases. In 1974, she had turned the directorship of the WRP over to Kathleen Peratis, who took the *Turner* case to the Supreme Court (and who had joined Ginsburg in writing the WRP's *Geduldig* brief). Fittingly, Peratis was visibly pregnant during the litigation. When her pregnancy was mentioned in the *New York Times'* coverage of the decision, ACLU Executive Director Aryeh Neier commented in amusement, "Only the queen of England and Kathleen Peratis have their pregnancies announced in the New York Times."

As of 1975, then, the court had held in *Geduldig* that it was not illegal for a pregnant woman to be excluded from a disability benefits system, but the justices had also declared in *Turner* that it was illegal to force her out of the workplace. What the Supreme Court effectively did in *LaFleur* and *Geduldig* was establish the male employee as the paradigm worker. To the extent that women workers could be seen as similar—that is, as able as men were to continue working no matter what their physical condition—they could not be treated differently. Where women differed from men, however, as in requiring time away from the workplace for pregnancy-related factors, they had no right to equal treatment. It appeared that if a pregnant woman was physically in the workplace, the court would view her as entitled to constitutional protection, but if she was not actually clocking in for work, she was not. The basis for that distinction was less than clear, unless the court was once again relying on a model of the "normal" worker as male. As long as a woman could emulate him, she was entitled to constitutional protection. If she was temporarily disabled for reasons outside the male experience, the Constitution did not apply. *Turner* notwithstanding, *Geduldig* was still a significant loss. The one consolation for proponents of gender equality was that while the court's decision jeopardized pregnancy-related insurance under a state-created system, such insurance in the private sector was still covered under the EEOC's guidelines.

The Supreme Court knocked that one out in 1976.

What became the case of *General Electric v. Gilbert* began when Martha Gilbert and current and former employees of GE's Salem, Virginia, plant, all of whom became pregnant while working but were denied disability benefits, sued the company. The G.E. disability plan, like the one at issue in *Geduldig,* covered a wide range of disabilities but excluded those relating to pregnancy, miscarriage, and childbirth. The case was a class action, brought by the International Union of Electrical Radio and Machine Workers (IUE) on behalf of thousands of women. Both the federal district court and the appeals court that heard the case agreed with the women that the exclusion violated Title VII. So did three other federal appeals courts, hearing similar cases, with all of them holding that the programs constituted sex discrimination. They specifically differentiated the Supreme Court's ruling in *Geduldig,* saying it was based on the Equal Protection Clause whereas cases arising from private employers' programs fell under Title VII.

The case was argued in the Supreme Court by Ruth Weyand, associate general counsel of the IUE. Given the lower courts' rulings, she had every reason to hope for a favorable decision. So did the WRP, which filed an amicus brief along with Wendy Williams's Equal Rights Advocates.

They were appalled when, on December 7, 1976, the court announced that it had voted 6–3 in favor of General Electric. Justice Rehnquist's opinion for the court relied on the justices' holding in *Geduldig,* finding once again that "there is no risk from which men are protected and women are not. Likewise, there is no risk from which women are protected and men are not." Justice Brennan, writing in dissent for himself and Justice Marshall, chastised the majority for assuming that G.E.'s rule was based on anything other than sex discrimination and for disregarding "a history of General Electric practices that have served to undercut the employment opportunities of women who become pregnant while employed." Justice Stevens dissented separately.

"The Supreme Court today legalized discrimination," Susan Deller Ross, a WRP lawyer, told the *New York Times.* Ginsburg called the decision "a disaster." She wrote to Herma Hill Kay, the California law school professor who was one of her coauthors on their gender law casebook, that she was "thinking now how to deal with the pregnant problem after the *Gilbert* disaster. Any ideas?" Ideas soon emerged. An outraged coalition of what became more than two hundred organizations, encompassing, as Ginsburg pointed out, "women's equality advocates, labor unions, civil rights proponents, pro-life as well as pro-choice groups," organized a Campaign to End Discrimination Against Pregnant Workers. Ruth Weyand was a driving force behind the campaign, of which she and Susan Deller Ross were cochairs. Weyand and Ginsburg worked on a draft of a federal law that would effectively overturn the decision; Ginsburg and Ross published an op-ed in the *New York Times* urging Congress to pass it.

The combined efforts of dozens of men and women resulted in the passage of the 1978 Pregnancy Discrimination Act, which provided that pregnant workers "shall be treated the same for all employment related purposes, including . . . benefit programs, as other persons not so affected but similar in their ability or inability to work." In passing the law, "Congress thus displayed an understanding that perhaps eluded the Court in Aiello and Gilbert," Ginsburg commented. She wondered if the justices were simply unable to deal with the reality of pregnant women. "I have a suspicion about the Court's diverse rulings in LaFleur and Turner on the one hand, and Aiello and Gilbert on the other," Ginsburg wrote in 2009.

> The pregnant woman ready, willing, and able to work met a reality check. She sought, and was prepared to take on, a day's work for a day's pay. But the woman who sought benefits for a disability caused by pregnancy may have sparked doubt in the Justices' minds: Was she really a member of the labor force, or was she a drop out who, post-childbirth, would retire from the paid labor force to devote herself to the care of her home and family?

Her analysis seemed to be borne out by the Supreme Court's 1977 decision in *Nashville Gas Company v. Satty.* Company policy both forced pregnant employees to go on unpaid leave and denied them their accumulated seniority when they returned to the workplace. With Justice Rehnquist writing for the court, the justices held that depriving pregnant women of disability benefits was legal but that denying them seniority when they returned to their jobs violated Title VII. As Ginsburg suggested, the justices could understand the need for equal treatment in the workplace, but not when a woman was physically out of it—even if her absence was not of her own choosing. Justice Stevens wrote a long, agonized concurrence in *Nashville Satty,* attempting to reconcile the court's contradictory pronouncements about whether or not pregnancy discrimination was sex discrimination. That led Ginsburg to comment, "When does disadvantageous treatment of a pregnant or formerly pregnant worker operate to discriminate on the basis of sex? Justice Stevens," she noted, "offered this summary of high Court precedent up to December 1977: while the Court's answer should be 'always,' it appeared in 1976 to be 'never,' and is now clearly 'sometimes.'"

* * *

Ginsburg referred repeatedly to the race/sex analogy in her litigation, hoping, as we have seen, that the Supreme Court would make classifications based on sex as suspect as those based on race. Pregnancy, however, pointed up the difficulty with the analogy. One could argue that non-Caucasian people were no different from Caucasians in every way that mattered legally. Men and women of all skin hues had the same ability to work, to be educated, and to participate in the political process. There was therefore no reason for non-Caucasians to be treated differently by the government, or by private employers, or by educational institutions, or by anyone else. Segregation and racial injustice could be eliminated, the argument continued, by wiping out provisions in the law and in practice that treated the races differently.

Where the analogy broke down, according to most of the justices, was in the ability to bear children. As men could not bear children, the law was reasonable in treating women differently in anything related to childbirth and child-rearing.

Ginsburg's job, in the 1970s, was to convince the justices that the Constitution required that individuals be treated equally. If some women could not do some jobs, neither could some men. If some women had to take temporary leave from the workplace during pregnancy, so did some men when they became temporarily disabled. The only legitimate way to interpret the Equal Protection Clause was to view it as giving equal opportunities to men and women. If a group of people was subjected to disadvantaged treatment because of reliance on stereotypes, that was unconstitutional discrimination.

The argument for "sameness"—the assertion that women had to be treated in the same way as men—was contested not only by some of the justices but by some feminists as well. Fair treatment, they believed, was not the same thing as sameness of treatment. Fairness did not mean only that women had to be given opportunities and privileges that men already had; that was merely the beginning. Fairness, however, meant treating human beings according to their needs, and women as a group had a right to expect the law to recognize their unique needs. Instead of arguing that the end of discrimination necessitated sex-blind laws, they maintained that sex discrimination would end only when the law became cognizant of and provided for women's differences. Pregnancy, they asserted, was not like anything else, and it was appropriate for the law to make the accommodations necessary for pregnant women. Formal equality meant that pregnant workers could not legally be treated worse than anyone else temporarily unable to work. At the same time, however, these critics asserted, it meant that women could be treated no better than men, and it therefore ignored their particular needs. To ignore them implied, once again, that the typical worker was male. Formal equality, to cite one small example, did not deal with the need for rooms in the workplace for nursing mothers.

It was a legitimate argument, but Ginsburg knew that it was not one likely to be successful with the US Supreme Court of the 1970s. Her only hope of success in the fight for Constitutional gender equality was to emphasize sameness of treatment. It would have been counterproductive to argue simultaneously that women had to be seen as the equals of men, so that laws that "protected" or "benefitted" their supposedly lesser selves were in fact harmful, and that women deserved differing treatment in some situations. The second step could come later, but only after the first had been achieved. "The feminist movement today is a house of many gables," Ginsburg would reflect, "with rooms enough to accommodate all who have the imagination and determination to think and work in a common cause. . . . Different styles of feminist analysis undeniably produce conflicting responses in some contexts; but the common ground merits attention and statement in ways the wider public can understand."

What much of the public and the judicial audience of the 1970s would not have been able to understand was an argument based on equity rather than equality: on accommodating people's needs in a way that served them as individuals and did not denigrate them as a group. Ginsburg had spoken of giving the justices the equivalent of an elementary school lesson in the history of gender discrimination and the need to interpret the Equal Protection Clause in the light of that history and current realities. She recognized that leaping into what might be seen as a post-graduate-level course would be counter-productive. Nonetheless, she believed that law, an inherently conservative institution, could be used for what might appear to be radical purposes. That was the key to Ginsburg's approach to reproductive freedom. She quietly advised Janet Benshoof, the director of the ACLU's Reproductive Freedom Project, on litigation strategy, even though the terms of the Ford Foundation grants meant that WRP could take no formal part in it.

Ginsburg had begun to think about the relationship among the right to be pregnant, the right not to be pregnant, and equal protection when she worked on Susan Struck's case. The right to control her body, Ginsburg would tell the congressional committee considering her nomination to the Supreme Court in 1993, was "central to a woman's life, to her dignity. It's a decision that she must make for herself. And when Government controls that decision for her, she's being treated as less than a fully adult human responsible for her own choices." The Equal Protection Clause was violated if women were denied the right to bodily autonomy.

Nonetheless, she decried what she viewed as overly radical and ill thought-out change that would encourage a backlash. In what became a well-known speech delivered in 1992, she argued that the court's 1973 decision in *Roe v. Wade* had been overbroad. Had the justices simply struck down the relevant Texas law on equal protection grounds and not made a sweeping ruling about abortion, she believed, its decision would not have encouraged the creation of a vibrant national anti-abortion movement, and the states would gradually have ended restrictions on reproductive rights. That analysis may or may not have been correct, but it reflected her deep belief that in order for social change to be lasting, it had to be achieved as evolution rather than revolution. Still, she hoped that the court would someday "take abortion, pregnancy, out-of-wedlock birth, and explicit gender-based differentials out of the separate cubbyholes in which they now rest, acknowledge the practical interrelationships, and treat these matters as part and parcel of a single, large, sex equality issue."

CHAPTER 7

Thirsty Boys and Uncertain Justices

Mark Walker just wanted a drink.

More precisely, he wanted to buy 3.2 percent beer. He couldn't do it legally in Oklahoma, however, where he was a twenty-year-old student at Oklahoma State University in the small city of Stillwater. Oklahoma law forbade the sale of the very low 3.2 percent alcohol "near beer" to anyone under the age of eighteen and to men aged between eighteen and twenty-one, but not to women between those ages. There was a good reason for treating eighteen-to-twenty-one-year-old men and women differently, the state said. Statistics showed that the preferred drink of men of that age was beer and that they were far more likely than their female counterparts to be arrested for driving under the influence. In Oklahoma City alone, 82 percent of eighteen-year-olds arrested for driving under the influence were men, and the figures for nineteen- and twenty-year-olds were 98 percent and 94 percent, respectively. Oklahoma was simply trying to protect the safety of its citizens.

Walker thought that the law nevertheless discriminated against men his age, in violation of the Equal Protection Clause. In 1972, he contacted attorney Frederick P. Gilbert, known as Fred. Gilbert agreed but wasn't sure Walker would be able to sue successfully. The law did not penalize men under twenty-one who bought near beer, but it did penalize anyone who sold it to them. In order to get what is called "standing," or the right to bring a case, a plaintiff must show that he or she has been or could be harmed by the law. Could Walker find a coplaintiff who could incur criminal penalties for a sale to a man his age? He did, and the lawsuit was brought in his name and that of Carolyn Whitener, an owner of and licensed beer seller at the Stillwater Honk-N-Holler drive-in convenience store. Walker turned twenty-one during the course of the litigation, however, and so his eighteen-year-old Lambda Chi Alpha fraternity brother Curtis Craig joined Ms. Whitener as a plaintiff. The case would eventually reach the US Supreme Court as *Craig v. Boren*, with "Boren" referring to David Boren, the governor of Oklahoma.

The three-judge federal district court that heard the case in 1975 agreed with the state. "Rational basis" as applied in *Reed v. Reed* was the proper test, the appeals court said, and the state's statistics clearly demonstrated the rational relationship between the objective of public safely and the law regulating the sale of near beer. In addition, the Twenty-First Amendment to the Constitution, which overturned prohibition, gave the states wide discretion to regulate the sale of alcoholic beverages. The court did not mention that since the law didn't penalize consumption of near beer, it was fine for an eighteen-year-old girlfriend or anyone else to buy it for an eighteen-to-twenty-one-year-old male, whether or not he then drove.

Fred Gilbert had corresponded with Ginsburg during the course of the litigation. After the appeals court handed down its ruling, she described herself to him as "bothered and bewildered" by the decision. It was "poorly reasoned . . . the precedent can't be left sitting." A precedent that upheld a law based on false assumptions about gender differences would hurt the march toward gender equality. Gilbert asked the US Supreme Court to hear the case, and when in January 1976 it agreed, Ginsburg offered the help of the Women's Rights Project. "Delighted to see the Supreme Court is interested in beer drinkers," she wrote to Gilbert. "Would you like ACLU to file as amicus?" "I don't invite, I implore your appearance as amica," Gilbert replied enthusiastically.

Ginsburg and Gilbert continued to exchange letters about the case, with Ginsburg giving Gilbert mini-lessons about the relevant precedents and advising him not to argue for suspect classification because there would not be five votes for it. That was one part of her advice that he did not take.

His brief went to the court early in March 1976. One wonders what the justices, used to restrained and formal prose, made of it. The brief featured italics, exclamation marks, large capital letters, and occasional purple prose. "THE DECISION BELOW IS SO TOTALLY CONTRARY TO ALL THE MODERN RULINGS ON THE SUBJECT, TO INCLUDE THE AUTHORITATIVE PRONOUNCEMENT OF THIS HONORABLE COURT, THAT IT SAFELY MAY AND SHOULD BE SIMPLY REVERSED, WITHOUT ANY NEED FOR A DETAILED AND EXHAUSTIVE REVIEW OF ITS BELABORED REASONING AND TENUOUS EVIDENCE," the brief proclaimed. The bulk of its fifty-five pages were nonetheless devoted to exactly that kind of "detailed and exhaustive" attack on Oklahoma's use of statistics. The brief also accused Oklahoma of treating men as inferior: "In this case, the state officials actually 'proved' the unfavored sex's 'inferiority' with respect to the subject matter of the discrimination (or 'demonstrated a difference,' or whatever we may want to call it)."

"Let's face facts," Gilbert urged the justices. "No rational man doubts the essential truthfulness of sexual equality-in-fact." Referring to the Constitution's promise of equality, he added, "What's fair for one is fair for all. What's sauce for the gender, etc. Does Equality mean Equality, or does it mean double-talk for something else? Whatever the Appellant Craig has gotten in this case, he has *not* gotten Equality!"

It was left to Ginsburg's amicus brief to make the argument in language that might be more persuasive to the court. She said privately that she thought it was "something of an embarrassment" for the nation's highest court to spend time on what she called the "beer case," involving a law she considered ridiculous. Ridiculous as the law was, however, and quirky as Gilbert's brief might be, she had the job of convincing the justices that they had no option but to rule for Craig. She began by writing that the appellate court had "relied upon overbroad generalizations concerning the drinking behavior, proclivities and preferences of the two sexes" in a manner inconsistent with the Equal Protection Clause. The generalizations were reminiscent of the reasoning the court had relied on in the woman bartender case of *Goesaert v. Cleary*, which had been "politely discarded by the nation's lower courts" and was now both "an embarrassment" and "a decision overdue for a formal burial." Continuing her attack on *Goesaert*, Ginsburg said that *Craig v. Boren* "provides an opportunity for this Court explicitly to overrule" the earlier case. The Oklahoma law, she added, was "a bizarre and paradoxical remnant of the day when 'anything goes' was the rule for line-drawing by gender." The court had made it clear in cases such as *Reed, Frontiero, Taylor v. Louisiana*, and *Wiesenfeld* that the "anything goes" rule was no longer good law.

Ginsburg included her own attack on Oklahoma's statistics, demonstrating that "the supposed legislative objective (protecting young men and the public from weaknesses male flesh is heir to)" was in no way furthered by the law. She also reminded the court that the only cases in which it had upheld a law with a sex-based differentiation—*Kahn v.*

Shevin and *Schlesinger v. Ballard*—were meant as compensation for past discrimination against women. No such compensation was involved here.

The brief did not mention strict scrutiny or suspect classification. One paragraph, however, referred to language in an earlier case about a standard for assessing gender classifications. Some legal commentators, analyzing the court's decisions from *Reed v. Reed* on, had wondered whether the justices weren't already relying on a test somewhere in between rational basis and suspect classification: a test that would subject gender classifications to "strict scrutiny" but would not automatically assume, as "suspect classification" would, that they were unconstitutional. That seemed to be born out not only by *Reed* itself but by a case that the court ruled on in April 1975, more than a year before *Craig* was argued.

The case was *Stanton v. Stanton,* and it involved a Utah law that required a parent to support a son until he reached the age of twenty-one but a daughter only until she turned eighteen. Justice Blackmun, writing the decision that struck down the law, declared that "if any weight remains in this day to the claim of earlier maturity of the female, with a concomitant inference of absence of need for support beyond 18, we fail to perceive its unquestioned truth or its significance." The court held that the law failed "under any test—compelling state interest, or rational basis, or something in between." The phrase "something in between" implied the possibility of an intermediate standard, halfway between the rational basis test and suspect classification. Ginsburg's brief in *Craig v. Boren* quoted Blackmun and pointed out repeatedly that the appeals court decision conflicted with the decision in *Stanton v. Stanton,* tacitly suggesting to Justice Blackmun and his colleagues that the "something in between" standard might guide the Supreme Court's decision here as well. Like any successful advocate, she was well aware of positions individual justices had taken in the past and tailored her arguments in part to appeal to them.

The argument was scheduled for October 5, 1976. Two weeks earlier, as the wheels of justice turned somewhat slowly, Curtis Craig also reached the age of twenty-one. The court refused to allow Fred Gilbert to add a different male plaintiff under twenty-one at that late date, which meant the only plaintiff remaining was Carolyn Whitener. Whether it was possible for her to make a claim under the Equal Protection Clause, as all potential sellers of near beer were treated alike whether they were male or female, would be something that troubled some of the justices.

As Fred Gilbert had requested, Ginsburg was at the counsel table on October 5, 1976, when he stood to make his oral presentation. It did not go well. He began by declaring that the law "says that all females even those that are the most drunk, most alcoholic, most immature, and most irresponsible, may purchase 3.2 percent beer at age 18 in absolutely unlimited quantities." Justice Potter Stewart immediately jumped in. "The law does not say it in quite those words, does it?" Gilbert admitted that it didn't, and after he acknowledged that 3.2 percent near beer made no one drunk, Justice William J. Brennan asked, "Well then, what is the relevance of the suggestion that women can get drunk on 3.2% beer?" Gilbert had to acknowledge, "Well, Your Honor, I am perhaps exaggerating the point there." That led Chief Justice Warren E. Burger to comment, "Maybe we could take judicial notice of some of these facts and you won't have to exaggerate then, counsel." One can imagine Ginsburg maintaining a stoic exterior while cringing internally.

Gilbert went on to say that no one knew the legislative purpose for the discrimination, which undercut his (and Ginsburg's) argument that it was based on outmoded stereotypes. The justices and Gilbert then had a long discussion about whether or not Carolyn Whitener had standing to sue on the basis of the Equal Protection Clause. Eventually Chief Justice Burger asked, "Are you going to mention Mr. Justice Douglas' opinion in Kahn v. Shevin sometime in your argument?" Gilbert jumped at the chance to distinguish the Oklahoma law from the compensatory one at issue in *Kahn*. "It was not really based upon any innate difference between male and female, and there is no basis in this record to say that the legislature even remotely thought of compensating for past discrimination." The chief justice, clearly skeptical about Gilbert's argument, nonetheless gave him the opportunity to get back to the heart of the case.

CHIEF JUSTICE BURGER: Assume for the moment that the legislature by an appropriate committee had conducted hearings and come up with findings that legislation of this character was required in the public interest about safety. . . . If it was perfectly clear, that the legislative purpose was safety on the highways primarily, would that change your position?

MR. GILBERT: Well, it's kind of a moot question because we know what the real reason was ... if they are concerned about safety from irresponsible young adults, they are going to have to say all irresponsible young adults regardless of race, breed, color, sex, and whatever. They can't single out one particular group of teenagers just on the accident of their birth and say, "We are going to say that these people are congenitally dangerous and deny them the right to buy non-intoxicating beer."

When Justice William H. Rehnquist continued to express skepticism to Gilbert, the attorney asked rhetorically whether it would be constitutional to "pass a law saying, 'No Negro will drive while intoxicated'? Now, this relates to the public thing that the thing is you can't discriminate even for something like public safety on the basis of certain criteria." Justice Rehnquist pushed Gilbert on whether the court had ever said that race discrimination was exactly the same as sex discrimination, and acknowledging that it had not, Gilbert nonetheless attempted to analogize race to sex by referring to *Goesaert v. Cleary*.

MR. GILBERT: I feel that Goesaert is to sex as Plessy v. Ferguson was to race and should be treated accordingly. In fact, as I read the Goesaert decision, it was considerably worse than Plessy ... because Plessy, while saying that the unfavored race would have to have its education and facilities and so forth separately, Plessy never went so far to say the unfavored sex could be denied these things all together. But Goesaert went so far to say the unfavored sex could be denied these things altogether.

There was a good deal of laughter in the courtroom during Gilbert's presentation, occasioned as much by his somewhat bombastic manner as by the subject of the case. Ginsburg herself had taken to calling it the "thirsty boys" case, and as Gilbert ceded the podium to Oklahoma assistant attorney general James H. Gray, the question was whether the lightheartedness would help or hurt Craig's case.

Gray was interrupted almost immediately by Chief Justice Burger, who pushed him at length about the reason the law was enacted. Gray could not answer; as he noted, Oklahoma state legislative committees did not keep detailed records.

CHIEF JUSTICE BURGER: If a boy and a girl of the same age go out together, the girl can go in and buy it and they can drink it together?
MR. GRAY: Yes.
CHIEF JUSTICE BURGER: But the legislature just did not think of that eventuality, is that your assumption?
MR. GRAY: No, sir, I am not saying they didn't think of it. I am saying that the statute—I would have to be candid to say it is not perfect.

The chief justice returned to the subject of legislative intent later on in the questioning.

CHIEF JUSTICE BURGER: But your theory then is that any rational basis is sufficient to sustain this discrimination?
MR. GRAY: Yes, if it is not based on a ground of difference which has no relation to the objective of the statute. And I think we have—
CHIEF JUSTICE BURGER: But how do we know what the objective of the statute was?

Gilbert was permitted a few minutes for rebuttal, and then the court rose for its lunch break. Ginsburg could not relax, however, because she had her own oral argument to present in another case an hour later.

Her client was Leon Goldfarb, and he was not at all like the "thirsty boys." The seventy-year-old had immigrated to New York City from Russia decades earlier. He and his wife, Hannah, raised a son and a daughter while he was a manager at the US Army Pictorial Center—the studio first used by the military during World War II to produce propaganda films—and Hannah worked as a public school secretary. When Hannah died, Leon Goldfarb applied for Social Security survivor's benefits. He had a federal pension of his own, because of his work at the Pictorial Center, and that would become an issue in his case.

Goldfarb's application was turned down. A widow would have received the survivor benefits automatically, whether or not she was also receiving another pension, but a widower had to prove that his deceased wife had provided more than half of his support. Hannah, however, had earned less than her husband.

If that sounds reminiscent of the situations that faced Sharron Frontiero and Stephen Wiesenfeld, it was. Like Paula Wiesenfeld, Hannah Goldfarb had contributed the required portion of her earnings to the

Social Security system. Leon Goldfarb's children, both teachers, urged him to challenge the decision, but it was not until he read about the *Wiesenfeld* case that he agreed. He then turned to Professor Nadine Taub, the director of the Women's Rights Litigation Clinic at Rutgers Law School, who agreed to represent him.

Goldfarb's situation paralleled that of Edgar Coffin. Coffin was a retired New Jersey police officer whose late wife, Edna, had been a public high school math teacher. The police department was not part of the Social Security system but the schools were, and Edna contributed to it. Like Goldfarb, Coffin's application for Social Security benefits was denied. He had read about Stephen Wiesenfeld's case when it was filed and now turned to the ACLU. "I think the guide line that prohibits me from receiving some of my wife's social security benefits is unfair and discriminatory," Coffin wrote. Referring to the 1973 revisions in the law, he continued, "I have written the President, Senators, Congressmen, and the A.A.R.P.... Although in each instance I received polite, sympathetic letters, I now find nothing was written into the new law to correct the different standards set for widow and widowers." Ginsburg saw Coffin's situation as a logical follow-up to Stephen Wiesenfeld's case and took his complaint into federal district court in the District of Columbia. Under Nadine Taub's guidance, Leon Goldfarb's case was being heard on a parallel track in New York. Before the district court in *Coffin* issued its opinion, the New York district court hearing Leon Goldfarb's case issued its ruling in *Goldfarb v. Mathews*, and so it was the government's appeal in the *Goldfarb* case rather than Edgar Coffin's case that was filed first with the US Supreme Court. (F. David Mathews was the secretary of Health, Education, and Welfare at the beginning of the *Goldfarb* case. He was replaced by Joseph A. Califano Jr. while the litigation was pending before the Supreme Court, which is why the case became *Califano v. Goldfarb*.)

Ginsburg had liked the Coffin case better than Goldfarb's, because Leon Goldfarb had his own federal pension but Edgar Coffin did not, and she was concerned that Goldfarb might be seen as attempting to "double dip." "Sometimes the best laid plans go awry" however, she commented, "and this one did," when the lower court hearing *Goldfarb* decided faster than its counterpart considering *Coffin*. It was yet another example, she said, of the way "you can't really plan [test case] litigation with security." Nadine Taub and Kathleen Peratis joined forces with

Ginsburg, who would draw on the work she had done for *Coffin* in taking the lead in *Goldfarb*.

The *Coffin* and *Goldfarb* cases didn't just happen to fall into Ginsburg's lap. Numerous possible challenges to state and federal laws were brought to the Women's Rights Project's attention, but Ginsburg was focused on exactly where she wanted her litigation efforts to go. After the *Wiesenfeld* decision, she had decided to make a determined assault on other provisions of the Social Security laws that differentiated between men and women on the basis of outmoded stereotypes. "Califano v. Goldfarb was the second step in a litigation campaign aimed at advancing the Frontiero judgment and containing the Kahn decision," she wrote. Her goal, as always, was to bring about social change through strategic litigation. The Women's Rights Project and ACLU affiliates were on the lookout for the right cases in which to do so. If they could bring a number of such cases, they would hope to succeed in all of them. But if they lost any, they could then appeal to the US Supreme Court. One way or another, they would force the federal courts to confront the inequities in the Social Security law. By the time *Califano v. Goldfarb* was due to be argued at the US Supreme Court, the court had already added four similar ACLU Social Security cases, including *Coffin*, to its docket. In all five cases, the lower federal courts had held the challenged provisions of the Social Security act to be unconstitutional gender discrimination. That, however, was no guarantee that the Supreme Court would do the same thing, and it almost didn't.

The *Califano v. Goldfarb* brief that the federal government submitted to the Supreme Court under the name of Solicitor General Robert Bork declared that the appropriate test for "social and economic welfare programs like social security" was "a rational basis reasonably related to the legislative purpose which motivated it." The sentence did two things. The more obvious was to indicate that the government was relying on a relatively loose test, and it went on to argue that the proper test could be found in *Reed v. Reed*. The second was the government's questionable insistence that the Social Security system was a matter of welfare benefits the government chose to confer on people, rather than a system of insurance to which people contributed and to the benefits of which they therefore had a right. It was rational for Congress to confer those benefits on widows, rightfully assumed to be needy, the government said, and not on widowers, equally rightfully assumed not to need government assistance. Unlike *Frontiero*, the government argued, the law did not "involve the denial to women in the same situation as men equal compensation for equal work"; unlike *Wiesenfeld*, it did not involve benefits meant for children.

It was rational for Congress to have decided in 1939, when the provision was first enacted, and again in 1950, when it was amended, that widows would be dependent but widowers would not, the brief continued. It drew on the court's decision in *Kahn v. Shevin* to argue that aged women were still more likely to be financially dependent. Giving widowers the same benefit as widows now would simply give them a "windfall." "As with all statutory classifications, there are imperfections," the government admitted. "But the Constitution does not require that statutory classifications be drawn with mathematical precision." Citing statistics, the brief argued that it was reasonable to conclude that it was a rare husband who was dependent upon his wife at the time of her death.

The brief came with a warning about the possible effect of a decision in favor of Leon Goldfarb on what it described as the "already overstrained financing for the social security system." Such a decision would cost the country $447 million (the equivalent, in 2022, of more than two billion dollars). It would be six times that if the decision was applied retroactively, and would be unrelated to the law's purpose, which was "to meet the differing probable social welfare needs of the current retirement generation of widows and widowers." To the government, all the case entailed was an assault on the US Treasury by a nondependent man, and it had nothing to do with women's rights.

Ginsburg, who wrote the brief (Mel Wulf, Kathleen Peratis, and Nadine Taub were also listed as being on it), saw it differently.

Were Leon Goldfarb the insured individual and Hannah Goldfarb the retired worker not covered by social security on her own account, both members of the family unit would qualify for social security benefits in addition to their civil service pensions. Since the insured individual in this case is female, although her contributions to social security were made on the same basis as a male worker's, the marital unit receives fewer benefits.... This scheme ... discriminates invidiously. It provides the family of a female wage earner less protection than it provides the family of a male wage earner, although the family needs may be identical.

Besides being unfair, the system was divorced from the real world. "The familiar and once pervasive legislative assumption . . . that women depend on men but not vice versa, never matched reality, and is today further than ever from the truth." The result went beyond the inequality of the law itself, and Ginsburg once again reminded the justices of the larger societal context. "By rewarding men's employment more than women's, the arrangement has all the earmarks of self-fulfilling prophecy: it impedes removal of artificial barriers to recognition of women's full, human potential, and retards society's progress towards equal opportunity, free from gender-based discrimination."

Ginsburg disputed the idea that overturning the law would result in a potential "windfall" for men. She also disagreed with the government's characterization of the Social Security payments as, in her words, "a public assistance, need-determined welfare program," calling it instead an "earned right." She quoted Caspar Weinberger, the former secretary of Health, Education, and Welfare, as telling the House of Representatives, "Social security is purchased insurance for retirement, and not welfare." She insisted that both *Frontiero* and *Wiesenfeld* were relevant: "Like the dependency test for male but not for female military spouses invalidated in Sharron and Joseph Frontiero's case, the virtually identical test in the case at issue 'deprive[s] women of protection for their families which men receive as a result of their employment.'"

The quote was from the court's decision in *Wiesenfeld*. Clearly going after Justice Powell's vote, she also quoted his concurrence in that case: "The statutory scheme . . . impermissibly discriminates again a female wage earner because it provides her family less protection than it provides for a male wage earner, even though the family needs may be identical." That, she added, was the conclusion reached by all five of the district courts that had heard cases involving the relevant clauses, and she quoted from the lower court in *Goldfarb*: "She paid taxes at the same rate as men and there is not the slightest scintilla of support for the proposition that working women are less concerned about their spouses' welfare in old age than are men." Do you really want to disagree, Ginsburg seemed to be asking the justices, with your own precedents, as well as all those lower courts? "Statutes that make convenient assumptions about 'the way women (or men) are,' were found to be infirm in Reed, Frontiero, Wiesenfeld and Stanton." And what about a memorandum that Solicitor General Bork himself wrote in another case, saying, "It is now settled that the Equal Protection Clause . . . does not tolerate discrimination on the basis of sex"? In that memorandum, she reminded the justices ironically, Bork relied not only upon *Reed* but upon the decision in *Frontiero* as well.

She added the usual pages of statistics, designed to undermine "the arrogant legislative presumption that women depend on men, but not vice versa." Once again emphasizing that the equal protection cases she brought were about specific human beings as well as inequities in the law, she named the women in all five cases: "The working lives of Hannah Goldfarb, Shirley Silbowitz, Edna Coffin, Bette Jablon and Mildred Abbott indicate a pattern documented for their generation": they were in the paid workforce full-time. This was quintessential Ginsburg, pulling together the big public policy picture and the lives of particular individuals.

Ginsburg had to confront the ever-present specters of *Kahn v. Shevin* and *Schlesinger v. Ballard.* In those cases, she said, the perception (she would not call it a reality) was that "some women were helped, and no women were harmed by the classification." That was not the situation here, where excluding husbands from benefits earned by their wives in no way compensated the wives for past discrimination.

Finally, there was the question of what the government feared might be the astronomical cost if the law were struck down. "Surely the Court's precedent[s] makes it clear that neither administrative nor fiscal policy considerations can justify invidious discrimination." Ginsburg cited a host of decisions to that effect. She also challenged the government's estimates. The government's brief itself admitted that the numbers were based on "a small sample of cases," "sketchy data," and "very rough" estimates. The figures, she added, were not the same ones the government had used in its affidavit to the district court, and they had mysteriously grown in their journey from that tribunal to the Supreme Court. She therefore urged the court to strike the part of the law that required men but not women to prove dependency while leaving the support for surviving spouses intact.

The justices heard oral argument in the case on October 5, 1976. Keith A. Jones, the deputy solicitor general, spoke for the government.

As Ginsburg had feared, he repeatedly referred to Leon Goldfarb as a "non-needy" man who "sought to tack . . . Social Security survivors' benefits on to his existing civil service pension," and he described the law as an attempt to "weed out non-needy widowers" who could cost the government $447 million a year.

> MR. JONES: There is no legislative motive here to discriminate against women . . . appellee is attempting to obscure the fact that what he seeks here is a double benefit, that is, it is a windfall in a nature of Social Security survivors' benefits on top of the civil service pension.
>
> JUSTICE STEWART: Yeah, but if he were—if the genders were reversed she would get this windfall, right?
>
> MR. JONES: That is correct Mr. Justice Stewart, that is the loophole. Widows would get the benefit.
>
> JUSTICE STEWART: Well, anytime if somebody does not like a provision of the law he calls it a loophole, this is a provision of the law.
>
> MR. JONES: Sometimes they call it unconstitutional.
>
> [Laughter]

Jones went on to charge that double-dipping was only one reason for Goldfarb's attempt to present the case as involving women's rights.

> MR. JONES: I think the second reason that the appellee seeks to characterize this as a women's rights case, is that the cause of women's rights is now a fashionable one and the appellee seeks to ride on its skirt-tails. . . . But the third reason the appellee may be characterizing this as a women's rights case is the one that disturbs me the most. Appellee may be implicitly suggesting that the rights of women are constitutionally entitled to higher protection than the rights of men.

Women needed no help from the court, Jones declared.

> MR. JONES: Women constitute a majority of the voting age population in this country, unlike racial minorities, for example, women have the political power, if they choose to use it to remedy any

statutory inequality of which they perceive themselves to be the victims. In short, women are not a discrete insular minority that requires special judicial protection against an indifferent or a hostile legislature.

Women had faced discrimination "in the past," however, and so as the court had held in *Kahn v. Shevin*, remedial legislation might be appropriate.

Justice Byron White asked whether the government was making unwarranted assumptions.

> JUSTICE WHITE: Aren't there some widowers who are needy even though they cannot pass the support test? ... Why is the fact that a widow or a widower may have received more than one half of his support during the lifetime of his spouse, from his spouse relevant to his present neediness?
>
> MR. JONES: As a statistical matter, Mr. Justice White, 85%, roughly, of the benefits we are talking about go to Civil Service pensioners. They are plainly not needy. And of the other percentages, we cannot say with certainty that no needy person would thereby be given benefits, but, as a practical matter, it is a rare member of the so-called disadvantaged class here who, in fact, is needy.

Jones spoke at length about the difference he saw between *Wiesenfeld* and *Goldfarb*, saying that there was no relationship between the law at issue in *Wiesenfeld* and the government's purpose of helping children, but that there was a clear line between the government's desire to restrict benefits "to those groups that may be largely presumed to be needy" and its insistence that men demonstrate their neediness.

When Ginsburg took her place at the podium, she began with Leon Goldfarb's name, seeking once again to demonstrate that discrimination hurt real people. Here it was the Social Security system that was at fault. It treated men and women alike when taking the equal amount of contributions from equal wages, but "in contrast to the gender neutral contribution system, the program draws a sharp line between the sexes on the payout side. Benefits to a spouse available under a male wage earner's account are not equally available under a female wage earner's account." Women workers were required to pay into the Social Security system at the same rate as men: why, then, should their families receive less protection? *Frontiero* and *Wiesenfeld* were controlling here, Ginsburg argued. Pointing out an irony, she reminded the court that when Solicitor General Griswold warned in *Frontiero* that striking down that provision of the law would have consequences for other federal statutes, the law he referred to as resting on the same premises was section 402 of the Social Security Act, which was at issue in *Goldfarb*. Her point, of course, was that if the court found the provision involved in *Frontiero* unconstitutional, then it logically had to do the same thing here.

Justice Stewart quickly interrupted, calling Ginsburg "Mrs. Bader" and referring to Keith Jones's claim that Leon Goldfarb regarded discrimination against women as more important than discrimination against men. If the law discriminated against women rather than men, Justice Stewart asked, would that make a difference? The court's gender decisions were premised upon a history of discrimination against women. Was discrimination against them of greater constitutional importance than discrimination against men? "Every gender discrimination is a two-edged sword," Ginsburg replied, "because most anti-female discrimination was dressed up as discrimination favoring the woman.... The point is that the discriminatory line almost inevitably hurts women."

> JUSTICE STEWART: No, my question is if this were purely an anti-male discrimination and let us assume it were, would you have a stronger constitutional argument in your view?
>
> MRS. GINSBURG: My argument would be the same because I do not know of any purely anti-male discrimination. In the end, the women are the ones who end up hurting.

Justice Stevens jumped in, and it became clear that some of the justices didn't quite know what to make of a case that seemed to them to rest on the assumption that men were being discriminated against. They were still not ready to acknowledge that gender classifications meant to compensate women could hurt them, and Ginsburg had to work hard to reiterate that they did.

> JUSTICE STEVENS: Can I interrupt you just to be sure to understand your position in response to Justice Stewart, is it your view that there is no discrimination against males?

MRS. GINSBURG: I think there is discrimination against males.

JUSTICE STEVENS: Now, if there is such a discrimination is it to be tested by the same or by a different standard from discrimination against female?

MRS. GINSBURG: My response to that, Mr. Justice Stevens, is that almost every discrimination that operates against males operates against females as well.

JUSTICE STEVENS: Is that a yes or a no answer? I just do not understand you and are you trying to avoid the question or . . .

MRS. GINSBURG: No, I am not trying to avoid the question. I am trying to clarify the position that I do not know of any line that does not work as a two-edged sword, doesn't hurt both sexes.

That was the point that Ginsburg hammered away at in all her cases: laws based on generalizations about the sexes inevitably hurt both. It was also the point that some of the justices found most difficult to accept. That became apparent once again when Justice Stevens, referring to the morning's argument in *Craig v. Boren*, continued his questioning.

JUSTICE STEVENS: But we heard a case this morning, just to be concrete, involving a law that would not permit males to make certain purchases that females could make, and it was attacked as a discrimination against males. . . . My question is whether we should examine that law under a same or a different standard than if it were a discrimination against the other sex.

MRS. GINSBURG: My answer to that question is no, in part because such a law has an insidious impact against females.

JUSTICE STEVENS: So, your case depends, then, on our analyzing this case as a discrimination against females?

MRS. GINSBURG: No, my case depends on your recognition that using gender as a classification, resorting to that classification, is highly questionable and should be closely reviewed.

The words "closely reviewed" appeared to be carefully chosen, as they avoided any mention of the standard by which gender classifications should be judged. Perhaps Ginsburg hoped to signal that an intermediate standard of the kind suggested by Justice Blackmun in *Stanton v. Stanton* would work here. The justices, however, did not permit Ginsburg to sidestep the hurdle she wanted to circumvent. As noted in chapter 4, she had deliberately stopped asking the court to decide on the basis of suspect classification after it became clear in *Frontiero v. Richardson* that a majority for that test didn't exist. The justices nonetheless remembered her earlier arguments for it, perhaps in part thanks to Justice Brennan's continued insistence that it was the proper standard to use in gender discrimination cases. It was therefore no surprise that the next question was whether she thought sex should be a suspect classification. As saying "yes" would take her where she didn't want to go, because it might lose the votes of the justices who had made it clear in *Frontiero* that they were disturbed at applying "suspect classification" to classifications based on gender, she had to squirm her way out of that one.

> MRS. GINSBURG: The equal protection principle is part of a Constitution intended to govern American society as it evolved over time and inevitably keeping pace with the nation's progress toward maturity. Notions of what constitutes the equal protection of the laws do change and as to sex discrimination, they have changed. . . . The Court has not yet acknowledged sex as a suspect criterion, but it has plainly identified the vice of legislative resort to gender pigeon-holing.

She also had to grapple once again with the compensatory-based decision in *Kahn v. Shevin*, which some of the justices asked about.

> MRS. GINSBURG: A law that benefits a woman as wife or widow, but does not denigrate woman as wage earner might be rationalized as benign and the gender criterion ranked as an appropriate means to a legitimate end, but the Section 402 differential cannot be rationalized as favorable to some women, harmful to none. The wage earning woman is disfavored, her work is devalued when the earnings dollar she contributes to Social Security is worth less in protection for her family than the earnings dollar of an identically situated male worker.

Asked if she believed that Congress could not legislate on the basis of the assumption that the man was the primary breadwinner in most families, she replied, "Congress can use a gender neutral standard, but it can't simply assume that the men are the breadwinners and that the women are the dependents."

There was then an extended discussion of how much treating men and women equally in this section of the law would cost the government, with Ginsburg again challenging the government's calculations. As she would write later, "*Califano v. Goldfarb* might be described as *Frontiero* revisited with a hefty price tag ... or *Wiesenfeld* without the baby." Given the government's figure of $447 million as the potential cost, and the substitution of what the government cast as the double-dipping man for the sympathetic baby, it was unclear how the court would decide.

* * *

The justices would consider both *Craig v. Boren* and *Califano v. Goldfarb* in light not only of the facts in those cases but of their past Equal Protection Clause decisions as well. As even legal experts found the sometimes seemingly contradictory decisions confusing, it might be wise to summarize them here.

In *Reed v. Reed* (1971), the court declared that to be found constitutional, a sex-based classification had to have "a ... substantial relation to the object of the legislation" and could not be "arbitrary." That raised the standard from "rational basis" to "substantial relation," but it was unclear how high the bar was now placed. The decision in *Frontiero v. Richardson* (1973) reinforced *Reed*'s holding that "administrative convenience" was no longer a sufficient justification. *Frontiero* also made it clear that while a plurality of the justices would have raised the standard even higher to make sex a "suspect classification," a majority would not. Sex-based classifications were to be subjected to "scrutiny," although how strict that scrutiny would be was also unclear. The court's holding in the pregnant schoolteachers case of *Cleveland v. LaFleur* (1974) indicated that employers could not use pregnancy as a reason to keep women out of the workplace, but its decisions in *Geduldig v. Aiello* (1974) and *G.E. v. Gilbert* (1976) indicated that a majority of the justices considered pregnancy to be sufficient grounds for excluding women from disability insurance plans. To add to the confusion, the court held in *Turner v. Employment Security* (1975) that pregnant women could not be blocked from receiving unemployment benefits. *Kahn v Shevin* (1974) and *Schlesinger v. Ballard*

(1975) rested on the willingness of the court to allow classifications that a majority of the justices saw as compensating women for past discrimination, whether or not the classifications were premised on the very view of women as dependent and unable to perform "men's jobs" that the court seemingly rejected in *Reed, LaFleur,* and *Frontiero,* as well as in the jury cases of *Edwards v. Healy* and *Taylor v. Louisiana* (1975) and the preschool children case of *Phillips v. Martin Marietta* (1971). At the same time, *Stanley v. Illinois* (the widowed and unmarried father custody case decided in 1972) and *Weinberger v. Wiesenfeld* (1975) suggested the court's rejection of the outmoded gender-role stereotypes that it accepted in *Kahn v. Shevin* and *Schlesinger v. Ballard*—although some of the justices in *Wiesenfeld* appeared to be concerned about children's well-being rather than any notions of gender equality.

There was, in short, a good reason for Ginsburg to title one of her articles "From No Rights to Half Rights to Confusing Rights." According to the Supreme Court, it was and was not legal for employers to treat pregnant women differently. It was and was not constitutional to base classifications on a perception of women as unable to operate equally in a world historically dominated by men. The appropriate test for deciding sex discrimination cases was or was not rational basis, an enhanced version of rational basis, strict scrutiny, suspect classification, or something as yet unarticulated. As the nine justices of the country's highest court returned to their chambers to consider the cases of the "thirsty boys" and the widowed civil servant, they had a cornucopia of conflicting precedents—all of them handed down in the preceding five years—on which to base their decisions. Which way they would go was anyone's guess. And from the conversations the justices then had among themselves, it was apparent that they weren't too sure either.

CHAPTER 8

"From No Rights to Half Rights to Confusing Rights"

When the justices of the Supreme Court meet in conference to discuss and vote on a case, that is not the end of the story. As has been mentioned, if the chief justice is in the majority, he assigns the writing of the opinion for the court; when he is not, that task falls to the senior justice in the majority. That practice proved to be particularly important as the justices hammered out their decisions in *Craig v. Boren* and *Califano v. Goldfarb*.

Chief Justice Warren Burger had made it clear during oral argument in *Craig v. Boren* that he was skeptical about Caroline Whitener's right to bring the "thirsty boys" case at all, and that had not changed by the time the justices met in conference. He therefore voted to sustain the law limiting the right of young men under twenty-one to buy "near beer," as did Justice Rehnquist. They were in the minority, however, which gave senior Justice William Brennan the opportunity to assign the opinion for the court. On October 12, Justice Brennan told the chief justice that he would write it himself.

The justice who authors an opinion for the court naturally wants to get as many votes behind it as possible. The more justices who sign on, the more authoritative the opinion appears to be. That is one reason a draft opinion is circulated. Its author hopes to keep his or her majority and, if the vote is not unanimous, possibly persuade others to join it. It is not unusual for another justice to respond to the author's draft with something along the lines of, "I can join if you would consider omitting . . ." or "I would suggest we add a statement that . . ."

In keeping with his consistent approach to gender classifications, Justice Brennan wanted to base the decision in *Craig* on "suspect classification." That approach, it will be remembered, means that the law is assumed to be unconstitutional, and the burden is on the government to prove that it's not. The justices would scrutinize the law strictly. Putting that stringent a test in his first draft, however, threatened his majority and made it doubtful he could pick up other votes. Chief Justice Burger had flirted briefly with the idea of reversing himself and voting to strike the law, writing to Justice Brennan on October 18, "I may decide to join you in a reversal, particularly if we do not expand the 'equal advantage' clause or 'suspect' classifications! In short, I am 'available.'" After seeing Justice Brennan's draft, though, the chief justice wrote to him on November 11, "I thought I might be able to join a reversal in this case and I may yet do so as to the result. However, your 'test' goes beyond what I could accept." A later draft did not convince him. A follow-up letter on November 15 said that "you read into Reed v. Reed what is not there. Every gender distinction does not need the strict scrutiny test applicable to a criminal case. Reed was the innocuous matter of who was to probate an estate. As written, I cannot possibly join."

Justices Lewis Powell, Harry Blackmun, and John Paul Stevens also suggested changes as successive drafts were circulated, and Brennan incorporated some of those. He was working to keep Justice Blackmun in the majority, and it seems fair to hypothesize that Justice Brennan's repeated references in the drafts to Justice Blackmun's language in *Stanton v. Stanton* were designed at least in part to keep Blackmun's vote.

The final version of Justice Brennan's opinion for the court rested on what he referred to as the test enunciated in *Reed v. Reed*. He interpreted that test, however, to mean not the "rational basis" standard but the "something in between" that Justice Blackmun had suggested in *Stanton*. His interpretation effectively created a third test that was more stringent than rational basis but less so than suspect classification. It wasn't sufficient for the Oklahoma law to meet the criterion of rationality, Justice Brennan said; it had to be "substantially related to achievement of the statutory objective" of public safety. He examined the statistics at length, drawing on Ginsburg's and Gilbert's discussions of them. He declared that the state's interpretation of the numbers was seriously flawed and called Oklahoma's reading of them "statistically measured but loose-fitting generalities concerning the drinking tendencies of aggregate groups." Even if the statistics were taken at face value, he continued, Oklahoma had shown that only 2 percent of men had been arrested for driving under the influence. "Certainly if maleness is to serve as a proxy for drinking and driving," he commented, "a correlation of 2% must be considered an unduly tenuous 'fit.'"

"It is unrealistic," Justice Brennan continued, "to expect either members of the judiciary or state officials to be well versed in the rigors of experimental or statistical technique." That sentence was a not very subtle reference to Justice Rehnquist, who made it clear in dissent that he accepted Oklahoma's reading of the statistics. "But," Brennan continued, "this merely illustrates that proving broad sociological propositions by statistics is a dubious business, and one that inevitably is in tension with the normative philosophy that underlies the Equal Protection Clause." That clause, in other words, had to be applied in light of constitutional values, not mere numbers. He also noted that the Oklahoma law didn't prevent young men from drinking near beer purchased by their female companions, so "the relationship between gender and traffic safety becomes far too tenuous to satisfy *Reed*'s requirement that the gender-based difference be substantially related to achievement of the statutory objective." He added in a footnote that Oklahoma could set any cutoff age it chose for the sale of 3.2 percent beer, "provided that the redefinition operates in a gender-neutral fashion."

By relying heavily on *Reed*, and occasionally on *Frontiero*, Brennan implied that he was merely following precedents and doing nothing new. That, however, was ingenuous—or, to put it more bluntly, untrue. Ginsburg understood the decision as creating an intermediate standard: it was "a new formulation," she commented. To pass constitutional muster, a gender classification now had to rest on an "important" legislative objective and "must relate substantially to the important objective." She noted that "important" was not as strong a word as "compelling," and "substantial" didn't mean "necessary," but the words went farther than the court's earlier reliance on "legitimate" objective and "rational" basis. "One might wish the Court had chosen a less frothy case for announcing the 'heightened' review standard," she would note, tongue in cheek, but the good news was that the decision represented "a key doctrinal advance."

She was not the only one to see the importance of the new test. Justice Powell concurred in the decision, writing that while "I view this as a relatively easy case," he disagreed with the test Justice Brennan laid out and his dismissal of the statistics. He added in a footnote that "the Court has had difficulty in agreeing upon a standard of equal protection analysis," and while he admitted that "there are valid reasons for dissatisfaction with the two-tier" approach, that approach "now has substantial precedential support." Powell was clearly struggling with the question of precisely what the approach ought to be. "Our decision today will be viewed by some as a 'middle-tier' approach," he said. "While I would not endorse that characterization and would not welcome a further subdividing of equal protection analysis, candor compels the recognition that the relatively deferential 'rational basis' standard of review normally applied takes on a sharper focus when we address a gender-based classification."

Or, to put it differently, while he didn't like the idea of a third test and rejected the idea that there was one, he also knew that in fact such a test did exist now. Justices of the Supreme Court can sometimes be as muddled in their pronouncements as lesser mortals. The bottom line for Powell, however, was that the law had to be overturned, because "this gender-based classification does not bear a fair and substantial relation to the object of the legislation."

Justice John Paul Stevens didn't like the three-test formula any better than Justice Powell did. "There is only one Equal Protection Clause," his concurrence began. "It requires every State to govern impartially. It does not direct the courts to apply one standard of review in some cases and a different standard in other cases." But he, too, found it hard to believe that the reason for the law was traffic safety. "It is objectionable because it is based on an accident of birth, because it is a mere remnant of the now almost universally rejected tradition of discriminating against males in this age bracket, and because, to the extent it reflects any physical difference between males and females, it is actually perverse." Justice Blackmun wrote a one-sentence concurrence indicating that he thought the Twenty-First Amendment, which left regulation of alcohol up to the states, more important than did Justice Brennan. Brennan had devoted a lengthy part of his opinion to debunking Oklahoma's argument that the amendment gave the states such extensive power over the regulation of alcoholic beverages that it justified the law. Justice Potter Stewart concurred in the decision while adding a few paragraphs calling the law totally irrational. Chief Justice Burger, adding his name to

Justice William Rehnquist's dissent, also indicated that he had finally decided that Carolyn Whitener did not have sufficient standing to bring the case at all.

Justice Rehnquist's dissent declared the court's ruling to be entirely unacceptable. *Wiesenfeld* notwithstanding, Rehnquist was adamantly opposed to the court's gender equality jurisprudence and wrote that "the only redeeming feature of the Court's opinion, to my mind, is that it apparently signals a retreat by those who joined the plurality opinion in Frontiero v. Richardson, from their view that sex is a 'suspect' classification.'" He would have decided the case using the rational basis test, and he considered the Oklahoma law to be entirely rational. Rehnquist declared that terms such as "substantially" and "important" were hopelessly vague and that even if the justices in the majority thought they understood exactly how those words were to be applied in other cases, "the thousands of judges in other courts who must interpret the Equal Protection Clause may not be so fortunate."

He was not alone in thinking so. Astute commentators agreed that the ruling did something new, but exactly what was not entirely clear. Only Justices White and Marshall joined Justice Brennan's entire opinion, although Justice Blackmun also accepted the middle-level test. The concurrences of Justices Powell, Stewart, and Stevens, however, each indicated their discomfort with the new standard. Justice Brennan's herculean attempt to keep his majority had paid off only in part. There was now a third test, somewhere in between rational basis and suspect classification. Whether the court would rely upon it in the future, however, or whether the court expected lower courts to adopt it, or whether those courts could even understand what it meant was far from certain.

"Supreme Court Sets New Judicial Sex Bias Rule," the *Los Angeles Times* reported on its front page. It quoted a civil rights lawyer, who preferred not to be named, as commenting, "For some reason the court seems afraid to make sex discrimination like race discrimination. They seem to be searching for a verbal formula that will clear the air . . . but now we seem to be stuck with a first-rate muddle."

Muddle notwithstanding, the justices had next to decide what to do with Leon Goldfarb's case, challenging the provision of the Social Security law that kept widowed men from benefiting from their late wives' contributions to the system. Some of them found that equally difficult.

Anyone who thinks that the justices inevitably decide cases on the basis of preconceived ideas and partisan leanings might be inclined to rethink after considering their correspondence as they wrestled with *Goldfarb*. The case was argued on October 5, and the justices voted in conference shortly thereafter. By October 18, Justice Stewart had changed his vote from one upholding the law to one affirming the decision of the lower court in Goldfarb's favor, but, he wrote, "I am not particularly happy with this result, however, and shall read with hospitable interest what is written on the other side." Justices Brennan, Marshall, and White voted to find the law in violation of the Equal Protection Clause. Justice Powell had tentatively decided to vote with them. The chief justice, who wanted to sustain the law, found himself in the minority, so Justice Brennan would once again assign the writing of the opinion for the court. On October 21, he told the chief that he would write this one, too, himself.

Then, as in *Craig v. Boren*, he had to struggle to keep his majority, and it was even harder this time around. Justice Stevens, who had voted for Goldfarb, told Brennan on October 21 that he had changed his mind and would vote to uphold the law, "subject to reading your opinion." His reason, he said, was that the discrimination in the distribution of benefits was "against males rather than females" and so was justified under *Kahn v. Shevin*'s ruling in favor of laws seen as helping women. As Ginsburg had predicted unhappily, the specter of that case would continue to loom in the thinking of those justices who remained unpersuaded that automatically treating all women differently from all men invariably hurt both. By early December, a number of Brennan's drafts had made the rounds, and Justices Marshall and White had asked him to add their names to his opinion. So did Justice Powell, although with some hesitation. As of the middle of the month, Justice Blackmun was undecided and was waiting to see the dissent that Justice Rehnquist planned to write. So was Justice Stewart, who had begun to wonder if the court's earlier gender equality decisions were wrong. "I think your proposed opinion for the Court is a remarkably fine job," he wrote to Justice Brennan, and "that given Weinberger v. Wiesenfeld, the result it reaches is close to unanswerable. . . . However, I have had some second thoughts about the Wiesenfeld decision, and for that reason shall await the dissenting opinion." One can only imagine how that tentative denial of an entire line of cases must have made Justice Brennan feel. In early January, acknowledging that it was "after considerable backing and filling," Justice Stewart decided to join the dissent. So did Justice Stevens—but only for the moment.

Chief Justice Burger also signaled that he would sign on to Justice Rehnquist's dissent. He thought the draft of the dissent "should convince even the most ardent 'equal protector'." In a memo to all the justices saying so, he added a note to Justice Powell: "Lewis, How *can* you not agree with WHR [Justice Rehnquist]!?" Justice Brennan, perhaps still hoping to bring one or two of the dissenters over to his side, wrote back, "I can find nothing in Bill's dissent that provides any principled basis for distinguishing Wiesenfeld and Frontiero.... This 'ardent equal protector,' at least remains unpersuaded." The dissenters remained equally unpersuaded, but Brennan's majority held—barely. Justices Marshall, White, and Powell joined his opinion, and although Justice Stevens did not, he had finally decided to vote with them. That meant that when the decision was published, it would indicate that Justice Brennan announced the judgment of the court, for a vote of five, but not the opinion of the court. His opinion commanded only a plurality of four.

The opinion repeated what he had written privately to the brethren: that he found *Wiesenfeld* and *Frontiero* "indistinguishable" from the situation in *Goldfarb*. In a sentence that could have been penned by Ginsburg, he declared that "*Wiesenfeld* thus inescapably compels the conclusion reached by the District Court that the gender-based differentiation ... that results in the efforts of female workers required to pay social security taxes producing less protection for their spouses than is produced by the efforts of men—is forbidden by the Constitution, at least when supported by no more substantial justification than 'archaic and overbroad' generalizations." He insisted that the Social Security system was one of insurance, not of welfare. Over and over again, he declared that he was doing nothing new, but simply deciding on the basis of facts and precedent.

> The only conceivable justification for writing the presumption of wives' dependency into the statute is the assumption, not verified by the Government in *Frontiero*, or here, but based simply on "archaic and overbroad" generalizations, that it would save the Government time, money, and effort simply to pay benefits to all widows, rather than to require proof of dependency of both sexes. We

{ *"From No Rights to Half Rights to Confusing Rights"* }   149 held in *Frontiero,* and again in *Wiesenfeld,* and therefore hold again here, that such assumptions do not suffice to justify a gender-based discrimination in the distribution of employment-related benefits.

Justice Stevens's separate lengthy and somewhat agonized concurrence reflected what he had written to Justice Brennan: that he saw the law as discriminating against widowed men, not their deceased wives. Stevens considered that to be the result not of a reasoned attempt to compensate women for past discrimination against them but to be "merely the accidental byproduct of a traditional way of thinking about females." He saw the same thought process behind the statutes at issue in *Kahn* and *Wiesenfeld* and was uncomfortable at the disparity between those decisions.

> The exclusion in *Wiesenfeld* was apparently the accidental byproduct of the same kind of legislative process that gave rise to *Kahn* and to this case. If there is inconsistency between *Kahn* and *Wiesenfeld,* as I believe there is, it is appropriate to follow the later unanimous holding rather than the earlier, sharply divided decision. And if the cases are distinguishable, *Wiesenfeld* is closer on its facts to this case than is *Kahn.*

Justice Rehnquist, in the dissent joined by the chief justice and Justices Stewart and Blackmun, argued that the law was rational. "Congress has here adopted a test of dependency as a reasonable surrogate for proof of actual need.... The differentiation in no way perpetuates the economic discrimination which has been the basis for heightened scrutiny of gender-based classifications, and is, in fact, explainable as a measure to ameliorate the characteristically depressed condition of aged widows."

The dissent was an extremely lengthy one, ranging over almost all the gender equality cases decided by the court in the 1970s and concluding that *Kahn v. Shevin* was properly decided. But it was a dissent; Leon Goldfarb won his case. The fear that the justices would balk at the possible price tag if the court decided against the government proved to be unfounded. Yet the unwillingness of five members of the court—the dissenters and Justice Stevens—to see the law as harmful to both men and women indicated that a majority was still struggling with the concept of outmoded stereotypes and the damage they could inflict.

The case, as Ginsburg would write, "was a cliff-hanger," and she was delighted at the outcome. "Won Goldfarb 5–4!" she wrote to Steven Wiesenfeld. "Without the precedent in your case, we would never have achieved this success." That was undoubtedly right, and it was indeed a success. Coupled with the decision in *Craig v. Boren* and the creation of an intermediate standard in gender discrimination cases, it meant that the law had come a long way from what it had been in 1971 before *Reed v. Reed*. Reading the two decisions together, Ginsburg declared that "one senses the justices' evolving appreciation that discrimination by gender generally cuts with two edges and is seldom, if ever, a pure favor to women." On March 21, the court handed down its rulings in the other widowers' cases mentioned by Ginsburg that were similar to Goldfarb's, deciding all of them in the widowers' favor.

Still, the fight for constitutional gender equality was very far from over. Sex had not been labeled a "suspect classification," and the court's decisions were in some ways so contradictory that what might happen in any other case was very far from clear. "As one federal district court judge said," Ginsburg commented, "'In dealing with Supreme Court 1970s sex-discrimination precedent, lower courts judges feel like players at a shell game who are not absolutely sure there is a pea.'"

Three weeks after the court handed down its decision in *Califano v. Goldfarb*, it issued a per curiam opinion in the case of *Califano v. Webster*. The part of the Social Security Act devoted to old-age insurance had established a formula for calculating benefits for retired women workers that was more favorable than the one used to calculate men's benefits. Congress changed that in 1972 to make the formula gender-neutral, but the change was not retroactive. Will Webster, a worker who had retired before 1972 and was therefore receiving benefits based on the old formula, sued on Equal Protection grounds. The Supreme Court upheld the classification under the old law, finding that the purpose for it was the "permissible one of redressing our society's longstanding disparate treatment of women" and that it served "the important governmental objective" of reducing "the disparity in economic condition between men and women caused by the long history of discrimination against women." It differentiated cases like *Frontiero v. Richardson*, *Weinberger v. Wiesenfeld*, and *Goldfarb*, saying that the laws at issue in those cases "in fact penalized women wage earners." Here, however, the law was not based on outmoded stereotypes but—quoting *Goldfarb*—on "'the permissible [purpose] of redressing our society's longstanding disparate treatment of women.'"

The court's opinion in *Webster* was drafted by Jerry Lynch, who had been a student of Ginsburg's and was now clerking for Justice Brennan. He proudly sent a draft to his former professor, who agreed that the law actually was compensatory and replied, "Had I been assigned the task, I could not have done better." She believed that "post-hoc rationalization was unacceptable for laws that ranked women as men's subordinates." At the same time, however, "when a law, in design and operation, attempts to ameliorate past disadvantage during an interim-catch-up period, and is narrowly tailored to that end, sex classification, as a transitional measure, is permissible." She saw "genuinely compensatory classification" as "(1) in fact adopted for remedial reasons rather than out of prejudice about 'the way women are,' and (2) trimly tailored in scope and time to match the remedial end."

The justices who had dissented in *Goldfarb*—Chief Justice Burger and Justices Stewart, Blackmun, and Rehnquist—concurred with the judgment but wrote that they found it "somewhat difficult to distinguish the Social Security provision upheld here from that struck down so recently in Califano v. Goldfarb." Others had the same problem. The author of the Ford Foundation's report on gender equality litigation commented, "the line is very narrow between the judicial sanction for legislation that seeks to protect particular women against specified dangers and judicial paternalism toward women because they as a group need protection."

Ginsburg's assessment, as she wrote in a 1978 article for the American Bar Association, was that while there had been some "remarkable gains" since 1970, "the Court's performance is characterized by vacillation, 5–4 decisions and a tendency to shy away from doctrinal development. The historic fact that our 18th- and 19th century Constitution-makers had women's emancipation nowhere on their agenda is an obvious source of the Justices' uneasiness, and their reluctance to provide the firmer guidance lower courts seek." She was somewhat more hopeful about Congress. Referring to the congresswoman from Michigan, she wrote to one of her staff in 1973, "How about asking Martha Griffiths to consider the retired widower's case ... along with Stephen Wiesenfeld's young father-widower case." Griffiths was sympathetic, and Ginsburg could tell Jane Lifset in 1974, "Martha Griffiths has a pending bill which would increase Social Security payments where both spouses have been members of the work force." But piece-by-piece legislation was inadequate, and, like Griffiths, Ginsburg had come to think that only ratification of the Equal Rights Amendment could end legalized gender inequality. Still, in its absence, there were more cases to be brought. That was the situation as, in November 1978, she turned to what would be the last case she argued before the Supreme Court.

*　*　*

In 1976, Billy Duren found himself facing an all-male jury. He and a companion had tried to hold up a US post office in Kansas City, Missouri. In the course of the botched robbery, Duren killed one person and wounded another. A Jackson County jury found him guilty of first-degree murder and assault with intent to kill, and Duren was sentenced to consecutive life imprisonments.

Duren's attorney repeatedly challenged the absence of women on the jury panel, saying their exclusion violated his right to be tried by a jury drawn from a cross-section of the community. Article I of the Missouri constitution directed its courts to "excuse any woman who requests exemption therefrom before being sworn as a juror." Duren and Lee M. Nation, his Jackson County public defender attorney, presented statistics showing that the result was that while more than half of the Jackson County population were women, they were only 15.5 percent of those appearing for possible jury duty. Duren relied on the Supreme Court's 1975 decision in *Taylor v. Louisiana*, discussed in chapter 5, which had overturned a law requiring women but not men to register if they chose to be eligible for jury duty.

Missouri's law was different, both the trial court judge and the Missouri Supreme Court said. It didn't require women to register; instead, it permitted them to opt out when called, either by saying they chose not to serve or by not answering the summons at all. *Taylor* applied only to opt-ins, Missouri said, but not to opt-outs. Besides, the state pointed out, Louisiana's opt-in system had resulted in a mere 10 percent of women in any jury wheel, but the situation in Missouri was between 29 and 30 percent of people receiving a notice to appear, before women exercised the right to opt out. That, it claimed, met the constitutional standard. The Louisiana law, the state argued, effectively excluded women, but Missouri's excluded no one.

Duren appealed to the US Supreme Court. Lee Nation, his twenty-five-year-old public defender, was only three years out of law school and working on a very limited budget. He remembered reading about Ginsburg and the *Frontiero* case when he was in law school, and so he turned to the Women's Rights Project for help. Ginsburg saw the case as a chance to bury *Hoyt v. Florida* once and for all. Billy Duren wasn't the issue; undervaluing women's service on juries was. *Taylor* "settles the jury service issue," she wrote to a law student, but "Missouri misread *Taylor*'s message and had to be told again." She and Kathleen Peratis were ready to fashion a brief and an oral argument that would do exactly that.

The brief stated the reason Ginsburg had been so determined to overturn *Hoyt v. Florida.* Jury service is a basic responsibility of citizenship, a principle form of participation in the democratic process of government. "By giving 'any woman' an automatic exemption, thus treating men's service as essential, women's as expendable, Missouri reinforces ancient prejudices harmful to women, to the jury system, and to the community at large."

She added that permitting an exemption for "any woman" was as unacceptable as would be "an exemption for 'any man,' 'any Jew,' 'any black.'" The Missouri law violated the Sixth Amendment's right to a jury, but it also flew in the face of the Equal Protection Clause, and she cited the gender equality cases from *Reed v. Reed* through *Califano v. Goldfarb* to make her point. She was struck by the irony that while pre-1970s jury cases had been decided on the assumption that women's domestic duties were an adequate reason for them to be excused, the Missouri Supreme Court now wrote in upholding the law that women had become so busy in the paid workforce that they would no doubt seek exemptions anyway under the other categories of people the Missouri law exempted, such as teachers or government workers.

Missouri's brief was submitted under the name of John Ashcroft, then the state's attorney general and later attorney general of the United States. The issue before the court, according to Missouri, was not the law's wisdom but its constitutionality. As women were not excluded from serving, there was no violation of either the Sixth or the Fourteenth Amendment. But even if the law did violate the right to jury by a cross-section of the community, Duren could not prove that he had actually been harmed by the absence of women from his jury, and he was therefore not entitled to a new trial. It appeared that the state was less concerned about the validity of the law than about the prospect of Duren and other prisoners going free. It is noteworthy that the brief repeatedly identified Duren and his colleague in the crime as "black."

By the time the case reached the court, Missouri was something of an outlier. Only it and Tennessee gave women automatic exemptions, a point that was made in the amicus brief submitted by the Carter administration, under the names of Solicitor General Wade McCree and Assistant Attorney General Drew Days.

Nation and Ginsburg agreed to share the time for oral argument before the Supreme Court. Ginsburg invited Nation to New York for a pretrial moot (practice) argument and, as he had no funds, to stay in her apartment. "She was like an old Jewish mother," Nation would remember. "I was sick, but young, and wanted to go out in New York City at night and drink a few beers. . . . She wanted me to stay in and eat some chicken soup." It's a bit hard to imagine Ginsburg, who did not cook, pressing chicken soup on anyone, but whether Nation was already prepared ("I was just ready for any really weird question anybody might ask," he said later) or the moot court did its work, his argument went well.

He was the first to step to the podium when the Supreme Court heard argument in *Duren* on the afternoon of November 1, 1978. As Nation told the justices, he would address the Sixth Amendment question, and Ginsburg would handle the Equal Protection argument. He began with a long description of the jury pool and jury selection process in Missouri, drawing on statistics to demonstrate that women were effectively excluded from most juries. It was unconstitutional to exclude any identifiable group from a jury, he argued.

Justice Rehnquist challenged that. "Where do you get that from?" he asked. The court's own decision in *Taylor*, Nation responded. "What other identifiable groups" beyond women could not be excluded, Rehnquist continued to ask. "Blacks, Mexican-Americans," came the reply. "How about lawyers and judges and dentists and doctors and clergymen and teachers? . . . Don't you think a lawyer can make a much bigger impact if he's a member of a jury than a woman as a woman or a Mexican-American as a Mexican-American?" Rehnquist clearly was not going to be any more sympathetic to the plaintiff's argument in *Duren* than he had been in *Taylor*. There wasn't much Nation could say in reply that would make any difference, and he soon turned the podium over to Ginsburg for her fifteen minutes.

"My argument addresses the citizen's duty tied to a defendant's fair cross section right and the complete absence of justification for exempting any woman," she began, after Chief Justice Burger had once again invited her to lower the lectern. That was what she wanted to emphasize: that citizens were expected to be available for jury duty and that exempting women from that requirement suggested they were less than fully respected citizens. The case, she said, involved both Billy Duren's right "to a fair chance" that the jury would be representative of the entire community, and the fact that treating potential women jurors differently had to be viewed against what was historically "a certain way of thinking about women."

Chief Justice Burger immediately jumped in. "That [way of thinking] wouldn't concern Mr. Duren, would it?" he asked. Ginsburg was determined to tie the Sixth Amendment right to the Equal Protection right and to the historical reasoning behind such jury laws. Her reply referred to Judge Robert Seiler's dissent in the Missouri Supreme Court's decision upholding the law, as he had "pointed out that a defendant's fair cross-section right can be meaningful only if it hinges on a correlative duty, the duty of the citizen to show up for jury services when summoned." She was not about to give up the race/sex analogy: "That right is real only when the obligation to service is placed on citizens without automatic exemption, based solely on their race, national origin, or sex."

Chief Justice Burger went back to Justice Rehnquist's point, noting that Missouri exempted doctors from jury service. "Exemptions that apply on the basis of one's occupations reflect determinations by the state that certain occupations for the good of the community should be pursued uninterrupted," Ginsburg responded, "and it makes no difference whether a person is male/female, black or white, it's the neutral, functional category that is excluded, doctor, lawyer, dentist, clergy not any woman—" What if the law exempted women with small children, the chief justice interrupted to ask. There were states that did exempt *parents* of small children, she replied, without limiting the exemption to *women.* "But by using the term assuming that it will be the woman here or in a more general, any woman excuse" she added, "the state is providing an ineludible message that the male citizens are counted by Government as the essential participants of the administration of justice but the female citizens are not so counted, their service is expendable."

Justice Blackmun asked Ginsburg about the state's assertion "that if Mr. Duren prevails here, the Missouri jailhouse doors might be open. Do you have any comment?" "I think it's certainly the case that this objection is available only to the defendants who have properly raised it below and pursued it on appeal," she said, and would be relevant only in Jackson County, as it was the only county that still used the questionnaire and summons inviting women to opt out. Still concerned about the possible floodgates, Blackmun asked what had happened to Billy Joe Taylor, after the court's decision in *Taylor.* The answer was that he was retried and convicted.

Congress had voted a month earlier to put suffragist Susan B. Anthony's likeness on a one dollar coin. That was clearly on at least one justice's mind as Ginsburg's turn at the podium ended with this colloquy:

> MRS. GINSBURG: To conclude, the unconstitutionality of Missouri's excuse for "any woman" as it operates to distort Jackson County jury panels is plainly established. Any sensible reading of this record juxtaposed with this Court's 8-to-1 judgment in *Taylor* leads ineluctably to that conclusion.
>
> JUSTICE REHNQUIST: You won't settle for putting Susan B. Anthony on the new dollar then?
>
> [Laughter]

Her allotted time was over, and Ginsburg sat down without a comment. Years later, she told a Columbia University audience, also to laughter, that on her way home, "I thought of a good comeback: 'No, Mr. Justice Rehnquist, tokens won't do.' . . . Unfortunately, I didn't say that."

Missouri Assistant Attorney General Nanette K. Laughrey stood up to argue for the state, essentially repeating what Missouri had said in its brief. One of her points would resonate with the justices as they later exchanged thoughts about the way to decide the case.

MISS LAUGHREY: I think we also have to find out what degree of disparity must be proven in order to make out a violation of the Sixth Amendment. . . . We know that one percent is too small, and we know that 54 percent would be an exact mirror. We never know where, in between that, the Sixth Amendment violation occurs.

For the moment, however, the justices focused on other things. Justice Marshall was no less obvious about his approach to the case than Justice Rehnquist had been, although he came out on the opposite side. In an extended colloquy, he asked how the state justified the exemption for women.

MISS LAUGHREY: The exemption originally was given because of the presumed role of women in the home and that there were so many women in that situation that they should be given an exemption.

Also, there was some intimation that women should be given a choice as to whether they wanted to participate in the selection of juries where certain details might be described that they were uncomfortable in hearing.

JUSTICE MARSHALL: And at a time when . . . they weren't even qualified to vote? . . . They just couldn't do anything but tend a home.

At that point, Nanette Laughrey must have found herself as uncomfortable as Ginsburg had at times in other oral arguments.

JUSTICE WHITE: What's the state's strongest argument . . . for treating women different than men in terms of excuse?
MISS LAUGHREY: We recognize that women still play a primary role in the home that even though women may in fact be working mothers does not mean that they have been relieved of the responsibilities of their obligations to the home or to their family.
JUSTICE WHITE: Is that—is that a—do you think that's the legislative decision?
MISS LAUGHREY: I don't know what the legislative justification was. We do not have any evidence. I submit that that is the strongest justification that the State of Missouri can make for the exemption.

As it turned out, that statement would resonate with the justices, but not to Missouri's advantage. Almost as if she expected the state to lose the case, Laughrey spent much of the remainder of her time urging the justices not to make a ruling against it retroactive.

If Laughrey did anticipate losing the case, she was right to do so. When the justices met in conference, almost all of them voted to overturn the law. Chief Justice Burger assigned the writing of the court's opinion to Justice Byron White, after the justices discussed the retroactivity issue at conference but came to no decision about it. The draft Justice White first circulated did not deal with the issue, and Justice Stewart quickly wrote to him, "I wonder if you have considered whether to say anything about that subject." White replied, "Essentially, my recommendation is that Duren reaches all cases where juries were sworn after Taylor and in which the issue was raised in timely fashion and rejected by the State courts." That troubled Justice Powell, who wrote in reply that while he thought *Taylor* was controlling and so he would stay in the majority, "I do not think this conclusion free from reasonable doubt. The Missouri statute did not foreclose participation by women. It merely accorded them the option, and the actual participation was not negligible. In view of these differences, I am not disposed to apply Duren retroactively to the date of our decision in Taylor."

Perhaps to keep Justice Powell's vote, Justice White did not mention retroactivity in the final opinion for the court—although the court would go on to make its ruling retroactive two weeks later. The opinion did, however, deal with the question of what percentage of jurors in the pool was low enough to violate the Sixth Amendment. "Today we hold that such systematic exclusion of women that results in jury venires averaging less than 15% female violates the Constitution's fair-cross-section requirement," he wrote. Quoting *Taylor*, he reiterated that "'the right to a proper jury cannot be overcome on merely rational grounds.' Rather, it requires that a significant state interest be manifestly and primarily advanced by those aspects of the jury-selection process, such as exemption criteria, that result in the disproportionate exclusion of a distinctive group."

To demonstrate that the fair-cross-section jury requirement had been violated, Justice White said, a defendant had to show three things: "(1) that the group alleged to be excluded is a 'distinctive' group in the community; (2) that the representation of this group in venires from which juries are selected is not fair and reasonable in relation to the number of such persons in the community; and (3) that this under-representation is due to systematic exclusion of the group in the jury-selection process."

Duren had met all those criteria, he concluded. *Taylor* had made it clear that women were a distinctive group in the jury context. Having only 15 percent of the prospective jurors come from a group that made up 54 percent of the population was not "fair and reasonable." Finally, Duren had shown that the underrepresentation of women was caused by their "systematic exclusion." And the justices were skeptical of the reason for the exclusion: "In response to questioning at oral argument, counsel for respondent ventured that the only state interest advanced by the exemption is safeguarding the important role played by women in home and family life. But exempting all women because of the preclusive domestic responsibilities of some women is insufficient justification for their disproportionate exclusion on jury venires."

Justice Rehnquist dissented, as he had signaled in oral argument that he would. The court claimed to base its decision on the defendant's jury right, he wrote angrily, but that was a "fiction." "The majority is in truth concerned with the equal protection rights of women to partici-pate in the judicial process rather than with the Sixth Amendment right of a criminal defendant to be tried by an 'impartial jury.'" He referred dismissively to "organized women's groups that have appeared as amici curiae in similar cases." The decision would make states wary, he thought, of establishing any categories of exemption, lest they be found to have based the exemption "on merely rational grounds" rather than "a significant state interest." In addition, the 15 percent floor gave states no solid guidance about what percentage would be acceptable and would, he thought, result in the elimination of all categories of exemption, such as those for doctors and nurses.

Rehnquist's dissent notwithstanding, Lee Nation was ecstatic. "Oh, man. It was like winning the Super Bowl!" he remembered. The state of Missouri had reason to be pleased as well, in spite of its loss at the court. The floodgates did not open: Duren was retried and convicted, and spent twenty years in prison. The Women's Rights Project sent a memo to ACLU affiliates in states that still had limitations on women's ability to serve on juries, including excusing those who were "women" or "moth-ers" with childcare responsibilities. The memo, written by Ginsburg, urged the affiliates to lobby for statutory changes. Ginsburg suggested that if a state's legislatures failed to act, then the affiliates should consider litigation and locate men with childcare responsibilities who were denied the childcare exemption. She wrote as well to Assistant Attorney General Drew Days, advising him to eliminate the women-only childcare provision from federal district court juries: "Has any effort been made by the Department" on gender-based assumptions? "Shortly after the decision was announced," Days replied, "we . . . concluded that certain of the federal excuse provisions appeared unnecessarily overbroad as well as unjustifiably restricted to women. . . . We will keep you informed about the results of our efforts to modify these provisions." The case had been won, but Ginsburg would not be satisfied until all the gender-specific limitations on women's jury service were ended.

* * *

What turned out to be Ginsburg's last months as a litigator were filled with additional cases and a series of court victories.

In March 1979, two months after its decision in *Duren,* the Supreme Court decided the case of *Orr v. Orr.* With Justice Brennan writing for a majority of six, the court held that an Alabama law requiring men but not women to pay alimony violated the Equal Protection Clause. The law, Brennan said, "use[d] sex as a proxy for need" and so was unacceptably based on outmoded stereotypes. Brennan relied on the middle-tier test that had been established in *Craig v. Boren* and cited the cases that Ginsburg had won. He also made passing reference to the race/sex analogy that the court had not yet accepted. Replying to the assertion that the divorced husband who brought the case had no standing to sue, he wrote, "There is no doubt that a state law imposing alimony obligations on blacks but not whites could be challenged by a black who was required to pay." Ginsburg, working with Margaret Moses, her former student and now a lawyer with the Women's Rights Project, had submitted an amicus brief in the case.

She and a number of women lawyers from other organizations— Diana A. Steele, Phyllis N. Segal, and Nancy Duff Campbell (Center for Law and Social Policy, soon National Women's Law Center)—also wrote an amicus brief in the case of *Califano v. Westcott,* which was argued at the Supreme Court in April 1979. It involved the section of the Social

Security Act that provided Aid to Families with Dependent Children benefits to families if the father but not the mother became unemployed. In May, Ginsburg wrote to Stephen Wiesenfeld that if the court decided for Westcott, she would be "satisfied that we have reached the end of the road, successfully, on explicit sex lines in the law." A month later, a unanimous Supreme Court held the section to be in violation of the equal protection of the laws. Ginsburg also wrote an amicus brief in *Wengler v. Druggists Mutual Insurance Company* (along with NOW, the Women's Equity Action League, and the Women's Legal Defense Fund), challenging Missouri's requirement that men but not women had to prove dependency in order to receive workers' compensation benefits after the death of a spouse.

By the time a Supreme Court majority of eight announced its decision for Mr. Wengler, on April 22, 1980, with Justice Rehnquist still insistently in dissent, Ginsburg was about to end her career as a litigator. On April 8, President Jimmy Carter nominated her to the US Court of Appeals for the District of Columbia Circuit.

Ginsburg's victory in *Duren*, the last case she argued before the Supreme Court, meant that she had finally managed to bury *Hoyt v. Florida* and the exclusion of women from juries. Title VII of the 1964 Civil Rights Act and the Equal Employment Opportunity Commission's 1969 declaration that gender-specific protective legislation was no longer acceptable, along with court decisions citing Title VII to strike down such laws, had for the most part taken care of *Muller v. Oregon*. The Supreme Court's decision in *Craig v. Boren* meant that *Goesaert v. Cleary*, keeping women out of lucrative jobs and treating them differently when alcohol was involved, had been tossed onto history's scrap pile. *Wiesenfeld* and *Goldfarb* had made it clear that sex differentials in the Social Security Act that were based on outmoded stereotypes could not stand.

Constitutional gender equality was far from complete, and the Supreme Court was steely in its refusal to judge gender discrimination by the same standard it used for racial discrimination. But the constitutional landscape was so different from what it had been when Ginsburg began litigating at the court that she could confidently move on to the next stage of her career, knowing that she left behind a record that had been almost unimaginable only ten years before.

Epilogue

On June 26, 1996, the Supreme Court announced its decision in the case of *U.S. v. Virginia*. It found that the Virginia Military Institute (VMI), a 157-year-old public college, had violated the Equal Protection Clause by refusing to admit women. In order to defend a sex-specific law or practice, the court held, the government or institution had to prove that it had an "exceedingly persuasive justification" for treating men and women differently. VMI had not done so.

The phrase "exceedingly persuasive justification" was taken from the court's ruling in the 1982 case of *Mississippi University for Women v. Hogan*. Joe Hogan, a registered nurse who wanted to pursue a baccalaureate degree in nursing, was refused admission by the university because it accepted only women. Justice Sandra Day O'Connor, who in 1981 became the first woman to serve on the Supreme Court, wrote the opinion declaring that excluding Joe Hogan was a violation of the Fourteenth Amendment's Equal Protection Clause. It was the first time the Supreme Court had ever issued an opinion about sex segregation in public education and, as Ruth Bader Ginsburg would note, it was also "the first time a woman has spoken from the Supreme Court on the issue of sex discrimination." Justice O'Connor based the decision on the precedents—in *Reed v. Reed*, *Frontiero v. Richardson*, *Weinberger v. Wiesenfeld*—that Ginsburg had established, and Ginsburg described O'Connor's opinion as "vigorously recapitulating the main themes of the 1970s." One paragraph in particular echoed Ginsburg's arguments in those years.

> Although the test for determining the validity of a gender-based classification is straightforward, it must be applied free of fixed notions concerning the roles and abilities of males and females. Care must be taken in ascertaining whether the statutory objective itself reflects archaic and stereotypic notions. Thus, if the statutory objective is to

exclude or "protect" members of one gender because they are presumed to suffer from an inherent handicap or to be innately inferior, the objective itself is illegitimate.

Now, fourteen years later, the Supreme Court reiterated the "exceedingly persuasive justification" criterion, and the precedents cited by Justice O'Connor, when it decided *U.S. v. Virginia*. The justice who wrote the 7–1 opinion for the court (one justice recused himself) was Ruth Bader Ginsburg. President Bill Clinton had nominated her to the court in 1993, thirteen years after she took her seat on the US Court of Appeals for the District of Columbia. Finally, Ginsburg could draw upon her own victories as a litigator in formulating a new standard for judging cases involving gender discrimination—even if it was not quite as stringent as she would have liked. "The heightened review standard our precedent establishes does not make sex a proscribed classification," her opinion acknowledged, referring to the test used for cases alleging racial discrimination. While she nonetheless nodded to the race/sex analogy by citing *Sweatt v. Painter*, the 1950 case in which the court held that states could not exclude African Americans from a publicly funded law school, she also wrote, "Inherent differences between men and women . . . remain cause for celebration, but not for denigration of the members of either sex or for artificial constraints on an individual's opportunity." A classification based on gender "may not be used . . . to create or perpetuate the legal, social, and economic inferiority of women." Any such classification had to be subjected to "skeptical scrutiny."

Ginsburg had heard about the case in its early stages, before it reached the court, and it reminded her of one of her more frustrating experiences as a litigator.

In 1974, Susan Lynn Vorchheimer, an outstanding student at a Philadelphia junior high school, applied to the prestigious public Central High School. The school accepted only boys, however, and Vorchheimer was told she could go instead to Girls High. As she had visited Girls High and found it inferior to Central, she and her parents sued the school district. They won in the federal district court but lost at the appeals level. Her lawyer, who initially solicited the involvement of Ginsburg and the Women's Rights Project, then declined to take their advice, and when the case went to the Supreme Court, the lawyer did what Ginsburg and Mel Wulf considered to be a "rather poor" job on the briefs and oral argument. Justice William Rehnquist was away when the case was heard; the eight justices who considered it divided four to four, and so the appeals court decision remained in effect. Susan Vorchheimer could not attend Central High, on account of sex.

Ginsburg had not been certain that the time was ripe for the case. "I knew, I knew that case was going to be a cliff-hanger," she said, and added that the decision "indicated a Court not yet fully secure in its grapplings with sex discrimination." But the loss, which she attributed as much to the incompetence of Vorchheimer's attorney, rankled. Finally, in 1996, she felt she had triumphed after all: "To me, it [the VMI decision] was winning the Vorchheimer case twenty years later. It never took me so long to win a case."

As Ginsburg announced the decision to a hushed courtroom, she glanced down the bench to Justice O'Connor, tacitly acknowledging the difference the court's first two women justices had made. In fact, Chief Justice Rehnquist had assigned the majority opinion to O'Connor, who then told him that Ginsburg deserved to be its author. "I regard the VMI case as the culmination of the 1970s endeavor to open doors so that women could aspire and achieve without artificial constraints," Ginsburg said later. She hadn't realized it would take that long. Back in 1978, she commented, "I believed, after Frontiero, that an effective 5 year plan could finish the job. That estimate was wrong." But now it was 1996, and while "exceedingly persuasive justification" was not "suspect classification," it was far from the permissive "rational basis" standard of 1971. "The VMI decision is a stunning change from the Court's rulings in 1873, in Myra Bradwell's case," Ginsburg commented, "that women could be excluded from the practice of law in Illinois, without offense to the Federal Constitution, and in 1961, in Gwendolyn Hoyt's case, that women in Florida need not be placed on lists from which jurors are drawn." Like her victories in the 1970s, the VMI case was a landmark in the law.

O'Connor and Ginsburg had not gotten the court to that point alone. Ginsburg gave a signed copy of her bench announcement to by-then-retired justice William Brennan, who had voted so consistently on her side back in the 1970s. "Dear Bill," she inscribed it, "See how the light you shed has spread! With appreciation, Ruth." She added, as she handed it to the ninety-year-old Brennan, "Without you this would not have been possible." The ballet performed by the two in the 1970s, with each of them building on the other's words, had finally achieved its intended result.

Six justices signed on to Ginsburg's opinion in the VMI case. William Rehnquist, who became the chief justice in 1980, wrote a concurrence. The relationship between Ginsburg and Rehnquist was quite as interesting as the one between Ginsburg and Brennan and was indicative of the enormous changes in society and the law between 1971 and 1996. Just a few months before Ginsburg was sworn in as a judge on the DC Circuit Court of Appeals in 1980, she submitted the Women's Rights Project's amicus brief in the Supreme Court case of *Wengler v. Druggists Mutual Insurance Company*. Justice Byron White wrote for the court in that case, striking down a Missouri statute that treated men and women differently in awarding worker's compensation upon the death of a spouse. The only dissent came from Justice Rehnquist, who, as noted earlier, had voted against Ginsburg in every case she argued before the court except *Weinberger v. Wiesenfeld*. It was also Rehnquist who, as the chief justice, swore her in when she joined the court.

As she told the story:

> Janet Reno, our Attorney General, is going to present the commission [certifying Ginsburg's appointment]. Attorney General Reno . . . did not want to be "General," as was the tradition; she wanted to be called "Ms. Reno." The Chief wanted to be sure that he could say "Ms." comfortably, so the day before he actually repeated her name a couple of times. And that difference, his consciousness, in 1993, and lack of consciousness in 1978, shows that yes, we have made real progress.

Ginsburg and the man she always called "the Chief" became and remained friends until his death in 2005.

Ruth Bader Ginsburg had become something of a popular icon before she died on September 18, 2020. In 2013, a New York University law student named Shana Knizhnik created a Tumblr blog called "Notorious R.B.G." Inspired by Ginsburg's dissent in *Shelby County v. Holder*, a case limiting the Voting Rights Act, the blog riffed on the name of a popular Brooklyn-born rap star. It quickly ballooned into an Internet sensation. The best-selling *Notorious RBG: The Life and Times of Ruth Bader Ginsburg*, written by Knizhnik and Irin Carmon, followed. So did "You Can't Spell Truth Without Ruth" T-shirts and socks, a biopic and a hit documentary about her life, and a book detailing her workout routine. Little girls dressed in RBG costumes for Halloween. Ginsburg was the subject of a *Saturday Night Live* skit and showed off her workout moves on *The Late Show*. Audiences stood and applauded whenever the opera- and theater-loving justice entered an auditorium.

Erwin Griswold, Ginsburg's former law school dean, acknowledged the late justice as "the Thurgood Marshall of gender equality law." That was what President Clinton had dubbed her in announcing her nomination to the Supreme Court. Legal scholar and former Supreme Court law clerk Geoffrey Stone called her "simply the most important woman lawyer in the history of the Republic." The woman who almost went to business school rather than law school became the attorney most responsible for the landmark cases that permanently altered the legal status of women in the United States.

1866	Ratification of the Fourteenth Amendment to the Constitution, one section of which prohibits states from depriving any person of due process of law or the equal protection of the laws.
1873	US Supreme Court decides *Bradwell v. Illinois*, holding that the Fourteenth Amendment does not prohibit states from excluding women from the practice of law.
1875	Supreme Court decides *Minor v. Happersett*, holding that states have the power to exclude women from voting.
1908	In *Muller v. Oregon*, the Supreme Court upholds a state law setting maximum hours for some women workers. The court cites a societal facts–conscious brief by attorney Louis Dembitz Brandeis—the first use of the "Brandeis brief."
1924	Supreme Court holds in *Radice v. New York* that prohibiting women from working at night does not violate the Equal Protection Clause.
March 15, 1933	Joan Ruth Bader is born in New York City.
1948	Supreme Court holds in *Goesaert v. Cleary* that prohibiting women from running bars does not violate the Equal Protection Clause.
1954	Ruth Bader graduates from Cornell University; marries Martin Ginsburg.
1956–1958	Ruth Bader Ginsburg (RBG) attends Harvard Law School, one of ten women in a class of roughly five hundred.
1959	RBG graduates from Columbia Law School; begins a two-year clerkship for District Court Judge Edmund L. Palmieri.
1961	In *Hoyt v. Florida*, Supreme Court holds that effectively keeping women from serving on state juries does not violate the Constitution's Sixth Amendment right to a trial by jury.
1961–1963	RBG works for the Columbia Law School Project on International Procedure; lives intermittently in Sweden.
1963	Passage of the Equal Pay Act.
1963	President John F. Kennedy creates the President's Commission on the Status of Women, chaired by Eleanor

	Roosevelt. Its report will lead to the creation of annual meetings on the subject.
1963–1972	RBG teaches at Rutgers University's School of Law; handles cases of gender discrimination for the ACLU of New Jersey.
1964	Passage of the Civil Rights Act, including Title VII, prohibiting employment discrimination on the basis of sex; creation of the Equal Employment Opportunity Commission.
1970	RBG and Martin Ginsburg begin work on *Moritz v. Commissioner*, challenging the section of the Internal Revenue Code that gives a deduction for dependent care to unmarried women but not to unmarried men.
1971	RBG begins teaching a course on women and the law; becomes coeditor of the first sex discrimination case book.
1971	Supreme Court holds in *Reed v. Reed* that preferring men to women as executors of an estate violates the Equal Protection Clause. The first time the court has held a sex-based classification to be unconstitutional, the decision declares that any such classification cannot merely be "rational" but must have a "substantial relation to the object of the legislation."
December 1971	The American Civil Liberties Union (ACLU) votes to establish a Women's Rights Project.
1972	RBG begins work as the director of the ACLU Women's Rights Project (WRP) and as a professor at Columbia University School of Law; Brenda Feigen Fasteau becomes codirector of the WRP.
1972	Air Force reinstates Susan Struck, whom it had dismissed for becoming pregnant and refusing to have an abortion, thereby mooting the case of *Struck v. Secretary of Defense*.
November 22, 1972	Tenth Circuit Court of Appeals holds in *Moritz v. Commissioner* that the federal tax deduction for dependent care by unmarried women but not unmarried men violates the Equal Protection Clause. It is the first time a section of the federal tax law has been held unconstitutional.
January 17, 1973	RBG argues *Frontiero v. Laird*, her first appearance before the Supreme Court.
January 22, 1973	Supreme Court decides *Roe v. Wade* and *Doe v. Bolton*.
May 4, 1973	The court holds in *Frontiero v. Richardson* (formerly

Frontiero v. Laird) that the Air Force's denial of specific benefits to women but not to men violates the Fifth Amendment's Due Process Clause. Four justices indicate that they would have decided the case using the "suspect classification" test, presuming that any law differentiating on the basis of gender is unconstitutional.

January 21, 1974   A divided Supreme Court holds in *Cleveland v. LaFleur* that states cannot require all pregnant teachers to leave the classroom by an arbitrary date nor forbid all new mothers from returning by an equally arbitrary date.

April 24, 1974   The Supreme Court rules in *Kahn v. Shevin* that a state law giving a tax deduction to widows but not widowers, on the assumption that widows are needier, does not violate the Equal Protection Clause. It is RBG's only Supreme Court loss.

June 17, 1974   In *Geduldig v. Aiello*, the Supreme Court holds that a state's denial of disability insurance payments to pregnant women does not violate the Equal Protection Clause.

January 15, 1975   The Supreme Court holds in *Schlesinger v. Ballard* that giving male naval officers less time than female officers to qualify for promotion does not violate the Equal Protection Clause.

January 21, 1975   *Taylor v. Louisiana*, holding that a state cannot make eligibility for jury service different for men and women, is decided by the US Supreme Court. It effectively endorses RBG's similar argument in *Edwards v. Healy*.

March 19, 1975   A unanimous Supreme Court rules in *Weinberger v. Wiesenfeld*, RBG's favorite case, that the Equal Protection Clause is violated by a Social Security regulation giving widows but not widowers "child in care" payments.

November 17, 1975   The Supreme Court's per curiam decision in *Turner v. Department of Employment Security* holds that a state cannot arbitrarily deny unemployment benefits during the last three months of pregnancy and six months after delivery.

December 7, 1976   In *General Electric v. Gilbert*, the Supreme Court rules that a private company's denial of disability benefits to a pregnant woman does not violate Title VII of the Civil Rights Act.

December 20, 1976   The Supreme Court rules in *Craig v. Boren* that a state law enabling women to buy alcohol at an earlier age than men violates the Equal Protection Clause. In doing so, the court creates an intermediate standard, between "rational relation" and "suspect classification," for deciding Equal Protection Clause gender cases.

March 2, 1977 In *Califano v. Goldfarb*, the Supreme Court strikes down the Social Security rule that set different gender-based standards of eligibility for survivor's benefits.

1977 The US Civil Rights Commission publishes *Sex Bias in the U.S. Code*, drafted by RBG's Columbia Law School students.

1978 Passage of the Pregnancy Discrimination Act, outlawing discrimination on the basis of pregnancy.

January 9, 1979 *Duren v. Missouri* effectively reiterates the holding in *Taylor v. Louisiana* that a state cannot make eligibility for jury service different for men and women. It is the last Supreme Court case argued by RBG.

April 8, 1980 President Jimmy Carter nominates RBG to the US Court of Appeals for the District of Columbia Circuit.

August 10, 1993 RBG takes her seat on the US Supreme Court, having been nominated by President William Clinton on June 22.

June 26, 1996 Justice RBG announces the court's decision in *United States v. Virginia*, holding that a publicly financed college violates the Equal Protection Clause when it refuses to admit women. The decision creates a new, higher standard for judging cases alleging state gender discrimination, requiring an "exceedingly persuasive" justification that can survive "skeptical scrutiny."

September 18, 2020 Ruth Bader Ginsburg dies in Washington, DC.

CASES CITED

Adkins v. Children's Hospital, 261 U.S. 525 (1923)

Ballard v. United States, 329 U.S. 187 (1946)

Barnes v. Costle, 561 F. 2d (1977)

Bradwell v. Illinois, 83 U.S. 130 (1872)

Brown v. Board of Education, 347 U.S. 483 (1954)

Coffin v. Secretary of Health, Education & Welfare, 400 F. Supp. 953 (D.D.C. 1975)

Califano v. Goldfarb, 430 U.S. 199 (1977)

Califano v. Webster, 430 U.S. 313 (1977)

Califano v. Westcott, 443 U.S. 76 (1979)

Cleveland v. LaFleur, 414 U.S. 632 (1974)

Craig v. Boren, 429 U.S. 190 (1976)

Daniel v. Louisiana 420 U.S. 31 (1975)

DeFunis v. Odegaard, 416 U.S. 312 (1974)

Doe v. Bolton, 410 U.S. 179 (1973)

Duren v. Missouri, 439 U.S. 357 (1979)

Edwards v. Healy, 421 U.S. 772 (1975)

Eisenstadt v. Baird, 405 U.S. 438 (1972)

F.S. Royster Guano Company v. Virginia, 253 U.S. 412 (1920).

Forbush v. Wallace, 405 U.S. 970 (1972)

Frontiero v. Richardson, 411 U.S. 677 (1973)

Geduldig v. Aiello, 417 U.S. 484 (1974)

General Electric v. Gilbert, 429 U. S. 125 (1976)

Goesaert v. Cleary, 335 U.S. 464 (1948)

Griswold v. Connecticut, 381 U.S. 479 (1965)

Hoyt v. Florida, 368 U.S. 57 (1961)

Jablon v. Secretary of Health, Education & Welfare, 399 F. Supp. 118 (D. Md. 1975)

Kahn v. Shevin, 416 U.S. 351 (1974)

Lochner v. New York, 198 U.S. 45 (1905)

Minor v. Happersett, 88 U.S. 162 (1875)

Mississippi v. Hogan, 458 U.S. 718 (1982)

Moritz v. Commissioner, 469 F.2d 466 (10th Cir. 1972)

Muller v. Oregon, 208 U.S. 412 (1908)

Nashville Gas Company v. Satty, 434 U.S. 136 (1977)

Obergefell v. Hodges, 576 U.S. 644 (2015)

Orr v. Orr, 440 U.S. 268 (1979)

Phillips v. Martin Marietta Corporation, 400 U.S. 542 (1971)

Plessy v. Ferguson, 163 U.S. 537 (1896)

Radice v. New York, 264 U.S. 292 (1924)

Reed v. Reed, 404 U.S. 71 (1971)

Roe v. Wade, 410 U.S. 113 (1973)

Sail'er Inn, Inc. v. Kirby, 485 P.2d 529 (1971)

Schattman v. Texas Employment Commission, 459 F.2d 32 (5th Cir. 1972)

Schlesinger v. Ballard, 419 U.S. 498 (1975)

Shelby County v. Holder, 570 U.S. 529 (2013)

Silbowitz v. Secretary, 397 F. Supp. 862 (S.D. Fla. 1975)

Stanley v. Illinois, 405 U.S. 645 (1972)

Stanton v. Stanton, 421 U.S. 7 (1975)

Strauder v. West Virginia, 100 U.S. 303 (1880)

Struck v. Secretary of Defense, 460 F.2d 1372 (9th Cir. 1971)

Taylor v. Louisiana, 419 U.S. 522 (1974)

Turner v. Department of Employment Security, 423 U.S. 44 (1975)

United States v. Virginia, 518 U.S. 515 (1996)

Vorchheimer v. School District of Philadelphia, 430 U.S. 703 (1977)

Weinberger v. Weisenfeld, 420 U.S. 366 (1975)

Wengler v. Druggists Mutual Insurance Company, 442 U.S. 256 (1979)

White v. Crook, 251 F. Supp. 401 (M.D. Ala. 1966)

There is a substantial body of literature about the gender equality cases as well as about Ruth Bader Ginsburg (RBG), and there will undoubtedly be even more in the future. RBG herself produced a copious number of articles and speeches. Those listed here are a sampling of the ones this author found most useful. Many others can be found by surfing the Web or using the platforms mentioned below.

In addition, there is a comprehensive if now somewhat dated bibliography: Sarah E. Valentine, "Ruth Bader Ginsburg: An Annotated Bibliography," 7 *New York City Law Review* 391 (2004). Many of the articles included there, and below, are in law reviews. They are available on platforms such as HeinOnline, Lexis-Nexis, and JSTOR. Readers without personal access to those can usually access them in local public and university libraries. Some of RBG's speeches can be found on the website of the US Supreme Court: https://www .supremecourt.gov/publicinfo/speeches/speeches.aspx.

The Ginsburg quotes in this volume come from her published speeches, articles, and interviews; my interviews with her; and the substantial Ginsburg archive at the Library of Congress (LC). The archive includes material such as correspondence, speeches, and briefs. As of this writing, researchers seeking to use the papers must obtain permission from the LC's Manuscript Reading Room reference staff, reached at https://ask.loc.gov/manuscripts. Some of the files, particularly those that are personal or refer to her service on the Court of Appeals and the Supreme Court, are not yet open.

———

Books about Ruth Bader Ginsburg

As this book goes to press, the biography that undoubtedly will be the default source for years to come has not yet been published. It is by Mary Hartnett and Wendy W. Williams, written with the cooperation of Justice Ginsburg. Readers may recognize Williams as the attorney in *Geduldig v. Aiello*, who later coauthored articles with Ginsburg. The authors collaborated with the justice in producing *My Own Words*, by Ruth Bader Ginsburg, with Mary Hartnett and Wendy W. Williams (New York: Simon & Schuster, 2016). It is an annotated collection of Ginsburg's writings that span the years from her childhood through the Supreme Court's 2015–2016 term. There is also a later collection of some of her oral arguments and judicial opinions: Ruth Bader Ginsburg and Amanda L. Tyler, *Justice, Justice Thou Shalt Pursue* (University of California Press, 2021).

Jane Sherron DeHart's *Ruth Bader Ginsburg: A Life* (New York: Alfred A. Knopf, 2018) is a comprehensive biography. Jeffrey Rosen's *Conversations with RBG: Ruth Bader Ginsburg on Life, Love, Liberty, and Law* (New York: Henry Holt, 2019) is exactly what the title indicates: conversations that began in 1991 between the president of the National Constitution Center and Justice Ginsburg. *Ruth Bader Ginsburg in Her Own Words*, edited by Helena Hunt (Chicago: Agate, 2018), has snippets from Ginsburg's writings and speeches. Linda Hirschman's *Sisters in Law: How Sandra Day O'Connor and Ruth Bader Ginsburg Went to the Supreme Court and Changed the World* (New York: HarperCollins, 2015) has some good information about RBG's pre–Supreme Court years, in spite of the hyperbolic title. Irin Carmon and Shana Knizhnik's *Notorious RBG: The Life and Times of Ruth Bader Ginsburg* (New York: William Morrow, 2015) is a nicely illustrated volume about Ginsburg's life and work, by a journalist and the former law student responsible for the "Notorious RBG" phenomenon.

———

Early Life and Education

RBG, "Remarks at the Genesis Foundation Lifetime Achievement Award Ceremony," Tel Aviv, July 4, 2018, https://www.supremecourt.gov/publicinfo /speeches/speeches.aspx, details some of the early influences on her life. RBG discusses the impact of two of her college professors in Joseph Kimble, "Interview with United States Supreme Court Justices," 13 *The Scribes Journal of Legal Writing* 133 (2010): https://legaltimes.typepad.com/files/garner-transcripts-1 .pdf. Gerald Gunther, one of her law school professors, reminisces in "Ruth Bader Ginsburg: A Personal, Very Fond Tribute," 20 *University of Hawaii L.R.* 583 (1998). (For the sake of brevity, the abbreviations *L.R.* and *L.J.* are used in this bibliography to denote *Law Review* and *Law Journal*.) Erwin N. Griswold describes what he meant at the law school dinner RBG attended in his *Ould Fields, New Corne: The Personal Memoirs of a Twentieth Century Lawyer* (St. Paul, Minnesota: West, 1992), 171. Ginsberg talked at length about her Harvard experience in a 2020 interview by Dahlia Lithwick: "It's Amazing to Me How Distinctly I Remember Each of These Women," https://slate.com/news-and -politics/2020/07/ruth-bader-ginsburg-interview-transcript.html.

RBG described her education and her experience in Sweden, as well as her early years as a litigator in Gilliam Metzger & Abbe Gluck, in "A Conversation with Justice Ruth Bader Ginsburg," 25 *Columbia Journal of Gender & Law* 6 (2013): https://digitalcommons.law.yale.edu/cgi/viewcontent .cgi?article=5910&context=fss_papers. This is also a good source for Ginsburg's descriptions of the Supreme Court cases she handled. Cary Franklin details the development of RBG's thought, with particular reference to

Sweden and Pauli Murray, in "The Anti-Stereotyping Principle in Constitutional Sex Discrimination Law," 85 *New York University L.R.* 83 (2010).

There is more about early influences in Deborah Jones Merritt and Wendy Webster Williams's "Transcript of Interview of U.S. Supreme Court Associate Justice Ruth Bader Ginsburg, April 10, 2009," 70 *Ohio State L.J.* 805 (2009). This, too, has information about her cases. Wendy Webster Williams's "Justice Ruth Bader Ginsburg's Rutgers Years, 1963–1972," 31 *Women's Rights Law Reporter* 229 (2010) and RBG's "Remarks on Women's Progress in the Legal Profession in the United States," 33 *Tulsa L.J.* 13 (1997) cover aspects of her life before the Women's Rights Project, including her work for the New Jersey affiliate of the ACLU. Elizabeth Langer, who cofounded and became the first editor-in-chief of the *Women's Rights Law Reporter*, discusses RBG's contributions to it in "The Birth of the Women's Rights Law Reporter," https://web.archive.org /web/20180525125706/https://barnard.edu/headlines/birth-womens-rights -law-reporter. Herma Hill Kay, in "Ruth Bader Ginsburg, Professor of Law," 104 *Columbia L.R.* 2 (2004), covers both the Rutgers and the Columbia years. Brenda Feigen reminisces about the early years of the WRP in "The ACLU, Ruth Bader Ginsburg, and Me," https://www.aclu.org/issues/womens-rights /aclu-ruth-bader-ginsburg-and-me. Stephanie Francis Ward's "Family Ties: The Private and Public Lives of Justice Ruth Bader Ginsburg" is a very accessible article about RBG's life and work: 96 *ABA Journal* 36 (October 2010). Ruth Rubio-Marín's "'Notorious RBG': A Conversation with United States Supreme Court Justice Ruth Bader Ginsburg," 15 *International Journal of Constitutional Law* 602 (July 2017), is a delightful, long interview, covering Ginsburg's years as a student, an advocate, and a jurist.

Specific Supreme Court Cases

RBG's overview of the cases she participated in can be found in a number of places, but see especially her "Sex Equality and the Constitution," 52 *Tulane L.R.* 451 (1978), https://www.jstor.org/stable/25726416?seq=1#metadata_ info_tab_contents, which argues as well for the Equal Rights Amendment (as does her "The Need for the Equal Rights Amendment," 59 *ABA Journal* 1013 [September 1973]); "Women's Right to Full Participation in Shaping Society's Course: An Evolving Constitutional Precept," in *Toward the Second Decade: The Impact of the Women's Movement on American Institutions*, edited by Betty Justice and Renate Pore (Westport: Greenwood, 1981); "The Burger Court's Grapplings with Sex Discrimination," in *The Counter-Revolution That Wasn't*, edited by Vincent Blasi (New Haven: Yale University Press, 1983); "Women as Full Members of the Club: An Evolving American Ideal," 6(1) *Human Rights* 1 (Fall

1976); "From No Rights, to Half Rights, to Confusing Rights: For Women, the Supreme Court's Decisions Are a Study in Male Hesitation and Legal Timidity," 7(1) *Human Rights* 12 (Spring 1978); "Gender and the Constitution," 44 *University of Cincinnati L.R.* 1 (1975); "Gender in the Supreme Court: The 1973 and 1974 Terms," 1975 *Supreme Court Review* 1; "Gender in the Supreme Court: The 1976 Term," in *Constitutional Government in America*, edited by Ronald K.L. Collins (Durham, NC: Carolina Academic Press, 1980), 217; "Remarks for the Celebration of 75 Years of Women's Enrollment at Columbia Law School," 102 *Columbia L.R.* 1441 (October 2002); "Sexual Equality Under the Fourteenth and Equal Rights Amendments," 1979 *Washington University L.Q.* 161 (1979); and "Foreword," 14 *Yale Journal of Law & Feminism* 213 (2002).

As noted above, Sarah E. Valentine's bibliography includes articles by RBG about specific cases. All of the major law reviews have their own articles about each of the cases. There is an excellent overview of the cases and an analysis of RBG's strategy in them in Deborah L. Markowitz's "In Pursuit of Equality: One Woman's Work to Change the Law," 14 *Women's Rights Law Reporter* 335 (1989). David Cole covers the same cases and also criticizes RBG's strategy in "Strategies of Difference: Litigating for Women's Rights in a Man's World," 2(1) *Law & Inequality* 33 (1984), https://scholarship.law.umn.edu/cgi/viewcontent.cgi?article=1283&context=lawineq. The article also covers *Mississippi v. Hogan*, at 85–92. There is an excellent analysis of the race/sex analogy and RBG's use of it in Serena Mayeri's *Reasoning from Race: Feminism, Law, and the Civil Rights Revolution* (Cambridge, MA: Harvard University Press, 2011).

Bradwell v. Illinois. Jane M. Friedman's "Myra Bradwell: On Defying the Creator and Becoming a Lawyer," 28 *Valparaiso University L.R.* 1287 (1994), is a good account of the case and the life of Bradwell. Richard H. Chused's "A Brief History of Gender Law Journals: The Heritage of Myra Bradwell's Chicago Legal News," 12 *Columbia Journal of Gender and Law* 421 (2003), details Bradwell's inclusion of feminist material in her *Chicago Legal News*.

Minor v. Happersett. There is an excellent article on the website of the National Park Service: "Virginia Minor and Women's Right to Vote," https://www.nps.gov/jeff/learn/historyculture/the-virginia-minor-case.htm.

Muller v. Oregon. RBG discusses the case, and Brandeis's influence on her, in "Lessons Learned from Louis D. Brandeis for Presentation at Brandeis University January 28, 2016," https://www.supremecourt.gov/publicinfo/speeches/Lessons%20Learned%20From%20Brandeis%20January%202016.pdf. I also tell the story of the case in *Louis D. Brandeis: Justice for the People* (Harvard University Press, 1984), chapter 8. For women already running for and winning political office, see "Her Hat Was in the Ring," https://www.facebook.com/herhatwasintheringbefore1920/.

Goesaert v. Cleary. Amy Holtman French covers the case well in "Mixing

It Up: Michigan Barmaids Fight for Civil Rights," 40(1) *Michigan Historical Review* 27 (Spring 2014), https://www.jstor.org/stable/pdf/10.5342/michhist revi.40.1.0027.pdf?refreqid=excelsior%3Af4c4ee856e706fb3df28d77467937f53.

Hoyt v. Florida: There is a full account in George B. Crawford's "Murder, Insanity and The Efficacy of Woman's Role: The Gwendolyn Hoyt Case," 89(1) *The Florida Historical Quarterly* 51 (Summer 2010), http://ucf.digital.flvc.org/islandora/object/islandora:1918/datastream/OBJ/view/The_Florida_his torical_quarterly.pdf. For a fine discussion of *Hoyt* in the context of the history of women and juries in the United States, see Linda K. Kerber's *No Constitutional Right to Be Ladies: Women and the Obligations of Citizenship* (New York: Hill and Wang, 1998), chapter 4.

Moritz v. Commissioner: Martin D. Ginsburg's short, humorous take on the case is "A Uniquely Distinguished Service," 10 *Green Bag* 2d 173 (2007): http://www.greenbag.org/v10n2/v10n2_articles_ginsburg.pdf. There is a longer version, "How the Tenth Circuit Court of Appeals Got My Wife Her Good Job," in *My Own Words*, at 126. It is the speech he wrote but did not live to deliver at the 2010 annual conference of the Tenth Circuit Court of Appeals, which was read there by RBG. Her presentation of it can be watched at https://www.c-span.org/video/?c4511853/user-clip-tenth-circuit-wife-good -job. (Although it is outside the purview of this book, readers might also enjoy Martin Ginsburg's comments about RBG becoming a justice: Martin D. Ginsburg, "Some Reflections on Imperfection," 39 *Arizona State L.J.* 949 (2007): https://heinonline.org/HOL/Page?handle=hein.journals/arzjl39&div=3 9&g_sent=1&casa_token=&collection=journals.

Reed v. Reed: There is a good summary in "Supreme Court Decisions & Women's Rights—Milestones to Equality" on the website of the Supreme Court History Society: https://supremecourthistory.org/lc_breaking_new _ground.html. "Reed v. Reed at 40: Equal Protection and Women's Rights," 20 *Journal of Gender, Social Policy & the Law* 2 (2011), http://digitalcommons .wcl.american.edu/jgspl/vol20/iss2/, is a transcript of a conversation among RBG, Emily J. Martin, Earl M. Maltz, Jacqueline A Berrien, Nina Pillard, and Nina Totenberg about *Reed v. Reed* and its impact. Allen Derr's take on the case is in "Reed v. Reed," 44 *Advocate* (Idaho State Bar) 20 (January 2001), https://heinonline.org/HOL/LandingPage?handle=hein.barjournals /adisboo44&div=11&id=&page=. It does contain mistakes, however, including the claim that Mel Wulf wanted the dying Dorothy Kenyon (whom Derr wrongly describes as Black) to argue the case.

The law review articles referred to in chapter 3 are Joan M. Krauskopf's "Sex Discrimination: Another Shibboleth Legally Shattered," 37 *Missouri L.R.* 377 (1972); Judith A. de Boisblanc's "Constitutional Law: The Equal Protection Clause and Women's Rights," 19 *Loyola L.R.* 542 (1972); and John P. Murphy Jr.'s

"The Reed Case: The Seed for Equal Protection from Sex-Based Discrimination, or Polite Judicial Hedging," 5 *Akron L.R.* 251 (1972).

Frontiero v. Richardson: The best place to start is Serena Mayeri's "'When the Trouble Started': The Story of Frontiero v. Richardson," University of Pennsylvania Law School, Public Law and Legal Theory Research Paper Series Research Paper No. 10–13 (2011), https://static1.squarespace.com/static/53f2077ce4bofe85d1632056/t/5422d1abe4b082f3c75ba4da/1411568043412/Mills+Frontiero+v.+Richardson.pdf. The article is also included in *Women and the Law Stories,* edited by Elizabeth Schneider and Stephanie M. Wildman (New York: Foundation Press, 2011), chapter 2. The interview in which Ginsburg called *Frontiero* more important than *Reed* is "Women and the Law: A Dialogue with Ruth Bader Ginsburg," 5(4) *Women's Studies Newsletter* 25 (Fall, 1977), https://www.jstor.org/stable/pdf/40042542.pdf?ab_segments=0%252Fbasic_search%252Fcontrol.

Kahn v. Shevin: "Kahn v. Shevin and the 'Heightened Rationality Test': Is the Supreme Court Promoting a Double Standard in Sex Discrimination Cases?" 32 *Washington & Lee L.R.* 275 (1975): https://scholarlycommons.law.wlu.edu/cgi/viewcontent.cgi?article=3063&context=wlulr, places the case in the context of the court's earlier gender equality decisions and discusses the question of what standard the court used in such cases.

Geduldig v. Aiello: Jane Swanson, "Exclusion of Pregnancy from Coverage of Disability Benefits Does Not Violate Equal Protection," 12 *Houston L.R.* 488 (1975); Diane L. Zimmerman, "Geduldig v. Aiello: Pregnancy Classifications and the Definition of Sex Discrimination," 75 *Columbia L.R.* 441 (1975).

General Electric v. Gilbert: Nicholas Pedriana's "Discrimination by Definition: The Historical and Legal Paths to the Pregnancy Discrimination Act of 1978," 21 *Yale Journal of Law & Feminism* 1 (2009), discusses both the case and the path to passage of the Pregnancy Discrimination Act. The *New York Times* op-ed that RBG and Susan Deller Ross wrote, urging Congress to pass the act, is "Pregnancy and Discrimination," January 25, 1977, p. 33, https://www.nytimes.com/1977/01/25/archives/pregnancy-and-discrimination.html.

Geduldig, G.E. v. Gilbert, and other pregnancy cases are covered in Wendy W. Williams's "Equality's Riddle: Pregnancy and the Equal Treatment/Special Treatment Debate," 13 *New York University Review of Law & Social Change* 325 (1984). Although *Struck v. Secretary of Defense,* the reproductive freedom case that RBG described as "the one that got away," was not decided by the Supreme Court, Neil S. Siegel and Reva B. Siegel's excellent "Struck by Stereotype: Ruth Bader Ginsburg on Pregnancy Discrimination as Sex Discrimination," 59 *Duke L.J.* 771 (January 2010), is a very full description of RBG's approach to pregnancy discrimination. The lecture in which she criticized *Roe v. Wade* was published as "Speaking in a Judicial Voice," 67 *New York University*

L.R. 1185 (December 1992): https://www.law.nyu.edu/sites/default/files/ECM _PRO_059254.pdf.

Schlesinger v. Ballard: Linda E. Boelhauf's "Schlesinger v. Ballard: Equal Protection Washes Out to Sea," 13 *California Western L.R.* 317 (1977), is a solid examination of the case, as well as a good explanation of the court's differing standards in gender equality litigation.

Weinberger v. Wiesenfeld: John D. Johnston Jr.'s "Sex Discrimination and the Supreme Court—1975," 23 *UCLA L.R.* 235 (1975) puts the *Wiesenfeld* decision in the context of the court's struggle to find a consistent standard and covers the other gender equality cases of the 1975 term as well. Barbara A. Burnett's "Family Economic Integrity under the Social Security System," 7 *NYU Review of Law & Social Change* 155 (1978), discusses *Wiesenfeld* and the court's subsequent Social Security decisions, as well as both the purposes of early Social Security laws and later changed societal conditions. Stephen Wiesenfeld's account of the case is "My Journey with RBG," 121 *Columbia L.R.* 563 (2021): https://www .columbialawreview.org/content/my-journey-with-rbg/.

Craig v. Boren: Jeremy Bressman, "A New Standard of Review: Craig v. Boren and Brennan's Heightened Scrutiny Test in Historical Perspective," 32 *Journal of Supreme Court History* 85 (2007). No author is listed for the good article on the website of the Supreme Court Historical Society: "Supreme Court Decision & Women's Rights—Milestones to Equality: Justice for Beer Drinkers," https://supremecourthistory.org/lc_justice_for_beer_drinkers.html. There is useful background material in R. Darcy & Jenny Sanbrano, "Oklahoma in the Development of Equal Rights: The ERA, 3.2% Beer, Juvenile Justice, and Craig v. Boren," 22 *Oklahoma City University L.R.* 1009 (1997).

Califano v. Goldfarb: The case is described in "Equal Protection and Sex Discrimination: Evolution of a Constitutional Safeguard in Califano v. Goldfarb," 4 *Women's Rights Law Reporter* 115 (1978) and John V. Nordlund, "Constitutional Law: Equal Protection—Gender Discrimination—Califano v. Goldfarb," 23 *New York Law School L.R.* 503 (1978). RBG's "Some Thoughts on Benign Classification in the Context of Sex," 10 *Connecticut L.R.* 813 (1978), discusses this and preceding cases, as well as *Califano v. Webster.*

Duren v. Missouri: Two useful law review articles are Harriet C. Wright's "Criminal Procedure: State v. Duren; The Missouri Supreme Court's Stand against Jury Selection Reform," 47 *University of Missouri-Kansas City L.R.* 246 (1978) and "Sixth Amendment: Right to Trial by Jury," 70 *Journal of Criminal Law and Criminology* 490 (Winter 1979): https://scholarlycommons.law.north western.edu/jclc/vol70/iss4/10/. Lee Nation's take on the case is reported in Charles Holt, "Mr. Chief Justice, and May It Please the Court," *Kansas City Business Journal*, October 19, 1997, https://www.bizjournals.com/kansascity /stories/1997/10/20/focus1.html.

Mississippi v. Hogan: see the David Cole article above, as well as Laura Wheeler, "Single-Sex State Nursing Schools and the U.S. Constitution: Mississippi University for Women v. Hogan," 2 *Population Research and Policy Review* 131 (May 1983).

United States v. Virginia (the VMI case): There are fine discussions of the case in Kenneth L. Karst, "The Way Women Are: Some Notes in the Margin for Ruth Bader Ginsburg," 20 *University of Hawaii L.R.* 619 (1998), and Julie M. Amstein, "United States v. Virginia: The Case of Coeducation at Virginia Military Institute," 3(1) *Journal of Gender, Social Policy & the Law* 69 (1994): https://digitalcommons.wcl.american.edu/jgspl/about.html. See also my *Women in the Barracks: The VMI Case and Equal Rights* (Lawrence: University Press of Kansas, 2002).

There are numerous interviews, now available on the Web, in which RBG discusses her cases. In addition to those mentioned elsewhere in this bibliography, see Linda Greenhouse, "A Conversation with Justice Ginsburg," 122 *Yale Law Journal* 2012–2013: https://www.yalelawjournal.org/forum/a-conversation-with-justice-ginsburg; M. Elizabeth Magill, "At the U.S. Supreme Court: A Conversation with Justice Ruth Bader Ginsburg," 89 *Legal Matters* (Stanford Law School) (Fall 2013): https://law.stanford.edu/stanford-lawyer/articles/legal-matters/; and Charlie Rose, "Justice Ruth Bader Ginsburg, Part I," October 10, 2016, https://charlierose.com/videos/29284.

Transcripts of RBG's oral arguments before the Supreme Court are on the Supreme Court's website, at https://www.supremecourt.gov/oral_arguments/argument_transcript/2019, listed by year. They are also available at the Oyez website: www.oyez.org. Search for them under the name of each case. The transcripts on the two sites differ somewhat, depending on what the transcribers made of the tapes. Anyone wanting to hear the originals can do so on the Oyez website. The National Archives also has a collection of the oral arguments.

The Justices

The comments by the justices, other than in their published opinions, are drawn from a number of sources. Many of the justices' papers, including those of Justice Harry Blackmun and Justice William Brennan, are archived in the Library of Congress. Some of the Blackmun papers are online at http://memory.loc.gov/diglib/blackmun-public/collection.html. Justice Lewis Powell's Supreme Court papers are available at https://law.wlu.edu/powell-archives/powell-papers. Professors Paul J. Wahlbeck, James F. Spriggs II, and Forrest Maltzman have collected and scanned some of the justices' in-house correspondence about the cases argued before them at http://supremecourt opinions.wustl.edu/?rt=pdfarchive.

There are numerous biographies of the justices. One that was particularly valuable for this volume is Seth Stern and Stephen Wermiel's *Justice Brennan: Liberal Champion* (Lawrence: University of Kansas Press, 2013). Short bits of information about the justices can be found on the Supreme Court website.

ACLU and the Women's Rights Project

The article by Pauli Murray and Mary o. Eastwood that was important in the ACLU's decision to create a women's rights project is "Jane Crow and the Law: Sex Discrimination and Title VII," 34 *George Washington L.R.* 232 (1965). The ACLU website has good information about the WRP in the 1970s, as well as about the contributions of Pauli Murray and Dorothy Kenyon: https://www.aclu.org /other/tribute-legacy-ruth-bader-ginsburg-and-wrp-staff?redirect=womens-rights/tribute-legacy-ruth-bader-ginsburg-and-wrp-staff#pioneer; and https:// www.aclu.org/other/about-aclu-womens-rights-project. RBG discusses the early years in "Advocating the Elimination of Gender-Based Discrimination: The 1970s New Look at the Equality Principle," https://www.supremecourt .gov/publicinfo/speeches/viewspeech/sp_02-10-06, and in RBG and Barbara Flagg, "Some Reflections on the Feminist Legal Thought of the 1970's," 1989 *University of Chicago Legal Forum* 1 (1989): https://chicagounbound.uchicago .edu/cgi/viewcontent.cgi?article=1047&context=uclf.

Aryeh Neier, then executive director, reminisces in "Reflections on Ruth Bader Ginsburg's Leadership of the ACLU Women's Rights Project," https://www.aclu.org/other/aryeh-neier-reflections-ruth-bader-ginsburgs -leadership-aclu-womens-rights. Susan Deller Ross's "Early Women's Rights Adventures with Professor Ruth Bader Ginsburg and Our Clinical Teaching at Columbia Law School," 121 *Columbia L.R.* 553 (2021), was written by one of her WRP colleagues. It is at https://columbialawreview.org/content /early-womens-rights-adventures-with-professor-ruth-bader-ginsburg-and -our-clinical-teaching-at-columbia-law-school/. Kathleen Peratis's "Memories of RBG," 121 *Columbia L.R.* 5413 (2021), is by the coworker who became the next director of the WRP; see https://columbialawreview.org/content /memories-of-rbg/.

There are a number of very good scholarly articles about the WPR in the 1970s, including Karen O'Connor and Lee Epstein's "Beyond Legislative Lobbying; Women's Rights Groups and the Supreme Court, 67 *Judicature* 134 (1983); Michael J. Klarman's "Tribute to Justice Ruth Bader Ginsburg," 56 *Harvard Civil Rights-Civil Liberties L.R.* 27 (2021); and Ruth B. Cowan's "Women's

Rights through Litigation: An Examination of the American Civil Liberties Union Women's Rights Project, 1971–1976," 8 *Columbia Human Rights L.R.* 373 (1976). The Cowan article was written with RBG's cooperation at the midpoint of her tenure at the WRP and is particularly useful for the early years. The Klarman article is a good overview of Ginsburg in the 1970s, by a scholar who became one of Justice Ginsburg's law clerks. There is also a fine discussion by Susan M. Hartmann in *The Other Feminists: Activists in the Liberal Establishment* (New Haven: Yale University Press, 1998), chapter 3.

The Ford Foundation's view of the WRP's litigation, as well as gender equality litigation by other Ford-funded organizations, is detailed in Margaret A. Berger, *Litigation on Behalf of Women: A Review for the Ford Foundation* (New York: Ford Foundation, 1980).

———

The Societal Background

William H. Chafe's *The American Woman: Her Changing Social, Economic and Political Roles, 1920–1970* (New York: Oxford University Press, 1972) is a key work about the changing roles of women in the twentieth century. See also Carl Degler, *At Odds: Women and the Family in America from the Revolution to the Present* (New York: Oxford University Press, 1981). Basic data about women's occupations in the twentieth century can be found on the websites of the Census Bureau and the Women's Bureau in the Department of Labor.

The changing demographic composition of Congress in the mid-to-late twentieth century is detailed in US House of Representatives, "A Changing of the Guard: Traditionalists, Feminists, and the New Face of Women in Congress, 1955–1976," http://history.house.gov/Exhibitions-and-Publications/WIC/Historical-Essays/Changing-Guard/Introduction/ and http://history.house.gov/Exhibitions-and-Publications/WIC/Historical-Essays/Changing-Guard/New-Patterns/.

For a history of the rise of the 1960s–1970s women's movement, see Jo Freeman, *The Politics of Women's Liberation: A Case Study of an Emerging Social Movement and Its Relation to the Policy Process* (New York: McKay, 1975); and Ruth Rosen, *The World Split Open: How the Modern Women's Movement Changed America* (New York: Viking, 2000). Freeman analyzes the movement's impact on the Civil Rights Act of 1964 in "How 'Sex' Got into Title VII: Persistent Opportunism as a Maker of Public Policy," which is chapter 12 of her *We Will Be Heard: Women's Struggles for Political Power in the United States* (Lanham, MD: Rowman & Littlefield, 2008) and is at http://www.jofreeman.com/lawandpolicy/titlevii.htm.

Joan Hoff's *Law, Gender, and Injustice: A Legal History of U.S. Women* (New York:

New York University Press, 1991) surveys women and the law throughout US history. *Sex Bias in the U.S. Code*, the report prepared largely by RBG's students for the US Commission on Civil Rights, is at http://www.law.umaryland.edu /marshall/usccr/documents/cr12se9.pdf. Information about the impact of the report is detailed in "Carol A. Bonosaro, President," July 11, 2014, https://docs .house.gov/meetings/GO/GO25/20140711/102504/HHRG-113-GO25-Bio -BonosaroC-20140711.pdf; and Mary Frances Berry, *And Justice for All: The United States Commission on Civil Rights and the Continuing Struggle for Freedom in America* (New York: Alfred A. Knopf, 2009), 176.

Author's interviews

Finally, some of the material in this volume came from the author's interviews:

Jane Booth, by telephone, July 23, 2020

Brenda Feigen, by telephone, November 17, 2020

Ruth Bader Ginsburg, New York City, March 29, 1979, and September 10, 1994; Washington, DC, September 23, 1995, May 23, 2000, May 21, 2002, and February 16, 2012; Waltham, Massachusetts, January 28, 2016

Elizabeth Langer, by telephone, August 1, 2020

Margaret Moses, by Zoom, July 28, 2020

Kathleen Peratis, by telephone, August 11, 2020

Patricia Ramsay, by telephone, September 4, 2020

Susan Deller Ross, by telephone, September 19, 2020

Mel Wulf, by telephone, August 12, 2020

INDEX

Goldmark, Pauline, 18
Gotcher, Emma, 16
Gray, James H., 129–130
Greenberger, Marcia, 57
Griffiths, Martha, 11, 25, 153
Grimké, Sarah, 71
Griswold, Erwin, 167
    and *Frontiero v. Richardson*, 67, 138
    at Harvard Law School, 7
    and *Moritz v. Commissioner*, 37–38, 80
    and *Struck v. Secretary*, 62–63
Griswold v. Connecticut, 62
Gunther, Gerald, 8

Halloway, William J., 36–37
Hames, Margie Pitts, 31–32
Harlan, John Marshall II, 24, 54
Hartmann, Susan, 30
Harvard University School of Law, 6–7
Haselbock, Joe, 16
Healy, Marsha B. See *Edwards v. Healy*
Heide, Wilma Scott, 31
Hirschkop, Philip, 80
Hoppe, Bill, 81–82, 86, 88
Howe, Florence, 90
Hoyt, Clarence. See *Hoyt v. Florida*
Hoyt, Gwendolyn, 23–24, 26 (see also *Hoyt v. Florida*)
Hoyt v. Florida, 23–26, 30, 31, 39, 40, 41, 80, 85, 95
    overturned, 98, 162
    RBG on, 46, 67, 71, 96, 98, 154
Hulette, Alta, 18
Huntington, Samuel, 72–73

Idaho Statesman, 54

Jablon, Bette, 135
"Jane Crow and the Law," 30–31
Janeway, Elizabeth, 44, 91

Jaramillo, Jacquelyn, 113. See also *Geduldig v. Aiello*
Jefferson, Thomas, 13, 67
Johnson, Esther, 18
Jones, Keith A., 106–107, 136–137
Jong, Erica, 91
Juries
    Black people and, 22, 31, 96, 155
    women and, 21–26, 31, 67, 95–99, 153–161

Kahn, Melvin. See *Kahn v. Shevin*
Kahn v. Shevin, 89, 97, 103, 105, 106–107, 128, 133, 148, 150
    RBG on, 99, 101, 104, 110, 126, 131, 135, 140
Kanowitz, Leo, 44
Karpatkin, Marvin, 39
Karst, Kenneth, 57
Kay, Herma Hill, 27, 119
Kelley, Florence, 17–18
Kelly, Joan, 90
Kennedy, Florynce, 90
Kennedy, John F., 10, 41
Kenyon, Dorothy, 25, 30–33, 39, 48
Kerber, Linda, 26
Khoury, Charles, 100
Kilpatrick, James, 110
King, Billie Jean, 91
King, Martin Luther, Jr., 10
Knizhnik, Shana, 166–167

Ladies' Home Journal, 91
Langer, Elizabeth, 27
Laughrey, Nanette K., 157–159
Law, Sylvia, 16
Lazarus, Emma, 5
League of Women Voters, 56
Lerner, Gerda, 89, 90
Levin, Joseph, 64–65, 70, 72–73
Lichtman, Judith, 57

Protective legislation, 19, 47, 162
Public Advocates, Inc., 36

Rabb, Harriet, 55
Rational relation test. *See* Equal
    Protection Clause
Redbook, 91
Reddy, Helen, 91
Reed, Sally. See *Reed v. Reed*
Reed v. Reed, 38–54, 66, 68, 74–77, 81, 87,
        100, 114, 116–117, 127, 141–142
    cited and discussed by RBG, 67, 70,
        80, 82–84, 96, 104, 135, 151, 154
    cited by justices, 144–145, 163
    cited by lower courts, 67, 96, 125
    cited by RBG opponents, 132
Rehnquist, William, 42, 165
    in oral arguments, 119, 155–157
    in RBG cases, 74, 77, 86–87, 99, 109,
        129, 143, 147–150, 152, 160, 162
    relationship with RBG, 165–166
    in women's rights cases not brought
        by RBG, 119, 120
Reproductive freedom, 55, 62
    abortion, 60
    pregnancy, 61–64
    sterilization, 63–64
Richardson, Elliot, 69
Riggs, Bobby, 91
Ringgold, Faith, 91
Roberts, John, 1
Rockefeller Family Fund, 36
Roe v. Wade, 32, 62, 63, 94, 123
Roosevelt, Eleanor, 10
Roosevelt, Franklin D., 41
Rosen, Ruth, 90
Ross, Susan Deller, 119–120
Rutgers Law School, 11–13, 27, 43, 55,
        130, 131

Sacks, Albert, 8
Sail'er Inn, Inc. v. Kirby, 47–48, 78

Salter, Susanna, 18
Sarah Lawrence College, 90
*Schattman v. Texas Employment
    Commission*, 111–112, 114
Schlafly, Phyllis, 92
Schlesinger v. Ballard, 99–101, 127, 135,
        141–142, 171
Schneider, Elizabeth, 104
Segal, Phyllis N., 161
Seidenberg, Faith, 31, 32
Seiler, Robert, 156
Seneca Falls Declaration of
    Sentiments, 67
Sex Bias in the U.S. Code, 92–93
Sex/race analogy, 30–31, 46, 66, 129, 147
    contested, 34, 49, 66, 75–77, 79, 87, 105
    RBG and, 33–34, 41, 45–46, 70–71, 84,
        86, 104, 121, 156, 164
    used by justices, 51, 78, 161
Shevin, Robert, 81
Silbowitz, Shirley, 135
Sixth Amendment, 21, 96, 98, 154–156,
        158–161
Social Security Act, 80–81, 93, 101–109,
        130–140, 147–153, 161–162
Southern Poverty Law Center, 64, 100
Spock, Benjamin, 91
Stanley, Joan. See *Stanley v. Illinois*
Stanley, Peter. See *Stanley v. Illinois*
Stanley v. Illinois, 49–50, 67, 142
Stearns, Nancy, 38, 104
Steele, Diana A., 161
Steinem, Gloria, 91
Stevens, John Paul, 119–121, 138–139, 144,
        146–150
Stewart, Potter, 41–42, 82
    in justices' deliberations, 75, 77, 86,
        148–149, 159
    in oral arguments, 85–86, 97–98, 128,
        136–138
    in RBG cases, 79, 85–87, 146,
        147–150, 152

Women
  attorneys in United States, 4, 13–14,
    18, 20
  elected officials, 11, 18, 20
  in the labor force, 45, 68, 90, 98, 120
  in the military (see *Frontiero v.*
    Richardson, Schlesinger v. Ballard,
    Struck v. Secretary)
  office-holders in the nineteenth
    century, 18
  political caucuses, 32, 93
  in U.S. Congress, 11, 20
Women's Equity Action League, 102, 162
Women's Law Fund of Cleveland,
    56, 112
Women's Legal Defense Fund, 57, 58, 162
Women's Rights Law Reporter, 27

Women's rights movement, 28, 91, 136
Women's Rights Project. *See* American
    Civil Liberties Union
Women's studies programs, 89–90
  National Women's Studies
    Association, 90
Wulf, Mel, 2
  and RBG cases, 32, 33, 39–43, 47–48,
    53–56, 66, 81–82, 133, 165

Yale University Law School
  creates women and the law
    course, 89
  students and RBG cases, 43

Zimmerman, Diane, 116